Joyce in Court

ADRIAN HARDIMAN was born in
Dublin in 1952 and educated at
Belvedere College and University
College Dublin. After a distinguished
career as a barrister, he was appointed
to the Irish Supreme Court in 2000.
He wrote a number of important
judgements for the court, and was
generally acknowledged as the most
brilliant lawyer of his generation.
He died in 2016.

Joyce in Court

ADRIAN HARDIMAN

HEAD
of ZEUS

First published in the UK in 2017 by Head of Zeus Ltd

Copyright © Adrian Hardiman, 2017

9 7 5 3   2 4 6 8

A catalogue record for this book is available from
the British Library.

ISBN (HB) 9781786691583
ISBN (E) 9781786691576

Typeset by Adrian McLaughlin

Printed and bound in Great Britain by
CPI Group (UK) Ltd, Croydon CR0 4YY

Head of Zeus Ltd
First Floor East
5–8 Hardwick Street
London EC1R 4RG
WWW.HEADOFZEUS.COM

To my grandchildren Vincent, Karen and Eva

Contents

Publisher's Note   *ix*

⌁ Part I ⌁

1 Contexts: Joyce, History, Law and England   3
2 Outrages in Ireland and England: Maamtrasna,
   Great Wyrley and Judicious Doubt   51

⌁ Part II ⌁

3 Law, Crime and Punishment in
   Bloomsday Dublin   91
4 'A Gruesome Case'   127
5 The Mortgaged Life   163
6 Political Violence: Emmet and
   the Invincibles   203

⌒ Part III ⌒

7   Attempts to Suppress *Ulysses*   241
8   The American Trials of *Ulysses*, 1919–1933   253
9   'This Disgusting Book': *Ulysses* in England   283

Appendix: The Trial of Robert Emmet   307

Notes   343
Image credits   362
Index   363

Publisher's Note

`

Adrian Hardiman was always destined for a brilliant career. To his contemporaries at University College Dublin in the early seventies, he seemed to arrive fully formed as an articulate, brilliant and combative scholar, a formidable polemicist and a merciless critic of the student left. There could not have been any doubt that he would move seamlessly from the Literary and Historical Society, where he ran rings around his opponents, into the law and politics.

As a disenchanted observer of the coming generation of the State's leaders, I could not have imagined finding enough in common with Adrian Hardiman to want to become his publisher (a career of which I knew nothing at the time).

My attitude was complicated when he offered, years later, to libel-read a book that many sensible people were advising me not to publish under any circumstances. The then editor of *The Irish Times* told me that the people called to account in the book 'would spend a hundred pounds to win a penny', which was not music to the ears of the very risk-averse senior executives at Random House to whom I answered for my enthusiasms. But the author was a rigorous researcher, and Hardiman gave the manuscript a clean bill of health. He thought that the book would contribute to puncturing the impunity of corrupt businessmen and politicians, and declined to bill us for his work. I realised that for him establishing the facts and telling the truth were more important than any apparent ideological differences.

In 2007, I had the pleasure of reading the manuscript of a book by my former history tutor Ronan Fanning. As we worked on *Fatal Path*, his masterly account of the high politics of the period between 1910 and 1920, which led inexorably to violent insurrection, guerrilla war and a bitter civil conflict, Ronan mentioned that his close friend Hardiman – by then a Supreme Court Judge – had a private passion: the work of James Joyce, and in particular Joyce's own obsession with the law. I like books that drive writers compulsively down strange byways, and I wanted to know more.

I wrote to the Justice cautiously suggesting that we might discuss his work. He responded by inviting me to dinner, which turned into a very convivial evening rounded off by large whiskeys in a pub off Grafton Street. I walked away with about two kilos of typescript – essays, lectures, drafts of articles for obscure legal and historical journals. He began work on a more coherent manuscript and sent me a first draft of the first third of the book, which I edited quite closely and returned to him. He was generously responsive. I looked forward to working with him. Here was a great lawyer reflecting on Ireland's greatest writer, and in particular on Joyce's suspicion of power and the need to be vigilant about the presumption of innocence, the manipulation of evidence and the danger of miscarriages of justice.

That enjoyable relationship was interrupted by the low politics of publishing. I resigned from Faber and Faber in the summer of 2014 and accepted a job with my former colleague Anthony Cheetham, a creative literary entrepreneur, at his new company Head of Zeus. In the late autumn of that year Adrian delivered an almost complete but still rough draft of his manuscript to Faber, where it sat – apparently unread – for the next four months. And that was the situation when the extraordinary mind of this wonderful, contrarian jurist was stopped by sudden death in March 2016.

Ronan Fanning became Adrian's literary executor, and managed at last to extricate the manuscript from my former colleagues, who perhaps understandably didn't know what to do with the book I had commissioned. My serious work on the book began towards the end of 2016. By then, Ronan was himself severely ill, and he passed away in January of the New Year. I sorely missed his counsel as I edited the book, since he not only understood Adrian's intentions but was also an acute critic of style and had a magisterial grasp of the historical hinterland to Joyce's work. Above all, I regretted not being able to discuss the language and tone of the book, and aspects of its structure, with its author.

What you have in your hands is as faithful a version of the book that I think Adrian Hardiman would have wished to publish as I could achieve without him. I recast sentences and deleted passages that I thought were repetitious or less than fully formed, but of course I was unable to submit my work for his approval, and he could not expand or revise his draft text. Because he responded so well to my initial edit of his partial manuscript, I can only hope that he would not have been dismayed by what my colleagues and I have done.

In this task I had the peerless assistance of another editor, Linden Lawson, who is superbly meticulous and caring of writers and manuscripts. She brought this book to its final form. Patrick Geoghegan and Michael Sinnott have been very supportive and were extremely helpful in tracking down missing historical references and citations. Luca Crispi's expertise on Joyce's work and other sources was crucial, and he showed great attention to detail in reviewing the manuscript. And Jean Coyle, for many years Adrian Hardiman's personal secretary, is probably more familiar with every word that Adrian wrote or uttered on the subject of Joyce than any of us.

Above all, my colleagues and I are deeply appreciative of the kindness and determination of Judge Yvonne Murphy, Adrian Hardiman's wife, whose own contributions to the discovery of historical truth in Ireland are so invaluable.

Neil Belton, 2017

Part I

I. Contexts: Joyce, History, Law and England

In Ulysses *I tried to keep close to fact [… to] reality which always triumphs in the end.*

James Joyce, *Conversations with Arthur Power*[1]

*U*lysses is the first great monument of modernist literature in English. Almost immediately on its publication in book form in 1922 it was acknowledged not merely as an immense literary innovation but as a work that transformed the meaning of literature itself. In 1923 T. S. Eliot recognized the paradox that the book which overturned traditional modes of representation and of narrative was nonetheless directly rooted in the mythic origins of Western literature, in Homer's *Odyssey*, which provided the structure of the novel and many of its tropes and references.

Eliot recognized *Ulysses* as 'a way of controlling, of ordering, of giving a shape and a significance to the immense panorama of futility and anarchy which is contemporary history'. He concluded: 'It is, I seriously believe, a step towards making the modern world possible for art.' Eliot perceived that the book was based on 'manipulating a continuous parallel between contemporaneity and antiquity' and said that this had 'the importance of a scientific discovery'.[2]

Over the next ten years of more or less clandestine circulation the book's reputation spread well beyond literary circles. In 1933, the novel and its American publishers were brought before the United States Court of Appeals for the Second Circuit (New York), one of the great courts of the common-law world and equivalent to the English Court of Appeal. In an action improbably entitled *US v One Book called Ulysses*, an attempt had been made to declare the novel obscene, thereby effectively preventing its mass-circulation. But the US Federal District Court (the principal federal trial court, comparable to the High Court in Ireland or England) had acquitted the work in a judgment of striking sophistication. The would-be censors appealed, but without success (see Chapter 8). The author of the appellate judgment, Judge Augustus Hand, quoted Milton in acknowledging the book's revolutionary novelty. It contained, he said: 'Things unattempted yet in prose or rhyme'. Still more strikingly, twenty years later, the great Argentinian writer Jorge Luis Borges described Joyce as being 'less a man of letters than a literature'.[3]

The tributes of Eliot, Hand and Borges are lavish praise for a novel whose entire action takes place in a single day – 16 June 1904 – in the neglected streets of Dublin, the author's native city and the capital of Ireland, an island at the western extremity of Europe and of the then United Kingdom. The book focuses narrowly on the mundane personal and local occurences, the oblique reflections of international events and on the recollections of past incidents that were still current on that day in that remote city.

The city itself was partly assimilated to the metropolitan culture of Great Britain, but discontented with the centuries-old rule of the English in Ireland, and lately torn between parliamentary nationalism in the tradition of Joyce's childhood hero, Charles Stewart Parnell (1846–91), and on the other hand a romantic form of separatism based on the revival of an ancient Gaelic language, culture and civilization. Ireland was also supine in the iron grip of the legally powerless but practically all-powerful Roman Catholic Church. This venerable but grasping institution cared little whether the English imperialists or the Gaelic revivalists reigned in Ireland, so long as she ruled the country in actual fact.

Joyce 'made the modern world possible for art' firstly by embracing that world as found in Ireland *in its entirety*, omitting nothing that was experienced by his characters, nothing even that was *thought* by them. The exposition of their private thoughts in all their disorderly variety is the most obvious literary novelty in *Ulysses*. But those internal reflections are rarely pretentious or mannered, except in the case of the youthful Stephen Dedalus himself, and are always specifically related to the events of 16 June 1904. On the printed page, events and thoughts mingle, just as they do now and always have done in every person's mind. Many academics refuse to acknowledge that the real events evoked by Joyce spark the thoughts and are elucidated by them.

Legal episodes are hardly the only, or even the dominant, events of 16 June 1904, but they are a discrete category and are more amenable to our scrutiny than much of the factual substratum of the novel. In many cases the legal incidents are intrinsically interesting: certainly Joyce found them so. A century later they have the added significance of preserving, incidentally and therefore accurately, many details of life at the beginning of the modernist era, and in the city where its literature in English began, which would otherwise have vanished under the receding wave of time and memory.

Ulysses: characters and action

Ulysses follows two characters, Leopold Bloom and Stephen Dedalus, as they make their odyssey through Dublin from early morning on 16 June 1904, a Thursday, until the pre-dawn hours of the next day. Bloom is a thirty-eight-year-old advertising canvasser who lives with his wife Marion (Molly) in Eccles Street in inner North Dublin. A Christianized Jew, he had been baptized both as an Anglican and later (in order to marry Molly) as a Roman Catholic. He does not much believe in either religion. He is an ordinary, decent, sanguine man of normal attainments and modest prosperity, but is something of an outsider in Dublin society. His wife Molly, née Tweedy, is a soldier's daughter born in Gibraltar. (It is never quite clear if her father was a major or a sergeant-major.) A well-known concert singer in Dublin, Molly is about to go on a concert tour of Ireland organized by her impresario, Hugh 'Blazes' Boylan, with whom she is having an affair. She is expecting an amorous visit from Boylan at 4 p.m. on that day; Bloom knows this, and carries the knowledge in the back of his mind throughout the day, but he cannot, or chooses not to, interfere.

Both Bloom and Molly are deeply if differently affected by the death of their son Rudy, just after his birth eleven years previously. They have a teenage daughter, Milly, whom Bloom thinks was encouraged by her mother to take up employment in Mullingar, sixty miles from Dublin, in order to give Molly space and privacy, and freedom from hurtful comparisons. But Molly thinks Bloom encouraged the girl to move 'on account of me and Boylan'.[4]

Stephen, introduced in the book's first three episodes, is a young arts graduate, back from Paris and without serious occupation. Sensitive, 'literary' and self-obsessed, not quite as clever as he thinks he is, at odds with his family, he has been staying in a Napoleonic-era fort, a disused Martello tower on the coast at Sandycove, eight miles south of Dublin, with two friends. June 16 is his last day of employment in a temporary job as a teacher in Dalkey; he has been paid off and is determined to spend his money on drink and other diversions. Still badly affected, with guilt as well as grief, by the death of his mother the previous year, he is also at loggerheads with his charming, self-regarding, hard-drinking and improvident father. He falls out with his housemates during the day. But he never for a moment doubts his own genius. The father figure, Simon Dedalus, represents Joyce's beloved father John Stanislaus Joyce (1849–1931), an important presence in his life and work.

Bloom and Stephen criss-cross the city all day. Their journeys, first separate and later together, are chronicled in seventeen episodes, each named for a stage in the ten-year odyssey of Homer's Odysseus, latinized as Ulysses. Bloom corresponds to Ulysses, a figure not heroic or godlike but practical, good-hearted and dog-gedly optimistic. Stephen corresponds to Ulysses' son Telemachus, who has not seen his wandering father for years. The pair end up, after midnight, in Bloom's house, occupied by the dozing Molly. In contrast to Ulysses' wife, Penelope, she has not resisted her suitor but has made love with Boylan in the matrimonial bedroom that very afternoon. *Penelope* is the title of Molly's very long and almost unpunctuated stream-of-consciousness soliloquy which ends the book. This eighteenth episode contains, perhaps, an inkling that *her* Ulysses may regain his domestic kingdom.

The two men travel through Dublin several times in the course of the day, walking or in horse-drawn cabs, as do other characters such as the Jesuit Fr John Conmee SJ, representing the Catholic Church, and the English Viceroy or Lord Lieutenant, William Humble, Earl of Dudley and his cavalcade, representing the Crown and State. The action of the novel includes a chaotic breakfast in the Martello tower on the coast (*Telemachus*), a class in a suburban school (*Nestor*), a typically prolonged Dublin funeral (*Hades*), a session of literary political and legal talk in a newspaper office (*Aeolus*), scholarly chat in the National Library (*Scylla and Charybdis*), a session in a pub with some hard-drinking Dublin patriots (*Cyclops*), a boozy nocturnal visit to a maternity hospital (*Oxen of the Sun*), a later visit by much the same personnel to the city's red-light district (*Circe*), and much more. An enormous cast of characters is encountered, historical and fictitious. The style of the book varies enormously, from straightforward narration in several voices to pastiche and parody, fantasy, dreamlike sequences and stream of consciousness, the styles sometimes interwoven. In the course of all this, a dazzling multiplicity of aspects of Dublin life – social, political, religious, commercial, intellectual, cultural, medical and legal – are glimpsed and preserved.

Ulysses is, amongst other things, an odyssey through the collective consciousness of the 'Hibernian Metropolis'.[5] None of the varied aspects of life noticed in the novel, however, is formally and individually explored in a single episode or paragraph with a beginning, middle and end; instead each facet of human affairs crops up incidentally, scattered through the narrative, just as it would in everyday life. A particular reference to any topic may be a few words or a few pages long, direct or indirect, and is often a sort of parenthesis to the main thrust of the action or an oblique, tangential theme in the dialogue. Such specific topics throw light on others which are less readily apprehensible: the *mentalités* of different groups, the formation of public opinion, economic activity, the position of women, the contrasting but congruent forces of British rule and of the Catholic Church, and many others revealed in the daily life of the city Joyce called 'the centre of paralysis'.[6]

Ulysses has been a preoccupation of mine for over twenty years, not merely as a hobby or an interest, but as a benediction. I am irked that the great paradox of the book's contemporary reputation is that it is widely recognized as the supreme masterpiece of modernist literature, yet it is left largely unread, even by those unlikely to ignore any other literary monument of our time.

This is mainly the result of the coincidence of the book's early reception with the rise in the United States, Britain and Ireland of the university English department. This would not in itself have cut *Ulysses* off from the mass of readers it deserves to attract. But the self-conscious obscurantism and the contrived terminology of all too many critics have induced in the reading public the view that Joyce is simply too difficult, too esoteric to be worth reading. This attitude is reminiscent of the despairing view of Anatole France on the publication of the first volume of Proust's *À la recherche du temps perdu*: 'Life is too short and Proust is too long.'[7]

The result of this fencing-off of *Ulysses* has been pointed out by one of the most clear-headed of literary academics, Professor Declan Kiberd:

> The book which set out to restore the dignity of the middle range of human experience against the false heroics of World War I was soon lost to the common reader. [...] A book which set out to celebrate the common man and woman endured the sad fate of never being read by most of them. [...] It was first lost to those readers even as it triumphed in bohemia and then in the academy; but today it is lost also to most students, lecturers and intellectuals. Many of the people who read Joyce now are called 'Joyceans' and appointed as specialists in university departments, most of whose other members would never dream of attempting *Ulysses*. [...] Even before that defeat, however, *Ulysses* was wrenched out of the hands of the common reader. Why? Because of the rise of specialists prepared to devote years to the study of its secret codes – *parallax*, *indeterminacy*, *consciousness-time* being among the buzz words.[8]

This is all too sadly clear and I agree with most of it, save that the terms Kiberd quotes are in the middle range of the jargon cultivated by so many Joycean critics.

Contrary to the impression fostered by such literary theorists,

Joyce's narratives, and especially *Ulysses*, are firmly rooted in mundane, day-to-day fact and in the experiences that make up the lives of ordinary people. He despised the merely theoretical and the fanciful. He mined a lifetime's material from the twenty-two years during which he lived continuously in his native city, and from the exceptionally vibrant legacy of knowledge he acquired from his father of the period just before and just after his birth. He excluded neither the stirrings of radical nationalism which marked that period in Ireland, nor the general contentment of the majority with Ireland's status as part of the old United Kingdom. He was more resentful of the imperialist posturings of the Catholic Church than of those of the mellowing British Empire. No one was more aware than he that he lived at a time of critical change in Irish history, but he saw it as part of a universal process.

My purpose is simply to rescue at least some of the hard facts of which so much of *Ulysses* is composed from the limbo of academic condescension to which certain critics have consigned them. After more than a century, these facts need some contextualization to be understandable.

'It seems history is to blame'

In the very first episode of *Ulysses*, *Telemachus*, Joyce, in his character as Stephen Dedalus, debates some of these issues with Haines, the visiting Englishman who has imposed himself as a guest in the Martello tower at Sandycove, where the protagonists are staying. This snippet of conversation is an interesting sidelight on the mentalities of both Stephen and Haines:

—I am a servant of two masters, Stephen said, an English and an Italian.

—Italian? Haines said.

A crazy queen, old and jealous. Kneel down before me.

—And a third, Stephen said, there is who wants me for odd jobs.

—Italian? Haines said again. What do you mean?

—The imperial British state, Stephen answered, his colour rising, and the holy Roman catholic and apostolic church.

Haines detached from his underlip some fibres of tobacco before he spoke.

—I can quite understand that, he said calmly. An Irishman must think like that, I daresay. We feel in England that we have treated you rather unfairly. It seems history is to blame.[9]

Much later in the book, in the cabman's shelter in *Eumaeus*, the sixteenth episode, a slightly drunken Stephen makes clear his rejection of the third master, who 'wants me for odd jobs'. This is the resurgent nationalist Ireland with its appeal to self-sacrificing patriotism. When Bloom urges Stephen to work hard in the interest of his country, as an act of pure patriotism, young Stephen demurs: 'Count me out, he managed to remark, meaning work.'[10]

After more paternalistic urgings on the part of Bloom, Stephen turns on him:

—You suspect, Stephen retorted with a sort of half laugh, that I may be important because I belong to the *faubourg Saint Patrice* called Ireland for short.

—I would go a step farther, Mr Bloom insinuated.

—But I suspect, Stephen interrupted, that Ireland must be important because it belongs to me.[11]

Mr Bloom blusters a little, pretending not to have heard the last remark. Then:

Stephen, patently crosstempered, repeated and shoved aside his mug of coffee or whatever you like to call it none too politely, adding:

—We can't change the country. Let us change the subject.[12]

Stephen is at odds with the three major influences in the Irish society of his time, 'the imperial British state', 'the holy Roman catholic and apostolic church' and the rising force of Gaelic and nationalist Ireland – 'Irish Ireland', as the contemporary ultra-nationalist journalist and controversialist D. P. Moran called it. The pronouncements Stephen makes in *Eumaeus* are of course immensely arrogant. Joyce was never much of an enthusiast for dogmas, establishments or ideologies: 'I fear those big words, [...] which make us so unhappy',[13] Stephen says in *Nestor*, but from a very early age Joyce recognized his own genius and never doubted it even in the years of poverty and literary rejection. Stephen is only twenty-two years old when he has the arrogance to speak as he does, half drunk, in a cabman's shelter on the Dublin Quays after he has been roughed up by two British soldiers, themselves the worse for drink, and rescued by a kindly Dublin Jew passing the time until he is sure that his Irish wife has finished entertaining her lover in the matrimonial home.

To illustrate the grounded, individualist nature of Joyce's procedures I intend to explore a theme that is more prominent than is
often realized in his work: the numerous law cases to which he refers.
In October 1899 James Joyce attended a murder trial in Dublin's
Green Street Criminal Court. It was the trial of Samuel Childs, a
sixty-one-year-old accountant, for the murder of his seventy-six-
year-old bachelor brother, a prosperous financier and company
director.[14] (The case is discussed in detail in Chapter 4.) More than
two decades later the case featured prominently in *Ulysses*. By then,
it was interwoven with thirty-one other legal cases, civil as well as
criminal, which Joyce had come across in the interval, the great bulk
of them from the Ireland and Britain of his youth.[15]

Other cases between 1900 and 1925 deepened and particularized
this preoccupation, many instances of which occur in his journalism
and in *Ulysses* and *Finnegans Wake*. They are based on actual
facts, drawn from life in the Dublin, Mayo, Liverpool, London or
Staffordshire of his time, and preserved accurately if randomly in
court reports. Joyce, as we shall see, was profoundly suspicious
of society's enforcers, and the cases he cited illustrate the basis of
this suspicion. The Irish cases, because Ireland was a politically
disturbed country for much of Joyce's youth, reflect the politics of
the time. But that is no more inaccessible to the interested reader
than is the need to grasp something of Dickens's London, Flaubert's
Paris, James's New York, Hardy's Wessex or Trollope's Barchester.

Though there is an abundance of criminal and other litigation
in *Ulysses*, it is emphatically not a crime novel in even the broadest
sense. The book, indeed, has no single theme other than the events,
conversations and recollections of one day in Dublin. The events
and images of that day are seen through the eyes of those imagined

to be living at that time and place, some fictional, some real and some, perhaps most, an amalgam of the two. Criminal and other litigation crops up in the novel principally as a topic of conversation between those people or as a theme in their private thoughts and is seen through the eyes of these characters.

The religious divide

An aspect of the reality to which Joyce refers was that Ireland in 1904 was a society very plainly divided along religious lines. In contemporary England and America as well, religious divisions were then much more marked than they have since become. But in Ireland, for historical reasons based on the wholesale land confiscations and plantations of the seventeenth century, religious affiliation overlapped very closely, but not quite precisely, with political affiliation. In the northern part of Ireland, especially in the six counties that later became the state of Northern Ireland, these divisions were especially acute because of the post-plantation demography, which created a local Protestant majority but never a particularly secure one. In such circumstances sectarianism was rife and not infrequently burst out in violence.

In the rest of the country, the Catholics were in so substantial a majority that the position was, comparatively, less acute. At the turn of the twentieth century Protestants made up perhaps 20 per cent of the population of Dublin; there were 237,645 Catholics and 52,966 other denominations, including 2,048 Jews.[16] While this included a significant Protestant working class, in general the Protestants were the most prosperous group in the community and dominated large business enterprises and the lucrative professions. By 1904, thanks in part to the resolute anti-sectarian policies of Gladstone's Liberal governments of the late nineteenth century, Catholics had begun to make inroads into the Bar, the medical profession and the commissioned ranks of the army and police, but the process was at an early stage. There were Catholic businessmen, some conspicuously successful, such as William Martin Murphy, proprietor of the *Irish Independent* and of much of the Dublin tram system, but they were in a distinct minority.

Against that background the fact that, in the Childs case, both the murdered man and the alleged murderer were Protestants was a highly unusual circumstance and one which added enormously to the impact of the case in its day. It is important to recognize that the Dublin Protestants, like the Irish Protestants generally, tended to favour the Union with Britain in the form it then took. They were a tightly knit group whose leading members were educated in a small number of schools such as the High School in Dublin, Kilkenny College, the Royal School in Enniskillen and frequently at English public schools. Those who went to university almost without exception attended Trinity College, Dublin. There were internal tensions within the group, such as that between the landed interest on the one hand and the business and professional classes on the other. The latter were rising and the former declining by the end of the nineteenth century.

It is equally important to realize that these religious divisions, although very pervasive, were not absolutely rigid. Since the end of the eighteenth century there had been a strong tradition of Protestant nationalism exemplified above all in tragic figures such as Wolfe Tone, Lord Edmund Fitzgerald and Robert Emmet. As the century wore on, the Protestants became increasingly reconciled to the Union but still produced figures such as Thomas Davis and, in Joyce's own youth, Charles Stewart Parnell, who despite their religion and economic background were widely accepted as leaders of the nationalist movement. Equally, there were Catholics such as Under-Secretary Thomas Burke, assassinated in 1882, Mr Justice William Kenny, the presiding judge at the Childs trial, and many others whose Catholicism was no obstacle to a commitment to Unionism. This group was quite accepted in the upper reaches of society, welcomed into its clubs and cultural organizations, but amongst their own co-religionists they attracted the derisive epithet 'Castle Catholics'.

The religious divisions were so well established in Joyce's day as scarcely to require comment from him. They are reflected in his works, for example in his great short story 'The Dead', where the main protagonist, Gabriel Conroy, a journalist who sees no contradiction in an Irish Catholic writing for the English press, is sternly rebuked by a nationalistic woman at a dinner party who accuses him of treachery.[17]

This sectarian aspect of Irish life at the turn of the nineteenth and twentieth centuries is not unduly emphasized by Joyce, though it is not concealed either. It is a characteristic of the society that is impossible to ignore. It goes to make up the tapestry of Dublin life as Joyce weaves it, confronting the reader with an enormous variety of circumstances, some now forgotten, relating to life in Dublin on 16 June 1904.

The law in *Ulysses*

Law is one part of this extraordinary factual matrix. Not 'Law' in the abstract, but the law of individual cases, the law as applied to the dramas and mysteries of human life, the law as laid down, practised and enforced in the society into which Joyce was born towards the end of Queen Victoria's reign. The thirty-two cases that feature in *Ulysses* involve eleven named judges and perhaps a further eight who are not specifically named, thirteen barristers, eleven named solicitors and more who remain anonymous. These practitioners are generally hard-headed, successful and prosperous. There are also two taxing masters, a cost accountant, a Master in Chancery, a briefless and impoverished barrister, a struck-off solicitor begging in the streets, statutes, law reports, disputed life policies, bills of exchange, marine collisions, divorces, murders, swindles, libels, orders of garnishee, an instalment order, an unlawful lottery and the Master of the Rolls's chef.

Joyce's aspirations to universality meant that, though *causes célèbres* in the form of treason, murder and political assassination receive due prominence in his work, he also concedes the significance of much smaller cases in the recorder's court or the police court, of charges, like being drunk and disorderly, trivial in themselves, but 'which simply spelt ruin for a chap when it got bruited about'.[18] He was intrigued by the odd case of a Poor Law authority which exceeded 'their ration of 15 gallons per day per pauper' and was prosecuted by the City Council.[19] Joyce's experience of such cases made him sceptical about the motives and practices of society's enforcers, uniformed or otherwise, and suspicious of the mobilized *Schadenfreude* of public opinion whipped up in what was then called the 'Yellow Press', the tabloids of their day. He was almost morbidly sensitive to the risks of miscarriage of justice.

As early as September 1903, when Joyce was twenty-one, he published in the Dublin *Daily Express* a review of a book about the 'Popish Plot' which occurred during the reign of Charles II and which involved the murder of a magistrate, Sir Edmund Godfrey. Two men, Greene and Berry, were hanged for this crime, 'of which posterity (unanimous in this one thing at least) has acquitted them'.[20] Reflecting on this, Joyce references with approval the *dictum* of the French monk and palaeographer Jean Mabillon (1632–1707), in which he urged historians *'Donner pour certain ce qui est certain, pour faux ce qui est faux, pour douteux ce qui est douteux.'*[21] The value of the last part, in particular, of this counsel is well illustrated by many of the cases glanced at so suggestively by Joyce.

These attitudes were not inbred in Joyce and neither did they arise from abstract reasoning on his part. They were rooted in his concrete experiences as a very young man and in his heritage of historical memory. This sense of the importance of doubt forms a major theme in *Ulysses* and also in *Finnegans Wake*. Its treatment in the novels is suggestive of Joyce's literary technique generally, especially of his unique intermingling of fact and fiction, thoughts and events.

Though *Ulysses* is rarely regarded as a murder story, or even a story that has murders in it, there are in fact plenty of them, and many other cases too.[22] Unlike many writers, Joyce was interested in civil as well as criminal law. The eighteen civil cases mentioned in the book include an action for breach of promise of marriage, a libel action, an action to enforce payment on a policy of life insurance and actions for debt in various forms. He seems to have been fascinated by the idea that one could insure against the one inevitable event, death, and even mortgage the insurance policy for ready cash. Many of the cases give the texture of Dublin life of the time; but others seem to illustrate one or other of Joyce's philosophical concerns:

how can one ever *know* the precise detailed truth of past events? Are those condemned by the law invariably the real villains?

The contemporary criminal matters to which Joyce made reference include, as well as the Childs case of 1899, the Henry Flower trial of 1900; the controversial English affair of Mrs Florence Maybrick (this trial occurred in 1889 but was kept in the public eye by the constant campaigns to have Mrs Maybrick's innocence recognized, and by her eventual release from prison in early 1904); a second English case, that of George Edalji, which ran from 1903 to 1907 (another *cause célèbre* resolved in the end by an official King's Pardon and one which seriously undermined confidence in the police and the criminal law system); the later cases of *R* v *Frederick Seddon* in 1912 and (in *Finnegans Wake*) the 1922 case of Bywaters and Thompson (see p. 30); and the Dublin murder of the prostitute Honor Bright, allegedly by a doctor and a superintendent of police, in 1925. These cases are all 'Crime Ordinary', in the Irish Police language of the day. Joyce treats somewhat differently such great political set-pieces as the trials of the Invincibles, the murderers of Lord Frederick Cavendish and Under-Secretary Burke (1882), the Parnell Commission of 1888 and the O'Shea divorce trial of 1890.

British Ireland

The fact that English and Irish cases mingle so easily in Joyce's treatment of famous crimes underlines an important aspect of the writer's cultural hinterland. Joyce was born in February 1882 and *Ulysses* was published in book form in February 1922. During the whole of that period Ireland was part of the old United Kingdom of Great Britain and Ireland, established by the notorious Act of Union of 1800. Ireland's government was appointed from London and it had no independent parliament or representative structures higher than a county council. Its culture, and particularly its popular culture, was assimilated, though by no means totally, to that of Britain. The law of Ireland was English common law, together with such statutes as the Westminster Parliament applied to the United Kingdom including Ireland (and that included the great majority of statutes), and others which that parliament applied to Ireland alone. Up to 1922, when Joyce or his Irish contemporaries thought of 'the law' they thought of British common law and Westminster statute law. Famous British murders like that ascribed to Mrs Maybrick of Liverpool were regarded as domestic cases.

Joyce, however, had a nuanced attitude to England. He leaped over the neighbouring island, both physically and intellectually. As a seven-year-old schoolboy at Clongowes Wood College, Stephen gives his address as:

Stephen Dedalus

Class of Elements

Clongowes Wood College

Sallins

County Kildare

Ireland

Europe

The World

The Universe[23]

Here, he simply ignores the United Kingdom of which Ireland was a part. Joyce never lived in England for any considerable period until he needed to establish residency for his very belated civil marriage ceremony to Nora Barnacle in 1931. But his reasons for eschewing England are themselves a sort of back-handed compliment. He said that he could never have become 'part of English life, or even have worked there, for somehow I would have felt that in that atmosphere of politics, power, and money, writing was not sufficiently important'. Speaking of the effect of English rule in Ireland in the days of his youth, he said: 'In the Dublin of my day there was a kind of desperate freedom which comes from a lack of responsibility, for the English were in governance then, so everyone said what he liked.'[24]

A similar paradox is reflected in the fact that Joyce, though sympathetic to Italian nationalism, preferred the Trieste which was ruled by the Austro-Hungarian Empire, where he lived for a decade from 1905, to the same city under its new Italian masters after the First World War. There was more individual freedom under the empire, he thought.

Joyce travelled on a British passport all his life even when he could have had an Irish one after 1922, and even at times (as when fleeing France in 1940) when a neutral passport might have suited his purposes. He declined suggestions that he visit Ireland in the 1930s, when his reputation was firmly established, claiming to fear physical assaults, as Parnell was assaulted by ultra-Catholics throwing quicklime in his face.

But Joyce was also acutely conscious of the more assertive, almost self-caricaturing aspect of the British nation's ratifying culture, as when he has the tipsy medical students in *Oxen of the Sun* march

off to 'annex liquor stores' while chanting the 'British beatitudes':
'Beer, beef, business, bibles, bulldogs, battleships, buggery and
bishops.'[25] In contrast, the *Cyclops* episode contains a similar, but
much more prolonged, send-up of Irish nationalism. In the end,
as Seamus Deane has said: '[Joyce] was no more impressed by the
Irish nationalist argument against colonialism than he was by
the colonialist argument itself.'[26]

The Ireland of Joyce's youth was, politically, a deeply discontented nation. Much of that discontent found a focus in Irish
political trials in which, it seemed to those of a nationalist bent,
English law was stretched and perverted, to an extent that would
not have been tolerated in England, to obtain convictions of those
regarded by the Irish as patriots; or if not patriots, at least victims.
The names of these victims entered Irish historical consciousness,
and Joyce accurately reflected them in his works. A wrongful or a
merely cruel hanging of fifty or a hundred years before was still the
stuff of ballads in Ireland. There were specific reasons for that. 'It
seems history is to blame', as Haines remarked to Stephen Dedalus.

William Pitt the Younger, the British Prime Minister responsible
for the 1800 Act of Union between Britain and Ireland, quite
genuinely saw the measure, which ended the old independent
Irish Parliament, as a new beginning in Anglo-Irish relations. He
believed that it was politically impossible to emancipate the Irish
Catholics (that is, free them from their legal disabilities, including
their exclusion from Parliament and government, from the judiciary
and from holding commissioned rank in the armed forces) in a
separate Irish kingdom. This was because, once emancipated,
the Catholics would dominate an Irish Parliament and would be
likely to expropriate the pro-British Protestant landowners as their

own Catholic forebears had been expropriated in the seventeenth century. But he believed that Catholic Emancipation *would* be possible in a United Kingdom of Great Britain (England, Wales and Scotland) and Ireland because the Catholics would be a small minority in the larger state. He intended to introduce Emancipation with the Act of Union. However, the episodically mad King George III (r.1760–1820) refused to countenance Emancipation, claiming that it would violate his coronation oath. Pitt resigned shortly after the abolition of the Irish Parliament.

The consequences of this were far-reaching. Emancipation was eventually conceded in 1829 after a titanic battle led by the first modern Irish democratic leader of significance, Daniel O'Connell. Though many of O'Connell's supporters were Protestants, the campaign, inevitably, took on a sectarian complexion, which cast long shadows forward. The prominence of priests in the organization of the campaign was the foundation of that clerical influence that dogged Irish politics until very recent times. Both of these developments could have been avoided by a timely concession of Emancipation in 1801.

In the aftermath of O'Connell's necessary but divisive campaign, the great famine of the late 1840s and the death or emigration of vast numbers of Irish people inculcated a sense of bitter, fatalistic grievance which also had very long-term consequences.[27]

By the early 1880s these feelings found political expression in a large, disciplined Home Rule Party. The greatest leader of this party was Charles Stewart Parnell, and under his influence the English Liberal Prime Minister William Ewart Gladstone introduced two Home Rule Bills. But Parnell himself was brought down, ironically, by a combination of English nonconformist morality and Irish

Catholic clerical power. These oddly allied forces took advantage of Parnell's decade-long affair with Mrs Katherine O'Shea to do so. Joyce reproached the Irish people: 'they did not throw him to the English wolves: they tore him apart themselves'.[28] Joyce as a small boy, under his father's influence, took a huge and emotive interest in Irish politics. At nine he wrote a poem, now lost, on the fall of Parnell in 1890 – the event preoccupied him all his life, and rendered him strongly anti-clerical.

The destruction of Parnell was accomplished by his oddly assorted enemies in 1891. The event split the Joyce family and many other families in Ireland. The impassioned row at the Christmas dinner scene in *A Portrait of the Artist as a Young Man* perfectly catches the poisonous atmosphere it engendered, the naked, sectarian triumphalism of the victorious Catholics and the bitter anti-clericalism of the routed Parnellites. The scene is set in the Joyce family home on the esplanade in the seaside town of Bray, a railway suburb of Dublin. The men in the group, led by Joyce's father, complain resentfully of the unconcealed anti-Parnellite campaign which had been conducted by the Catholic Church, but they are answered, in increasingly hysterical terms, by 'Dante', Mrs Riordan, a sort of great-aunt figure to the Joyce children (though not actually related) who espouses the position of the priests:

—It is religion, Dante said. They're doing their duty in warning the people.
—We go to the house of God, Mr Casey said, in all humility to pray to our Maker and not to hear election addresses.
—It is religion, Dante said again. They are right. They must direct their flocks.

—And preach politics from the altar, is it? asked Mr Dedalus.

—Certainly, said Dante. It is a question of public morality. A priest would not be a priest if he did not tell his flock what is right and what is wrong.[29]

The conversation is then discountenanced by Mrs Dedalus on the basis that there is a child present, but it soon flares up again:

—O, he'll remember all this when he grows up, said Dante hotly—the language he heard against God and religion and priests in his own home.

—Let him remember too, cried Mr Casey to her across the table, the language with which the priests and the priests' pawns broke Parnell's heart and hounded him into his grave. Let him remember that when he grows up.

—Sons of bitches! cried Mr Dedalus. When he was down they turned on him to betray him and rend him like rats in a sewer. Lowlived dogs! And they look it! By Christ, they look it!

—They behaved rightly, cried Dante. They obeyed their bishops and their priests. Honour to them![30]

Stephen's mother intervenes again and there is peace for a few minutes. The row flares up a third time at the mention of Cardinal Cullen, a former Archbishop of Dublin:

Dante bent across the table and cried to Mr Casey:

—Right! Right! They were always right! God and morality and religion come first. [...]

—God and religion before everything! Dante cried. God and religion before the world!

Mr Casey raised his clenched fist and brought it down on the table with a crash.

—Very well then he shouted hoarsely, if it comes to that, no God for Ireland!

—Blasphemer! Devil! screamed Dante starting to her feet and almost spitting in his face. […]

At the door Dante turned round violently and shouted down the room, her cheeks flushed and quivering with rage:

—Devil out of hell! We won! We crushed him to death! Fiend![31]

This poisonous atmosphere continued at least until the year 1900, when the Irish Parliamentary Party was nominally reunited under Parnellite leadership. But no one who participated in the 'split' of 1890–91 ever forgot it and Joyce himself addressed it in all of his novels. The well-known, brilliant but astonishingly bitter Irish barrister and politician Tim Healy was the most vocal leader of the anti-Parnellite faction. He popularized the appellation 'Kitty' O'Shea for Parnell's lover; at the time, the shorter version of the name carried a suggestion of prostitution. Healy was a member of the British Parliament from the early 1880s until 1918 and when the Irish Free State came into being he was, by agreement between the new government and Lloyd George, created Governor General of Ireland: in other words, the King's representative. This merely confirmed Joyce's jaundiced view of the new State, whose capital he dubbed 'heliopolis' in *Finnegans Wake*. '*Et cur Heli*', he makes a character remark in *Finnegans Wake*.[32] '*Cur*' means 'why', but there is another implication as well.[33]

Election after election in the late nineteenth and early twentieth centuries demonstrated the desire of the great majority of the Irish population for Home Rule. But that wish was constantly frustrated by the Unionist bastions of the House of Lords and the Tory Party, together with the large section of English liberal opinion which formed the Liberal Unionist Party after the defeat of the First Home Rule Bill of 1886. The long-term result of this blockage was the hollowing-out of Irish commitment to an apparently futile parliamentary politics and the early stirrings of revolutionary nationalism, which was making itself felt in 1904. When the armed Ulster Unionists excluded their province from the Home Rule eventually granted (but deferred) in 1914, the lesson for nationalists seemed obvious.

A by-product of this painfully long, slow process was that past events had a personal, social and political resonance in Ireland which time would have eroded anywhere else. The execution in 1803 of the impossibly romantic revolutionary Robert Emmet features surprisingly often in conversations and in the protagonists' thoughts in Joyce's version of June 1904. Emmet's famous speech from the dock resonates in *Ulysses* a hundred years and more after it was delivered. (See Chapter 6.)

Equally, the Maamtrasna murders of 1882, which led to the execution of a peasant called Myles Joyce, universally believed (and now proven) to have been innocent, is a significant theme in *Finnegans Wake*. (See pp. 49–59.)

The historical hinterland, then, forms a larger part of the cultural awareness of the Dubliners of 1904 than it would have done for similar people in most European or American cities at that time. Moreover, because so many of the Irish historical protagonists died on the scaffold, or were imprisoned or transported for long periods, the Irish attitude to the law was generally sceptical, even when individual practitioners were admired.

Very strikingly, the dubious nature of many of the convictions of Irish convicts, like Myles Joyce, tended to undermine faith in the process of the law in criminal trials, even when it was impartially applied. When Joyce saw a similarly flawed process played out in England, in a case with no Irish connection, it raised epistemological concerns for him that loom so large in his writing. The English case was the so-called 'Great Wyrley Outrage', where a half-Indian solicitor, George Edalji, son of a vicar, was jailed for seven years for cattle-maiming, on the basis of flawed evidence and a huge fund of prejudice (see pp. 65–71). This led Joyce to a firm conviction of the moral necessity of doubt.

In this sense, the seventeen-year-old Joyce's attendance at the Childs murder trial in September 1899 marked the beginning of a lifelong preoccupation with guilt, innocence, proof, framings and officials who were 'unscrupulous in the service of the Crown'.[34]

Over the next few years the young James Joyce was exposed to several other cases, English as well as Irish, which strengthened these impressions. Many people, the man in the street as well as officials, seemed all too willing to jump to conclusions, to despise doubt, even reasonable doubt, as weakness, and to work on the basis that there could be no smoke without fire. These issues became major themes in his writing. His legal concerns are in part an oblique but persistent assertion of the need for philosophical and judicial doubt as a proper, moral and humane reaction to the inadequacy of evidence. Joyce's epistemological concern was centred on how the law resolved the uncertainties of a case.

Although these legal preoccupations are a significant theme in

Ulysses (and offer an illuminating approach to the understanding of Joyce's literary technique), they are little explored by critics. This is mainly because, for reasons devastatingly exposed by Declan Kiberd, too many of these critics feel a professional need to obfuscate what Joyce has written, and for the promotion of arcane theory in a vocabulary still more arcane, and (above all) are dedicated to the sedulous avoidance of hard fact.

Joyce was never totally literal-minded, still less pedantic, about facts and tended, in the novels, to deploy them sparingly. But he recognized that they represent 'reality which always triumphs in the end'[35] so that, especially in *Ulysses*, they governed the recorded events of the day and entered the thoughts of his protagonists.

Localism and hard fact

Every year thousands of people determine to 'tackle' Joyce's *Ulysses*. If such an enthusiast goes to one of the large multiple booksellers he or she will immediately confront the problem of categories. He or she is unlikely to seek *Ulysses* under the banner of 'popular fiction', for that would be an obvious misdescription, and still less under 'crime fiction' or 'true crime', which, though still a distortion, would be less inaccurate. The usual euphemistic antithesis of 'popular' fiction, 'literary fiction', may seem more promising. But it too is a poor fit – Joyce was the least 'literary' of writers.

'Fiction', at least as it was understood in 1922, is a dubious characterization of a book in which a vast amount is culled from history, memory, anecdote, ballad, newspapers, directories, gazetteers, maps and charts, law reports, bus schedules, stories from the author's rumbustious old father and the local topographical research he imposed from afar on his devoted aunt, information from visiting friends and from more recent exiles. Joyce never left Dublin in his mind, though he emigrated in 1904. Thirty years later, as Seamus Heaney writes: 'Blinding in Paris, for his party-piece / Joyce named the shops along O'Connell Street'.[36]

The role of Joyce's father, John Stanislaus Joyce, is central here: according to his son he provided thousands of stories and hundreds of characters for *Ulysses*. For twenty ruinous years he had lived as high as he could off the property his own father had left him. He was involved without noticeable profit in various commercial ventures and was at one time locally prominent in nationalist politics. This led to his appointment to a privileged and congenial 'outdoor' position in the Dublin Corporation Rates Office. But he was made redundant in 1892. He never worked seriously again. During the four decades of almost total idleness that preceded his death in December 1931, he witnessed without obvious upset his family's descent into poverty while vaingloriously recalling the days of his youth and *quondam* prominence. He never thought of himself as a poor man, but as a rich man who had suffered reverses. Many of Joyce's themes and preoccupations are rooted in his father's time, and the time of his own childhood and youth. Alone in the Joyce family, John Stanislaus was vocally proud of his eldest son. Joyce in turn loved him fiercely and was greatly upset by the old man's death. 'I hear my father talking to me. I wonder where he is,' he told a Parisian friend sadly, some months later.[37]

Thirty years after Joyce's legal preoccupations began with the Childs case, they continued to be manifest in his 'Work in Progress', which evolved into *Finnegans Wake*.

Finnegans Wake embraces, as a major theme, the question of what crime, if any, can be laid by his enemies at the door of its main protagonist, HCE, a crime that has been committed by him (so rumour alleges) in the Phoenix Park; there is the question, too, of what evidence, real or contrived, can make the charge stick. It also contains, as an archetype of the trials and framings of the violent West of Ireland of Joyce's childhood years, the trial of Festy King ('of a family long and honourably associated with the tar and feather industries')[38] on an 'incompatibly framed indictment',[39] and several asides, with varying degrees of obliquity, on the false accusations against Captain Dreyfus,[40] and the 1925 Dublin murder of Honor Bright.[41] There is also the case of Bywaters and Thompson, an English case of the 1920s which preoccupied Joyce for a long while, in which a respectable married woman had induced her younger lover to dispose of her husband, who had become surplus to her requirements. Both were hanged.[42] That other married woman no longer attracted to her husband, Mrs Florence Maybrick of Liverpool, escaped hanging by her reprieve in 1889 and went on to earn her place in *Ulysses*, and to help break down the resistance of English jurists to the innovation of a Court of Criminal Appeal in 1907.[43]

These cases came to have a very significant role in Joyce's literary practice and in his thinking. They led him to evolve an elaborate sense of the need not to jump to conclusions and of the necessity of philosophical and judicial doubt. They led him to reflect deeply on epistemology, on how one can know the truth of any past event. But he never carried doubt so far as to doubt the existence of the originating event, merely the (often self-interested) narratives and versions of it.

Joyce's sense of the moral necessity of doubt arose from personal experiences between his eighteenth and his twenty-sixth years.

The Childs trial, as we have seen, was the earliest of the four criminal trials that made an impression on Joyce, three in Ireland and one in England in the years between 1899 and 1904. He was also affected by a civil action tried in Ireland in 1904, and by his own arrest and brief detention in Trieste, then part of Austro-Hungary, in 1905.[44] These events left him with a sense of personal vulnerability, of the fallibility of human reasoning, most especially in a political or forensic context where passion, prejudice and the felt political need to find *someone* to blame for outrageous crimes risk grotesque miscarriages. Once Joyce was sensitized to these possibilities, he saw examples of them everywhere and alluded to them in all of his works. And indeed, examples were not wanting.

Joyce's legal preoccupations were facilitated by his connections, through his father, with the lawyers who were so prominent in Irish constitutional nationalism. The best known of these was John Stanislaus, Joyce's great friend Timothy Harrington, barrister and MP, who wrote the book which established Myles Joyce's innocence and who was Constable Henry Flower's successful defence counsel. Joyce was deeply impressed by the intellectual, oratorical and forensic abilities of Harrington and of such notables, who became characters in *Ulysses*, as Lord Justice Gerald Fitzgibbon,[45] Timothy Michael Healy, QC, MP,[46] John F. Taylor, QC and Seymour Bushe, QC,[47] while not at all empathizing with their politics.

Roads not taken

When the young Joyce emerged as a prominent speaker in the Royal University's Literary and Historical Society, essentially a debating society, his father urged him repeatedly and very seriously to become a barrister. John Stanislaus Joyce was impressed by the prosperity, fine houses and lavish lifestyle enjoyed by the leading practitioners who patronized Dublin's clubs and private societies. The blandishments his father held out to him about the life of a successful Dublin professional man at the end of the nineteenth century are mentioned throughout *Ulysses*: the enormous wealth of the Lord Chancellor of Ireland is mentioned in *Scylla and Charybdis*;[48] in *Lestrygonians* Bloom thinks of the feast prepared by the Master of the Rolls's chef at his house in Merrion Square as well as the convivial luncheon of Sir Frederick Falkiner, Recorder of Dublin.[49]

Joyce preferred to follow his father's example, rather than his advice, by enrolling as a medical student but also by dropping out. The two professions remained roads not taken, in which he maintained a lifelong interest, however. The knowledge of legal and medical technicalities occasionally apparent in the novels is indicative of these interests.

Two other features of Joyce's forensic preoccupations deserve mention. He was keenly conscious of the nature of a trial as a contest between rival narratives, and of how much depended on the way in which those competing narratives were expressed. This was the skill of the advocates. Credit for the acquittal of Samuel Childs is several times accorded to his leading counsel, Seymour Bushe; in Joyce's *schema* for *Ulysses*, 'Eloquence' is the art illustrated in the *Aeolus* episode.[50] There, the men in the newspaper office compare tales of great orators and quote from their speeches. With 'his blood wooed by grace of language and gesture', listening to one such, Stephen thinks: 'Could you try your hand at it yourself?'[51] This is reflective of Joyce's own flirtation with the idea of a legal or political career, which he seems to have considered quite seriously, though he eventually rejected his father's advice.

Shards in wild earth

The obscure cases, such as those of Childs, Harvey, Flower and others, rescued from utter oblivion only because of their use in *Ulysses*, also operate like time capsules convincingly (because randomly) preserving the texture of a time that is gone, that of Joyce's youth. Mr Bloom is uncommon amongst the characters in *Ulysses* in doing any work at all on 16 June 1904. The city's idlers, *flâneurs*, a numerous class in the Dublin of that time, greet the pomp and circumstance of the viceregal cavalcade with indifference but without hostility.[52] The Jew Leopold Bloom can live and work in Dublin and achieve modest prosperity, but his standing as an outsider is made all too clear to him many times during the day.[53] The novel thus recalls many aspects of life beyond the reach of the conventional histories of the time, and evokes the *mentalité* of different groups – which are hard for the conventional historian to access.

Joyce did not make the mistake of considering that his own notably liberal views on crime and punishment were replicated in society as a whole or in the characters in *Ulysses*. Leopold Bloom, as we shall see, takes a strongly liberal view of such things. He notes that the man in the street is always calling for more severe sentences but thinks that 'if the man in the street chanced to be in the dock himself penal servitude with or without the option of a fine would be a very *rara avis* altogether'.[54] His wife, Molly, on the other hand, makes it perfectly clear that she is a strong proponent of both hanging and flogging, but on the strict understanding that neither of them is applied to women. Thinking of a notorious case, she reflects: 'they ought to be all shot or the cat of nine tails a big brute like that that would attack a poor woman to murder her in her bed Id cut them off him so I would'.[55]

But one of the cases that she thinks of in her long soliloquy in the final episode of *Ulysses*, *Penelope*, is that of Mrs Maybrick. This lady was an American married to a Liverpool cotton broker who had fallen on hard times. In 1889 she was convicted of poisoning him. The evidence against her was extremely thin and she was reprieved from hanging, to serve penal servitude for life. She was eventually released in 1904, a few months before the first Bloomsday. Molly Bloom, however, has no doubt whatever about the guilt of Mrs Maybrick but is strangely forgiving about what she was alleged to have done. (See pp. 87–8.) This book takes Joyce at his word: in *Ulysses*, despite verbal, literary and structural innovation, he stuck close to fact.

Though Joyce took a detailed interest in the events of the day on which the book is set, he knew that, just as an individual cannot be understood without some sense of their personal history, the Dublin of that day cannot be understood without a sense of its past, its politics, its controversies, divisions and scandals. But these are rendered in the novel not (necessarily) as they appeared to the citizens of 16 June 1904, as they might have spoken of them on that day, in their homes, offices, public houses and newspapers, on the streets, on public platforms and in the churches.

Joyce's core facts are mostly local and directly contemporary with the action of his fictions. But that action has a surprisingly wide and deep hinterland, for reasons I have mentioned in this chapter.

They range from the rebellion of 'Silken Thomas' in the 1530s to contemporary foreign events such as the assassination of General Count Bobrikov, the Tsar's Governor of Finland, and the sinking of the *General Slocum* in New York Harbour, both of which happened in June 1904.

Similarly, the legal cases range from those of purely local interest to those of enormous political significance, such as the 1882 assassination of Lord Frederick Cavendish and Under-Secretary Thomas Burke (see pp. 212–20). A third category is that of non-political crimes which for some reason became notorious either in Ireland or in the English-speaking world more generally. Mrs Florence Maybrick's case is one of these, as is that of Frederick Seddon, accused of poisoning his lodger in 1912 and anachronistic-ally mentioned in *Ulysses*; and so is the sad case of Honor Bright. These cases caught Joyce's imagination for a number of reasons – their striking facts, the genuine uncertainty of guilt or innocence, their demonstration of the ever-present risk of miscarriages of justice, or simply their dramatic significance in the minds of Joyce's characters, as Mrs Maybrick resonates with Molly Bloom.

The political, legal and historical themes just discussed are an important part of the context of *Ulysses*. But however controversial they were, the novel never takes sides. Strong opinions are expressed by characters but never endorsed by the author. Usually, the strongest opinions – like Molly Bloom's empire loyalism and deep respect for the British Army and Navy – are grounded in their own background and self-image.

Their views are assumed by other characters in the novel to be those appropriate to their background, and the reader is often told of these obliquely. The topic of Molly Bloom comes up in *Sirens* as the gentlemen gather for an informal concert in the Ormond Hotel. With her mixed background and foreign upbringing, she is a somewhat exotic figure, leading some of the men to question whether she is Irish at all.

The political views of a number of the characters, and the way in which Joyce treats them, are illustrated in the following paragraphs. In reported conversation, and still more in the stream-of-consciousness sequences, spoken words and thoughts have to be identified by the reader and distinguished from descriptions of the events which accompany them, such as the lighting of a cigar in the first extract given.

Molly is proud to be a 'daughter of the regiment', proud of her father's status as an officer and a gentleman and uneasy at the resentment she knows these aspects of her persona arouse in women more inclined to an Irish nationalist point of view. Molly is recognized in this way in her Dublin circle.

—What's this her name was? A buxom lassy. Marion…?
—Tweedy.
—Yes. Is she alive?
—And kicking.
—She was a daughter of…
—Daughter of the regiment.
—Yes, begad. I remember the old drummajor.
　　Mr Dedalus struck, whizzed, lit, puffed savoury puff after
—Irish? I don't know, faith. Is she, Simon?
　　Puff after stiff, a puff, strong, savoury, crackling.
—Buccinator muscle is… What?… Bit rusty… O, she is…
My Irish Molly, O.

He puffed a pungent plumy blast.

—From the rock of Gibraltar... all the way.[56]

But Molly suspects her career as a concert singer in Dublin suffers from her Unionist and imperialist attitudes. In her long, silent soliloquy in *Penelope* she reflects:

> the last concert I sang at where its over a year ago when was it St Teresas hall Clarendon St little chits of missies they have now singing Kathleen Kearney and her like on account of father being in the army and my singing the absentminded beggar and wearing a brooch for Lord Roberts when I had the map of it all and Poldy not Irish enough[57]

The Boer War (1899–1902) sharply polarized opinion in Ireland, the nationalists being strongly opposed to it and seeing it as evidence of imperialist pretentions. The 'Absent-minded Beggar', written by Rudyard Kipling, was regarded as a pro-British song; Lord Roberts (1832–1914) was a famous imperialist soldier with Waterford connections who was Commander-in-Chief during the Boer War. He was subsequently Commander-in-Chief of the British Army. In wearing a brooch for him, Molly was making no secret of her political affiliations.

Molly's discourse on these subjects in *Penelope* is complex. She fears she has been supplanted as a concert performer by 'little chits of missies', who are of course much younger. She attributes this not to any falling-off in her musical and dramatic talents, but to her pro-British feeling, which she does not conceal; she looks down on the lowly background and employment of the fathers of these 'missies', contrasting this to her status as an officer's daughter. She thinks with nostalgia of the experience and *savoir faire* she acquired in one of the most emblematic outposts of the empire:

> Kathleen Kearney and her lot of squealers Miss This Miss That and Miss Theother lot of sparrowfarts skitting around talking about politics they know as much about as my backside anything in the world to make themselves someway interesting Irish homemade beauties soldiers daughter am I ay and whose are you bootmakers and publicans [...] theyd die down dead off their feet if they ever got a chance of walking down the Alameda on an officers arm like me on the bandnight [...] I knew more about men and life when I was 15 than theyll all know at 50[58]

Molly spent her youth in Gibraltar, where her father was apparently stationed. Some of her early romances, lovingly remembered in her soliloquy, were with British Army officers; her first lover, Lieutenant Mulvey, who kissed her 'under the Moorish wall' in Gibraltar;[59] and, later in Dublin, Lieutenant Stanley Gardner, who subsequently died of disease in the Boer War. She wishes Gardner had been 'decently shot' instead of dying of enteric fever.[60] Her recollections of Gibraltar and the British presence there are affectionate:

> I love to see a regiment pass in review the first time I saw the Spanish cavalry at La Roque it was lovely after looking across the bay from Algeciras all the lights of the rock like fireflies or those sham battles on the 15 acres the Black Watch with

their kilts in time at the march past the 10th hussars the prince of Wales own or the lancers O the lancers theyre grand or the Dublins that won Tugela his father made his money over selling the horses for the cavalry well he could buy me a nice present up in Belfast after what I gave him theyve lovely linen up there[61]

The first Bloomsday was exceptionally hot and this puts Molly in mind of her time in Gibraltar:

I thought it was going to get like Gibraltar my goodness the heat there before the levanter came on black as night and the glare of the rock standing up in it like a big giant compared with their 3 Rock mountain they think is so great with the red sentries here and there the poplars and they all whitehot and the smell of the rainwater in those tanks[62]

Molly is comparing the noble mass of the Rock of Gibraltar with Dublin's rather puny Three Rock Mountain. Another loyalist is Mr Garrett Deasy, the headmaster and proprietor of the Clifton School in Dalkey, where Stephen Dedalus has been employed. He represents a Unionist of a different kind. He is proud both of his ancestry and of his own experience:

—You think me an old fogey and an old tory, his thoughtful voice said. I saw three generations since O'Connell's time. I remember the famine in '46. Do you know that the orange lodges agitated for repeal of the union twenty years before O'Connell did or before the prelates of your communion denounced him as a demagogue? You fenians forget some things.[63]

Speaking of himself, he declares:

—I have rebel blood in me too, Mr Deasy said. On the spindle side. But I am descended from sir John Blackwood who voted for the union. We are all Irish, all kings' sons.[64]

But he adheres to what he considers to be the principles of England. He refers to Shakespeare: '*Put but money in thy purse*'. He continues:

—He knew what money was, Mr Deasy said. He made money. A poet, yes, but an Englishman too. Do you know what is the pride of the English? Do you know what is the proudest word you will ever hear from an Englishman's mouth?

The seas' ruler. His seacold eyes looked on the empty bay: it seems history is to blame: on me and on my words, unhating.

—That on his empire, Stephen said, the sun never sets.

—Ba! Mr Deasy cried. That's not English. A French Celt said that.

He tapped his savingsbox against his thumbnail.

—I will tell you, he said solemnly, what is his proudest boast. *I paid my way*.

Good man, good man.

—*I paid my way. I never borrowed a shilling in my life*. Can you feel that? *I owe nothing*. Can you?[65]

Stephen, of course, mentally reviewing his debts, can say nothing of the kind. Deasy is delighted at this and laughs uproariously, then gazes admiringly at the picture of Albert Edward, Prince of Wales and future King Edward VII, but a little later he becomes depressed and says:

England is in the hands of the jews. In all the highest places: her finance, her press. And they are the signs of a nation's decay. Wherever they gather they eat up the nation's vital strength. I have seen it coming these years. As sure as we are standing here the jew merchants are already at their work of destruction. Old England is dying.[66]

The first actual English figure encountered in *Ulysses* is Haines. It is with Haines that Stephen has the conversation quoted above, about the three masters wanting him to serve them. Haines is unambiguous about his own identity:

—Of course I'm a Britisher, Haines's voice said, and I feel as one. I don't want to see my country fall into the hands of German jews either. That's our national problem, I'm afraid, just now.[67]

Haines is in fact modelled on Samuel Chenevix Trench, scion of an old Anglo-Irish family but educated in England. He had passionately embraced the Irish revival:

—He's English, Buck Mulligan said, and he thinks we ought to speak Irish in Ireland.[68]

He is patronizing to Stephen and intends, he says, 'to make a collection of your sayings if you will let me'.[69] He attempts to engage him in conversation on politics, religion and literature to that end but he is rebuffed by an angered and quarrelsome Stephen Dedalus. His statement, quoted above that 'We feel in England that we have treated you rather unfairly. It seems history is to blame'[70] is typical of the well-meaning but rather vacuous English sentiment that Joyce encountered all his life. But it is also typical that Haines is able to address the old woman who comes to deliver milk to the Martello tower in Irish, a language which neither she nor Dedalus can understand, although, as the old woman remarks, 'I'm told it's a grand language by them that knows.'[71]

It may not be without significance that Haines spent part of the night raving in his sleep and threatening to shoot an imaginary black panther with a gun which he had with him. This leads Stephen to threaten Mulligan: 'If he stays on here I am off.'[72] Mulligan purports to agree with him:

> —God, isn't he dreadful? he said frankly. A ponderous Saxon.
> He thinks you're not a gentleman. God, these bloody English!
> Bursting with money and indigestion. Because he comes from
> Oxford.[73]

But while agreeing with Stephen, he asks: 'Why don't you play them as I do?',[74] and this is perhaps the fundamental difference between Stephen and Mulligan.

There are of course other views expressed in *Ulysses* on Anglo-Irish affairs, some pretty obvious caricatures. The medical students' drunken caricature of the English, quoted above, is in this category;

so too, perhaps, is the drunken and self-pitying patriot the Citizen's drunken snarl in the *Cyclops* episode:

—We'll put force against force, says the citizen. We have our greater Ireland beyond the sea. They were driven out of house and home in the black '47. Their mudcabins and their shielings by the roadside were laid low by the batteringram and the *Times* rubbed its hands and told the whitelivered Saxons there would soon be as few Irish in Ireland as redskins in America. Even the Grand Turk sent us his piastres. But the Sassenach tried to starve the nation at home while the land was full of crops that the British hyenas bought and sold in Rio de Janeiro. Ay, they drove out the peasants in hordes. Twenty thousand of them died in the coffinships. But those that came to the land of the free remember the land of bondage. And they will come again and with a vengeance, no cravens, the sons of Granuaile, the champions of Kathleen ni Houlihan.[75]

The final treatment of Anglo-Irish tensions in the action of *Ulysses* occurs in the surreal, dreamlike fifteenth episode set in Dublin's red-light district, *Circe*. The format of this episode on the printed page seems to resemble a play with the names of characters, real and fictitious, preceding speeches attributed to them. There are also long stage directions which considerably amplify the content. But to read the episode at any length is to become convinced that it simply could not be acted on a stage; the technique is instead cinematographic, veering from events taking place in the brothel or in the streets immediately around it to things that happen, if at all, only in the characters' heads and from conversations between small groups to vast crowd scenes. The characters include people who are dead, such as Patrick Dignam and Stephen's mother, who reproaches him in strong terms, and Bloom's father; and also the merely absent, such as the reigning King Edward VII. Many characters encountered earlier in the day also appear again; these notably include the raucous Irish patriot, the Citizen, and the imperialist ex-officer Major Brian Tweedy, father of Molly Bloom.

Stephen Dedalus is drunk when he leaves the brothel swinging his ashplant stick and shouting incoherently. In this condition, in Tyrone Street in the centre of the red-light district, he comes face to face with two drunken British soldiers, Privates Carr and Compton. These two believe that Stephen has been making up to their lady friends. Stephen addresses the drunken soldiers on philosophical themes: 'Struggle for life is the law of existence but human philirenists, notably the tsar and the king of England, have invented arbitration. (*he taps his brow*). But in here it is I must kill the priest and the king.'[76]

Private Carr demands: 'What's that you're saying about my King?', which leads to a spectral appearance of the King himself. Stephen sees that he has annoyed the soldiers: 'I seem to annoy them. Green rag to a bull.'[77] Bloom tries to get Stephen to leave quietly, muttering ineffectually to the soldiers that the Irish troops, the Dublin Fusiliers, had fought with the British during the Boer War. The Citizen then arrives, wearing a green scarf and carrying a shillelagh. He sings the following provocative doggerel:

May the God above
Send down a dove
With teeth as sharp as razors

To slit the throats
Of the English dogs
That hanged our Irish leaders.[78]

The diction of the Citizen is perfectly suggested in the way in which
he makes the words 'razors' and 'leaders' to rhyme.

Just as the soldiers are going to 'do him one in the eye', on the
basis that 'he's a pro-Boer', Major Tweedy arrives to confront
the Citizen. As the stage direction says:

*Casqued halberdiers in armour thrust forward a pentice of
gutted spearpoints. Major Tweedy, moustached like Turko the
terrible, in bearskin cap with hackleplume and accoutrements,
with epaulettes, gilt chevrons and sabretaches, his breast bright
with medals, toes the line. He gives the pilgrim warrior's sign
of the knights templars.*[79]

That is, he gives a Masonic sign. Major Tweedy then '*growls gruffly*':
'Rorkes Drift! Up, guards, and at them! Mahar shalal hashbaz.'[80]
Rorke's Drift was a famous military action during the first Zulu
War of 1879. Although only a relatively small number of troops
were involved, more Victoria Crosses were awarded to the British
participants than in any previous action.

To this outburst the Citizen responds: '*Erin go bragh!*' A telling
stage direction then requires that '*Major Tweedy and the Citizen
exhibit to each other medals, decorations, trophies of war, wounds.
Both salute with fierce hostility.*'[81] Each of these heroes is, apparently, supported by a large military band. Private Carr declares:
'I'll wring the neck of any fucker who says a word against my

fucking king.'[82] And his military companion urges the Major to 'Make a bleeding butcher's shop of the bugger.'[83] At that point the stage direction requires that the '*Massed bands blare* Garryowen *and* God save the king.'[84]

This confrontation, drunken and risible as it is, is obviously a parody of the presumed hostility between British and Irish characters, not least when both are fuelled with drink. The notion of each being supported by a massed band blaring their respective tribal anthems emphasizes the pure parody of the confrontation.

Emer Nolan has noted this role of the respective bands, but she considers that 'Garryowen' is merely an Irish drinking song, thus rather oversimplifying the musical aspect of the confrontation. 'Garryowen' did indeed start life as a drinking song, but it was a drinking song of Irish soldiers in the British Army. It has a quick tempo, is markedly upbeat and was adapted as a marching tune of the Irish regiments and, sometimes, for the British Army in general. It was the regimental march of the Ulster Defence Regiment until 1992.

The musical accompaniment to the pastiche confrontation is thus rather more complicated than it might appear at first glance. The other obvious observation to be made about this passage in *Circe*, the last Anglo-Irish confrontation in the novel, is of course that nothing actually happens. The whores from the brothel and the drunken British privates are excited at the thought of a fight and cheer on the prospective protagonists, but no battle actually occurs. Wiser counsels prevail: the drunken soldiers sidle off in fear of what the sergeant-major might say, the sober and sensible Bloom, with the aid of Corney Kelleher, whisks the intoxicated Stephen away none the worse for having been knocked down by the also drunken soldiers. Everyone has expressed his opinions strongly and made clear his contempt for his would-be opponents. The whores have convinced themselves that the fight is really about their favours. No one emerges with credit, but there is no harm done.

2. Outrages in Ireland and England: Maamtrasna, Great Wyrley and Judicious Doubt

There were attacks on livestock, but these did not even happen in Ireland, where the mob contented itself with opening the stalls and driving the livestock a few miles down the road, but in Great Wyrley in England where barbaric, insane criminals have been rampaging against livestock for six years to such an extent that English companies will no longer insure them.

Five years ago, in order to quieten public anger, an innocent man, now freed, was condemned. But even while he was in prison, the attacks continued. Last week two horses were found dead with the usual cuts to the base of the stomach and their guts spilt out over the grass.

JAMES JOYCE[1]

the unfacts, did we possess them, are too imprecisely few
to warrant our certitude, [...] if it be true that any of those
recorded ever took place for many, we trow, beyessed to
and denayed of, are given to us by some who use the truth
but sparingly

JAMES JOYCE[2]

It is a capital mistake to theorize before one has data.
Insensibly one begins to twist facts to suit theories, instead of
theories to suit facts.

SIR ARTHUR CONAN DOYLE, 'A Scandal In Bohemia' (1892)

In 1907, fifteen years before Joyce published *Ulysses*, thirty-two
years before he published *Finnegans Wake*, he first addressed in
print the question of notorious criminal trials that went wrong
either for technical reasons or because of a misunderstanding of
the evidence. There were also some trials that were never intended
by the prosecuting authorities to be a proper inquiry into guilt
or innocence, but simply a response to society's felt need to have
someone found guilty of a notorious crime.

Joyce first addressed these questions in a piece of journalism
entitled 'L'Irlanda alla Sbarra', usually translated as 'Ireland at the
Bar', but which is perhaps more correctly rendered 'Ireland in
the Dock'.[3] It was the third in a series of articles about Ireland
commissioned by Joyce's friend and English-language pupil,
Roberto Prezioso. Prezioso was 'an intelligent, dapper Venetian'[4]
and the editor of the Triestine nationalist newspaper *Il Piccolo della*

Sera, which favoured the 'Irredentist' (Italian nationalist) cause and ardently wished to 'redeem' Trieste from the Austro-Hungarian Empire. According to Richard Ellmann, Joyce's articles were commissioned to examine 'the evils of empire as found in Ireland', leaving readers to supply the Austrian parallel.[5]

The article itself is a notably forceful and beautifully written piece of polemical writing. The significance of 'Ireland in the Dock' from the point of view of Joyce's legal interests, and the influence they had on his writings, is apparent on a first reading. The short article begins with a notorious Irish case of miscarriage of justice and ends with an equally notorious English case of the same sort. If the Irish case stood alone it might be regarded as merely another example of the grievances of the Irish against the English, albeit one which, tragically, ended in the hanging of an innocent man. But the English case with which the article ends makes it clear that Joyce does not believe that miscarriages of justice occur only to Irish people at the hands of English officials and packed juries. Rather, the temptation to find evidence somewhere to convict a suitably vulnerable person for a notorious crime is universal. At the start of his article, Joyce immediately foregrounds the notorious Irish case:

> Several years ago a sensational trial took place in Ireland. In the western province, in a remote place called Maamtrasna, a murder was committed. Four or five peasants from the village were arrested, all of them members of the ancient tribe of the Joyces. The eldest of them, a certain Myles Joyce, sixty years of age was particularly suspected by the police. Public opinion considered him innocent then, and he is now thought of as a martyr. Both the old man and the other accused did

not know English. The court had to resort to the services of an interpreter. The interrogation that took place through this man was at times comic and at times tragic. On the one hand there was the officious interpreter, on the other, the patriarch of the miserable tribe who, unused to civic customs, seemed quite bewildered by all the legal ceremonies.[6]

Joyce might have added that the sole interpreter, who reduced long answers by the defendant to monosyllables, was a uniformed police officer.

There could (as we shall see below) be only one end to this procedure. As Joyce writes:

the poor old man was found guilty and sent before a high court which sentenced him to be hanged. On the day the sentence was to be carried out, the square in front of the prison was packed with people who were kneeling and calling out prayers in Irish for the repose of the soul of Myles Joyce. Legend has it that even the hangman could not make himself understood by the victim and angrily kicked the unhappy man in the head to force him into the noose.

Joyce moves then to his main theme:

The figure of this bewildered old man, left over from a culture which is not ours, a deaf-mute before his judges, is a symbol of the Irish nation at the bar of public opinion. Like him, Ireland cannot appeal to the modern conscience of England or abroad. The English newspapers acted as interpreters

[...]. So the Irish figure as criminals, with deformed faces, who roam around at night with the aim of doing away with every unionist.[7]

Joyce, then, began and ended his 1907 article with terse references to two notorious cases of miscarried justice, one in Ireland in 1882 and one in England in 1903. From a literary point of view the treatment of these cases is very similar. It is extremely succinct, stating no more than is required to make the political point of his article. As we shall see, in both cases he omits, as irrelevant to his argument, many salient details which almost any other writer about the cases would have considered important.

The Maamtrasna murders

Joyce's opening statement, quoted above, is true as far as it goes. But a great deal more could be said. The Maamtrasna trial took place not 'several years ago' but almost twenty-five years before Joyce's article was published. The location of the outrage was in the heart of the 'Joyce country', remote barren uplands, then unserved by any road, on the border between Mayo and Galway, above the south-western corner of Lough Mask. So remote is the place that when, in the aftermath of the crime, the Lord Lieutenant visited the spot it was thought necessary to bring him by destroyer into Killary Harbour, a large fjord-like inlet in the west coast of Ireland and to convey him from there on horseback the twenty miles to Maamtrasna with an escort of dragoons. So miserable was the crime scene at Maamtrasna that the Lord Lieutenant wrote to a fellow member of the British Cabinet: 'I could not have believed that six human beings could have lived in such a hole.'[8]

Nor was it simply that '*a* murder was committed'; no less than five miserably poor peasants, all members of one family, were shot or beaten to death on the night of 17–18 August 1882. These were John Joyce, his wife, his elderly mother and two teenagers, a boy and a girl. A sixth victim, a ten-year-old boy, was viciously assaulted but survived.

A historian would put this brutal crime, the murder of five people living at or below the level of subsistence, apparently by their neighbours or relatives, in a particular historical context. This has been admirably done more than once in recent times.[9] But the background to the crime in social and political history need not detain us here. The feature that Joyce seized upon was the hanging of an ageing peasant, Myles Joyce, despite the fact that he was believed to be innocent, and after a trial conducted in a language which he could neither speak nor understand.

It is instructive for an assessment of Joyce's legal preoccupations to look in a little detail at his assertion that Myles Joyce was 'considered [...] innocent then, and [...] is now thought of as a martyr'.[10]

The trial at which he was convicted was an extraordinary one. Unlike most agrarian murders of the time, where a strict *omertà* was the rule and neighbours of the accused could not be induced to testify, evidence was available in great profusion. Firstly, the police were approached the day after the crime by a cousin of the murdered Joyces and other relatives. This family was known as the 'Maolra' Joyces in order to distinguish them from the many other Joyces involved. Maolra was the name of their father.

This group of witnesses, referred to by the prosecution as 'the independent witnesses', said that they had been awoken in their houses some three or four miles from the murder scene by the barking of dogs and saw six men out in the middle of the night, calling to the house of the Casey family. There the party was joined by four other men. The Maolras claimed that they had followed this augmented group, whom they recognized, and whom they said were clad in dark clothes, and saw them approach the murder house, several miles away, and then heard a great commotion and screaming from that house.

This evidence, if believed, was obviously fatal to the people implicated, including Myles Joyce. The authorities accepted the evidence unquestioningly. It was a curious feature that four of the men identified by the Maolras were also Joyces, cousins of the 'independent witnesses'. This group were the sons of Seán Joyce and were known as 'the Seáns' and included Myles Joyce. There was considerable evidence of feuding between the two groups over grazing rights, stolen sheep and the like.

When the authorities arrived at the murder house on 18 August they found two boys, Michael aged seventeen and Patrick aged ten. Both of these youths were grievously wounded and the doctors who attended them advised that they could not survive. Accordingly, a magistrate in attendance took from each of them a 'Dying Declaration'. This is a statement made by a person with a 'settled and hopeless expectation of death' made as to the cause of his death. Such a declaration is admissible at a trial as an exception to the law against hearsay. This is done on the basis that a person who knows that he is going to die very soon is unlikely to make a false statement as to the reason for his death. As it happened, however, the younger boy survived his grievous wounds and would have been available to give evidence at the trial. But the prosecution decided that they could not call him because his evidence contradicted that of the 'independent witnesses'. To avoid this contradiction the lead prosecutor, Sir Peter O'Brien, QC (later, as Lord O'Brien of Kilfenora, Chief Justice of Ireland), informed the court that he could not call the boy. The reason O'Brien gave was that the boy did not sufficiently understand the meaning of the oath. The actual reason was that the boy had stated that the men who attacked his family had been dressed in white *bainin* (white flannel jackets – the usual garb of Galway mountaineers) and had blackened faces so that he could not identify them. This, if accepted, absolutely contradicted the evidence of the Maolra Joyces, who had purported to identify all ten men and had said nothing about disguise.

A further difficulty with the dying declarations was that they described the crime as having been committed by three or four people only, whereas the Maolra Joyces' account described an attacking party of ten men, each of whom they named.

The Crown made every effort to hide the dying declarations and they were not part of the court, but it was not possible entirely to conceal them. This was because they had been taken by the local magistrate, Mr Newton Brady, at the scene of the crime and had been proved in the police court proceedings at Cong a few days later. These proceedings had been extensively reported in the newspapers. It must have tormented the prosecution in the run-up to the trials that the defence solicitor, Mr Henry Concannon of Tuam, might have noticed the reports and told his counsel about them. If that were so, the Maolra witnesses risked being utterly discredited from a credible and appealing source.

The prosecution had another, quite separate problem. Anthony Philbin was one of the men identified by the Maolra Joyces as part of the group of ten. But he appeared, on further investigation, to have an impressive defence. There were several witnesses to show that he had spent the night of 17 August at the wake of a man called Quinn. This could not be accepted by the prosecution because the Maolras were adamant that Philbin had been part of the murder gang. If the prosecution dropped the case against him it would tend to discredit their evidence in general. Accordingly, the Crown solicitor, George Bolton, took a very bold step indeed. He recruited Philbin, who could speak English very well as a result of years spent in northern England, as a prosecution witness.

It is important to stress the remarkable nature of this prosecution tactic. It involved Philbin giving up his alibi defence and he would only do this, naturally, in exchange for immunity. This the prosecution gave him. They granted immunity to an admitted murderer. When he gave evidence against the Seán Joyces he denied that he had been at the wake, denied that he had met his own mother there, denied that he had walked home with two neighbours, one a relative of the dead man.

Philbin also assisted the prosecution in recruiting his brother-in-law Tom Casey, another of the ten implicated men, to turn Queen's evidence the day before the trial. His evidence, also in return for a promise of immunity, sealed the fate of Patrick Joyce: he was sentenced to hang.

What happened next was even more extraordinary. After the conviction of Myles Joyce and Patrick Casey, two more of the ten original defendants, five other prisoners agreed to withdraw their pleas of not guilty and to plead guilty instead. This followed discussions between their lawyers and the prosecution but also followed an extraordinary intervention by their parish priest, Fr Michael McHugh. He admitted that he had brought about four pleas of guilty and justified himself as follows:

> I argued with myself thus – if the men were guilty their plea of guilty can do them no harm, and will save their lives; and that if they were innocent I felt that the truth would leak out, as from my knowledge of the locality and the people, I believed such a huge wrong could not continue. This was the argument I made use of to the men themselves in the cell of Green Street Courthouse; and I dare say it was the argument which induced them to withdraw their plea of 'not guilty' and enter a plea of 'guilty' […] I rather believed that they were innocent.[11]

This is an absolutely extraordinary statement by the priest which was brought to light within a short time of the convictions, as described below. One of the recent books on the case, cited above, was written by Jarlath Waldron, who was himself a priest. It appears from the account of events in Fr Waldron's book that he was embarrassed at his predecessor's actions, even after the lapse of a century. Fr McHugh frankly admitted that he had induced four men whom he 'rather' believed to be innocent to plead guilty in order to save their lives. But their action in pleading guilty, of course, tended to quiet any concern that may have been felt at the conviction of Myles Joyce on evidence which was partly that of 'approvers', that is witnesses who had participated in the crime and were swearing away the lives of others in order to save their own, and partly of his family's tribal enemies, the Maolra Joyces.

It appears that the Crown prosecutors had promised the five men their lives in return for pleas of guilty. But it also appears that the prosecutors had made this offer without authority from their political masters. This was significant because, once pleas of guilty were entered, the judge had no option but to impose the death sentence and it was up to the politicians to decide whether or not they should be reprieved. It was a notable fact that the judge, Mr Justice Barry, did not put on the black cap, which was customary at the time, before sentencing the men. The Lord Lieutenant, Lord Spencer, informed the Home Secretary in London:

> I gather from what the judge said that although he left the case free for me, he considered that the five men having pleaded guilty should make me commute their sentences. He purposely delivered sentence without assuming the black cap that is an outward form, but I do not know what interpretation is to be put on it. He must have done it with a meaning.[12]

In a subsequent letter to no less than Queen Victoria herself, Lord Spencer reported:

> the law officers, though they had not pledged him [Spencer], had allowed the idea to prevail both with the Counsel for the prisoners and with the Judge, that the death sentence would not be carried out, if they pleaded guilty.
>
> The Judge acted on this and most earnestly pleaded for mitigation of sentence. Lord Spencer felt constrained to follow his advice. Had he allowed any of these men to be hung after what took place there would have been such an outcry

in the country, and the idea would have been spread that the men were made, on a false representation, to plead guilty.[13]

Convictions obtained in this way would never have been accepted without controversy. Just before the scheduled hangings of Patrick Joyce and Patrick Casey, they made dying declarations which, like the similar declarations of the two boys mentioned above, were duly concealed by the authorities. The men admitted their own guilt but asserted the innocence of Myles Joyce. They also said that the witness Anthony Philbin, who had claimed to have been party to the crime in order to bolster his evidence against Myles Joyce, was not present at all. They said that the Maolra Joyces 'did not and could not have seen us the night of the murder and that they had never been to the Casey house on the night'.[14]

It is evident that the Lord Lieutenant was greatly disturbed by these statements. He wrote to the judge, Mr Justice Barry, on 19 December 1882: 'I need not tell you what great anxiety these statements caused me: I may now have made a mistake, but I do not think I did. I have written you a very imperfect account of the last episode in this dreadful business. I think no advantage will be gained by any official statement.'[15]

This was not the end of the matter. In 1884 the barrister, Timothy Harrington MP, published a book which destroyed the case against Myles Joyce.[16] Harrington had been alerted to the Crown's malpractice in the Maamtrasna case by what a Dublin barrister, Edward Ennis, who had told Tim Healy, the Dublin barrister and Nationalist Party MP. In his memoirs, published in 1928, Healy recorded:

A month later the late Edward Ennis, a barrister, who was a frequenter of Green Street Courthouse, Dublin came to me with a bundle of papers. He had gained access to a room where Crown briefs were carelessly thrown after the trial and found the brief held in the Maamtrasna case by Peter O'Brien Q.C. (afterwards Lord O'Brien, Chief Justice). Taking the printed 'informations' from it he gave them to me. It was the right of the accused to be furnished with 'deposition' moreover, Lord Justice Barry declared from the Bench at Limerick in July 1891, that as Attorney General his practice was to hand a copy of the entire Crown briefs to the prisoner's counsel.

In the Maamtrasna case the accused had not been furnished even with the 'informations'. The chief witness against them was an informer named Casey, who swore that Myles Joyce was one of the murder party with himself and that all of them came to their victim's cabin dressed in black or with black overalls. The Crown brief, however, contained printed copies of an 'information' by the surviving boy who had been brought to Dublin to make it.

He swore that the murderers wore 'baunyeens'. This testimony, straight from the scene of the assassination, was in complete conflict with Casey's evidence.

The Prosecution not only suppressed it, but did not produce as a witness the sole survivor of the tragedy.[17]

This was a devastating point against the safety of Myles Joyce's conviction, though perhaps more impressive to a lawyer than to a layman.

On 8 August 1884 the approver Patrick Casey attended Mass at the parish church in Tourmakeady, on the banks of Lough Mask. He was free to do so because all charges against him had been dropped when he turned Queen's evidence. There, the Archbishop of Tuam, Dr John MacEvilly, was presiding at a confirmation ceremony. Casey addressed the congregation, apparently from the foot of the altar, and while holding a candle confirmed the dying declarations of Patrick Joyce and Patrick Casey, exonerating Myles Joyce. He said that he had made a full confession of his own guilt to the Crown solicitor George Bolton but that this had been rejected and he had been required, as the price of saving his neck, to make a statement which was consistent with that of Anthony Philbin.

The Crown were badly shaken by Harrington's book and Casey's declaration but decided to do nothing about them because three men had been hanged, and to accept Myles Joyce's innocence would bring the entire legal proceedings into disrepute.

This, then, is the explanation of James Joyce's statement in his 1907 article that Myles Joyce was believed to be innocent at the time and by the early twentieth century was regarded as a martyr. As we shall see, in the English case widely known as the 'Great Wyrley' outrages, mentioned at the end of Joyce's article, the processes of English law convicted a man later proved to have been innocent, even without any political imperative to do so. The linkage between the two cases is significant for a consideration of Joyce's legal interests. As we shall see, the English case fed into the decades-long agitation for a system of appeal from convictions in criminal cases.

In 1907, then, Joyce wrote as a journalist about certain legal themes that become major topics in *Ulysses* and *Finnegans Wake*.

There is a marked degree of continuity between this first written exploration on the one hand, and the themes as developed in Joyce's works, notably an uneasy concern that the solemn processes of the law may lead to miscarriages of justice due to prejudice, sloppy thinking, perjury or to a feeling on the part of the public that the man charged must be guilty, since the police obviously think so. Joyce's 1907 article shows him in an Irish patriotic mode, rather untypically, responding in a spirited way to English media caricatures of the Irish and using an archetypally English miscarriage of justice case as a *tu quoque*, a response in kind.

The second epigraph to this chapter is taken from *Finnegans Wake*, published more than thirty years after the Italian newspaper article. It is part of the conclusions of the four annalists who act as judges on the question of what crime, if any, was committed by HCE in the Phoenix Park; they are unable to come to any conclusion because of a lack of evidence, conflict in evidence, the unreliability of the evidence-givers and inconsistent variations in the allegations made, all difficulties with which courts, then and now, are very familiar. This major theme in the *Wake* illustrates the continuance of Joyce's preoccupation with questions of knowledge, proof and epistemology. Joyce's view of these topics is remarkably consistent over the years between his early Italian journalism and his last publication. It is also reflected in his treatment of certain contemporary Irish law cases which took place between the years 1899 and 1925. The third epigraph is from Sir Arthur Conan Doyle, whose exculpatory role in the famous English miscarriage of justice, the Edalji case, is discussed below.

Joyce's piece in *Il Piccolo* is a powerful polemic, expressed in his usual highly compressed journalistic style. The dominant image is that of the helpless Myles Joyce, whose hopeless position as an illiterate monoglot Irish speaker questioned in English before the magistrates, a policeman the sole interpreter, is vividly portrayed. So too is his sadistically botched execution.[18]

In the second part of the article, Joyce likens the position of Myles Joyce in the dock to that of Ireland herself at the Bar of international public opinion. The country and its people, says Joyce, are perceived entirely through British eyes, just as Myles Joyce's answers were conveyed or distorted by the police interpreter.

This is a perfect description of one of the most famous English political cartoons of the late nineteenth century. 'The Irish Frankenstein' was published in the London satirical journal *Punch* on 20 May 1882. It shows a masked monster, bursting out of his clothes in a manner reminiscent today of the Incredible Hulk, holding a bloodstained knife in one hand, and appearing to be about nine feet tall. The figure is masked and features a protruding simian jaw and a dark cloak. His attitude is one of aggressive prowling and he towers over a cowering, top-hatted Englishman. Under the title there are the words: 'the baneful and blood-stained Monster... yet was it not my Master to the very extent that it was my Creature?... had I not breathed into it my own spirit?'. This cartoon was published in the immediate aftermath of the Phoenix Park murders on 6 May 1882. But it and other cartoons based on it appeared frequently in England from then onwards and were especially prone to appear after any outbreak of political violence. Moreover, they evoked a tradition stretching back to the 1830s when Daniel O'Connell and other nationalist leaders were frequently portrayed as having huge bodies consisting of potatoes with excrescences bursting out of them. One such image famously accompanied a piece of doggerel about O'Connell: 'Scum, condensed of Irish Bog / Monster, liar, demagogue.'[19]

This approach was not adopted generally in the English press but it was common and represented the default position of certain populist politicians. It is in this sense that Ronan Fanning refers to British political opinion on Ireland in the early twentieth century as being 'coloured by the racial and religious prejudice that had perennially characterised English attitudes to Ireland'.[20]

In this sense, too, Lord Salisbury opposed Home Rule for Ireland on the basis that 'We are to have confidence in the Irish people. Confidence depends on the people in whom you are to confide. You would not confide free representative institutions to the Hottentots for example.'[21]

Fifteen years later, in a similar mood, the Liberal Prime Minister H. H. Asquith echoed the prejudices of the Tory Lord Salisbury in expressing outrage about a Eucharistic procession in the streets immediately around Westminster Cathedral, as part of the celebrations of the London Eucharistic Congress in September 1908. He wrote: 'Such a procession appears to be clearly illegal, and there is a good deal of quite respectable Protestant sentiment which is offended by this gang of foreign Cardinals taking advantage of our hospitality to parade their idolatries through the streets of London: a thing without precedent since the days of Bloody Mary.'[22]

The point about Salisbury and Asquith is that they were both prime ministers, leaders of their parties and spokesmen for an enormous swathe of public opinion when they made these statements. The less censored views of their subordinates, such as Winston Churchill, can all too easily be imagined.

The Great Wyrley case

The last portion of Joyce's 1907 article is devoted to a rebuttal of this caricature. Examples of the unfair and distorted nature of coverage of crime in Ireland are discussed, and the argument builds up to the example of the Great Wyrley case, seen by Joyce as a knockout blow in his critique of British judicial standards. The Great Wyrley outrages were a series of savage, indeed as Joyce says 'barbaric', attacks on livestock that took place in the Great Wyrley district of Staffordshire, quite close to Birmingham in the West Midlands of England. They were of a depraved nature that was unparalleled in Ireland, even during the worst outbreaks of rural unrest. Yet they happened in the heart of the English countryside. A man – a solicitor and the son of a vicar – was convicted of the crimes in 1903 but the attacks continued after his imprisonment, suggesting to many that he was innocent. Moreover, as Joyce portrays it, this 'innocent' was convicted 'in order to quieten public anger', implying at best a rush to judgment and at worst the outright framing of an innocent man. And all this, Joyce notes, committed by people who assiduously portray the *Irish* as unreconstructed savages!

Joyce's 1907 article represents his first published engagement with the topic of notorious contemporary crimes. Sensational crimes and trials, however, feature largely – more largely than is often recognized – in both *Ulysses* and *Finnegans Wake*. It appears significant that his early Italian article focuses on two cases of apparent miscarriages of justice, each procured at best by a gross over-interpretation of the available evidence and at worst by inventing that evidence. In each case it can be demonstrated that Joyce had available to him ample and detailed sources of information about the evidence on which the prosecution case was built, and about the way in which that evidence turned out to be fatally flawed. This large body of material, however, underpins a very attenuated journalistic treatment by the writer, though one which accurately represents the substance of the cases in question. But it is highly significant that the doubt Joyce expresses about the official version of these sensational trials anticipates the epistemological concerns which he felt about various Irish and English cases to which he refers in his great works. These examples of legal miscarriage vindicate in quite a dramatic way the validity of philosophical (and judicial) doubt where certainty is not properly attainable. This is less obvious a point than one might think. There was in Joyce's time, and still is today, a tendency in sections of the media to think that an acquittal represents a failure of the system or a purely technical deficiency in evidence, and that the defendant is almost invariably guilty as charged. Joyce was emphatically not of this view.

Several of the cases Joyce discusses or alludes to in his novels are very doubtful ones. A small amount of ambiguous evidence was produced which it was hoped would act on a fund of prejudice (sometimes deliberately created) to produce a conviction. This happened in the two cases that were the subject of the 1907 article. In the other historic cases of unnatural death mentioned in *Ulysses*, which occurred in Ireland between 1899 and 1925, the trials all ended with the acquittals of the accused precisely because, as Joyce has Martin Cunningham say of the Childs case in *Hades*, the Crown had only circumstantial evidence.[23]

There is ample indication that Joyce preferred the 'maxim of the law' to the hotter-blooded conclusions of the man in the street or in the pub. There are various reasons for this. For example, Joyce had no confidence in or liking for the police: 'Nasty customers to tackle';[24] 'unscrupulous in the service of the Crown'.[25]

But it is evident from the terms of his 1907 article that the Great Wyrley case in particular made a huge impression on him and raised much more fundamental questions which he asked all his life: How do we know that which we think we know? Can we prove it?

It seems that the Great Wyrley case attracted Joyce's attention in the first place because its sheer barbarity made it an appropriate response to the British media's treatment of Ireland. The fact that an innocent man was convicted and later officially pardoned proved that British justice was far from infallible and that it could perpetrate obtuse or even malicious miscarriages of justice even on loyal British subjects in the heart of England.

The 'innocent man' in the Great Wyrley case was the twenty-seven-year-old son of the Vicar of St Mark's, Great Wyrley, George Edalji, himself a solicitor practising in Birmingham.[26] But Joyce omits entirely two salient facts of human interest about Edalji and his case. First, Edalji was half Indian, the son of the Rev. Shapurju Edalji, a Parsee convert to Anglicanism who became the first, and up to that time the only, such person to hold a benefice in the Church of England. The Rev. Edalji was a narrow and rigidly orthodox Anglican and his son's upbringing was a Victorian one in every sense. The Rev. Edalji's installation as vicar had not been universally welcomed in Great Wyrley. The family had been the victims of anonymous hate mail, vandalism and of strange advertisements placed, and letters sent, in the vicar's name.[27] These things occurred in bursts, first in the late 1880s and again in 1892–3. George himself, born in 1876, was an earnest, rather humourless boy whose bulging eyes were evidence of severe myopia; it was a considerable achievement for him to qualify as a solicitor. After he did so, he continued to live at home and commuted by train to his office in Birmingham each day. His plodding earnestness is illustrated by an extra-curricular task he undertook as a young solicitor: he wrote a layman's guide to the rights of the railway passenger, 'The Man in the Train'.

Commencing in early 1903, an extraordinary outbreak of cattle-maiming occurred in the Great Wyrley area. The victims were cows, horses and pit ponies from the nearby mines. The stomachs of the animals were cut from the base with what was thought to be a specialized tool, whose strong blade had a semicircular protuberance towards its end. The animals' guts would spill out, leaving them to die painfully over a long period. No motive of malice against the owners of the animals could be identified.

After the eighth of these episodes, an attack on a pit pony in August 1903, George Edalji was arrested and charged with cattle-maiming. He was convicted of this offence after a trial in October 1903 and sentenced to seven years in prison. He was also struck off the Roll of Solicitors. In short, he was ruined, his life destroyed. Suspicion had fallen on him because anonymous letters had identified him as the culprit.[28] As a result, his house was under surveillance by six policemen on the night of the pit pony attack. He would have had to avoid these watchers on leaving the house and again on re-entering it. They did not claim to have seen him coming or going.

The case against George Edalji was circumstantial only; there was mud on his shoes, he was said to have shown no surprise when arrested and it was alleged that he himself had written the anonymous letters. But the attacks, and the anonymous letters, continued after he was locked up.[29] His case was championed by various luminaries after his conviction and a petition for his release was signed by 10,000 people. After three years in prison he was set free without pardon, explanation or excuse. This occurred in October 1906.[30] He was 'free' to lead the miserable life of the ex-convict; stigmatized by his conviction, expelled from his profession, unemployed and unemployable, ruined in fortune and reputation, and undermined in health.

Desperate to clear his name, and if possible to return to his profession, the newly released Edalji took a step which catapulted his case to international prominence and thereby brought it to Joyce's attention. He appealed to Sir Arthur Conan Doyle, creator of Sherlock Holmes, to investigate his misfortunes and to state his opinion of the true position. Doyle was at that time one of the most famous men in England, and one of the most famous Englishmen in the world. He was at the very height of his career, a 'celebrity' in the modern sense of the term *avant la lettre*. He concluded that there was no case against Edalji and determined to prove it. He worked day and night on the case for three months and in January 1907 his 18,000-word article was published over two days in the *Daily Telegraph*, proclaiming Edalji's innocence.

The timing was very conducive to Conan Doyle's success. Captain Alfred Dreyfus had recently been exonerated in France, the contrived case against him exploded by the great writer Émile Zola. Conan Doyle's mighty destruction of the case against Edalji seemed another 'J'accuse'. In the article Conan Doyle took apart the forensic evidence against Edalji, pointing out that the soil on his shoes was of a quite different composition to that of the field where the attack had occurred. Conan Doyle, before he created Sherlock Holmes, had qualified as an ophthalmic doctor and he argued that Edalji's well-established and acute myopia would have precluded his participation in the crimes, committed in open country and in the middle of the night. He had the nature and severity of the condition independently verified. He ridiculed the handwriting evidence linking Edalji to the anonymous letters and this, indeed, turned out to be the very weakest point of the Crown's case.

Conan Doyle emphasized that, just as in the case of the Jewish Captain Dreyfus, Edalji's status as an outsider made him vulnerable to being set up. Dreyfus, he said, had been made a scapegoat because he was a Jew; Edalji because his father was an Indian. He said that he himself, because of his Irish/Scottish background, and the half-Indian Edalji were at best merely 'honorary Englishmen'.

Within the month *The Times*, organ of the English establishment, published an article 'by a legal correspondent' acknowledging the strength of Conan Doyle's attack.[31] Two weeks later the Home Office appointed a three-man Committee of Inquiry.[32] The brilliant and flamboyant Tory MP F. E. Smith, KC (later Lord Birkenhead, and a signatory of the Anglo-Irish Treaty of 1921) pointed out in the House of Commons that the Crown's handwriting expert was the same 'expert' who had made a vital error in the notorious wrongful conviction of Adolf Beck in 1904. He erred in Edalji's case, too, but it took more than thirty years for this to be recognized.

The triumvirate concluded that Edalji was innocent. He received a full pardon, which was a complete acknowledgement of his innocence. But he was given no compensation, as the committee very oddly thought that he had brought about his own misfortune by writing the anonymous letters. Why precisely a man who was innocent of the crimes would nonetheless write anonymous letters accusing himself was never explained. Conan Doyle then referred the letters to Lindsay Johnson, the handwriting expert who had shown the evidence against Captain Dreyfus to be a forgery. Johnson was adamant that the letters had not been written by Edalji.

In 1934, thirty-one years after Edalji went to jail, an elderly local man called Enoch Knowles was convicted of writing the anonymous letters.[33] Long before this, Edalji had been pardoned and restored to the Roll of Solicitors and he practised that profession, in London, until his death in the 1950s.

Doyle wrote a book on the case, *The Story of Mr George Edalji*, which went into a second edition in 1907 and which was reissued in expanded form in 1985. In 2005 Julian Barnes wrote a novel about the case, *Arthur and George*, which was shortlisted for the Booker Prize. More recently still, Roger Oldfield wrote *Outrage: the Edalji Five and the Shadow of Sherlock Holmes* (2010).

Joyce's source for the case, however, is obviously in part at least based on newspaper reportage: only thus could he have been aware of what had happened recently. The London *Times*, available in the port city of Trieste, had coverage of the case almost every day from 28 August 1907 to 16 September 1907, which was the period during which Joyce must have been writting the article. Specifically, on 29 August *The Times* covered the attack on two horses that Joyce described as happening 'last week'. There had been many mentions of the case in *The Times* since the legal correspondent's article on 29 January 1907.

This, then, is the probable source for Joyce's reference to the Great Wyrley case. From *The Times*, or from any of a number of other British papers, Joyce could have gleaned all he needed for his literary purposes. Indeed, the question is rather why he omitted so much of human or journalistic interest from his terse account of the case. Edalji's race, his father's unique position in the Church of England and the involvement of the celebrated Sir Arthur Conan Doyle are all passed over in silence. But this is of a piece with Joyce's treatment of other law cases and indeed of historical events generally: he says no more than is needed to make his point.

In the Great Wyrley example that point is a very simple one and might be summarized as follows. There was a *factual* episode of cattle-maiming but, unexpectedly, it took place in England and not in Ireland. To appease public anger, an innocent man was condemned for the crime. But he was freed when the continuance of the crimes after his incarceration made his guilt difficult to credit. This also suggests the contrived nature of the original case against him. Indeed the crimes continued right up to the time that Joyce's article was published.

That was all Joyce needed. The Great Wyrley case was the climax of his article, the bulk of which is a protest against the abuse by the British media of highly dramatized 'sensational trials' to portray the Irish as sadistic savages. Joyce uses Great Wyrley to show that mindless cruelty can be found in England too, as can abuses of the legal system to convict innocents.

But for us, considering 'Ireland in the Dock' in the context of Joyce's work as a whole and of his treatment of the 'crime cunundrum'[34] in particular, a different approach may be taken. The Great Wyrley case prefigures the concerns Joyce expressed about contemporary cases of unnatural death in *Ulysses* and in *Finnegans Wake*, which include those of Samuel Childs,[35] Constable Henry Flower,[36] the mysterious death of Charles Harvey, Secretary of the Cork Yacht Club,[37] and the Honor Bright case of 1925, apart altogether from the recurrent concern in *Finnegans Wake* as to what, if any, crime was committed in the Phoenix Park.

Sometimes the parallels between the cases in the novels and the two cases in the 1907 article are uncanny. One essential point relevant to the Edalji case is that the prosecution in *R* v *Childs*, the Dublin murder trial that Joyce witnessed, decided to suppress, in a capital case, a vitally important letter written by the deceased about a year previously to the Commissioner of the Dublin Metropolitan Police (DMP).

The effect of this was very similar to that of the proof that Edalji had not written the anonymous letters. In a phrase which could equally be applied to the Childs case, Conan Doyle criticized the Staffordshire police because they had 'commenced and carried on their investigation, not for the purpose of finding out who was the culprit, but for the purpose of finding evidence against [one] whom they were already sure was the guilty man'.[38] They first decided who was guilty and only then looked for evidence, carefully omitting any that suggested a different outcome.

The significant role played by handwritten letters in the Edalji case, in the Childs case and in the case against HCE in *Finnegans Wake* will be obvious. In the *Wake*, the never-produced letter is certainly part of the 'unfacts' which lead the judges to conclude 'the unfacts, did we possess them, are too imprecisely few to warrant our certitude'.[39] There are obvious parallels as well with the suppressed declarations in the Maamtrasna case.

Here too are echoes of the forged letter used to attempt to implicate Parnell in the Invincibles murders of 1882, which features largely in *Finnegans Wake*,[40] and the forged *bordereau* used to implicate Captain Dreyfus, which is also mentioned in the *Wake*. This reference occurs in Chapter 5 of Book 1,[41] which is devoted to a study of a letter written by Anna Livia Plurabelle, her

'Mamafesta' memorializing her husband. There is a three-page list of the names given to her document,[42] a soiled letter with a lost signature, dug up by a neighbour's hen. The document, which it is optimistically believed will reveal the truth of the allegations against HCE, is virtually illegible. It is amalgamated with the forged letters attributed to Captain Dreyfus by the use of the term *bordereau*:

> Closer inspection of the *bordereau* would reveal a multiplicity of personalities inflicted on the documents or document and some prevision of virtual crime or crimes might be made by anyone unwary enough before any suitable occasion for it or them had so far managed to happen along. In fact, under the closed eyes of the inspectors the traits featuring the *chiaroscuro* coalesce, their contrarieties eliminated, in one stable somebody similarly as by the providential warring of heartshaker with housebreaker and of dramdrinker against freethinker[43]

This obscure passage ends with the oddly phrased but unmistakable query: 'Say, baroun lousadoor, who in hallhagal wrote the durn thing anyhow?'[44]

When James Joyce was born, and for many years after, there was no right to appeal the decision of an English criminal court, even in a capital case. This in itself seems almost incredible in our time, one hyper-conscious of the possibility of error or injustice committed by churches, banks, the police, the courts, the medical profession, the media and many others. But the Victorians were more self-confident in their institutions.

Certainty and doubt

The period 1880–1920 was what George Orwell called the 'golden age of English murder'.[45] People like Doctor Crippen, Doctor Crean, Mrs Maybrick and Mrs Bartlett committed or were taxed with murders, often in genteel circumstances, which are still familiar to aficionados. Their trials filled the newspapers and the pages of popular literature. These trials were often legally and logically crude in the extreme. Four cases around the end of Queen Victoria's reign caused widespread public disturbance because of apparent bias, over-interpretation of slight evidence and societal prejudice against the accused. These were the cases of Israel Lipski (1887), Mrs Maybrick (1889), Adolf Beck (1904) and of course George Edalji (1907). It may not be irrelevant that all of these defendants were foreigners – two Jews and a Parsee, and the other an American woman.[46]

These egregious cases exploded the notion of the infallibility of the English criminal court and led to the introduction of the Court of Criminal Appeal. Of the four cases which brought about this important reform, two are mentioned by Joyce (Edalji and Maybrick), together with a third case, that of Myles Joyce which, since it was an Irish case, had no influence on the English imperial legislature.

Joyce was demonstrably preoccupied with questions of certainty and doubt, not merely about criminal cases but about history and life generally. Especially in *Finnegans Wake*, he was deeply concerned with what is true, what we (or they) wish to be true and what we (or they) can prove to be true, and with a vital distinction between these three things.

Joyce distinguishes sharply between past 'headline' events whose truth he rarely questions, and accounts or narratives of these events, which he questions all the time. Thus, when Stephen, a part-time history teacher in Mr Deasy's school, teaches the boys about the Battle of Asculum in 279 BC, an event which he himself knows about only from a dog-eared book on Roman history, he reflects: 'Fabled by the daughters of memory. And yet it was in some way if not as memory fabled it.'[47] This line of thought leads him to reflect on other momentous events of ancient Rome, particularly the deaths by assassination of the great soldiers Pyrrhus and Julius Caesar. Were these events inevitable? Could they have been avoided, or did they for ever oust all other possibilities?

> Had Pyrrhus not fallen by a beldam's hand in Argos or Julius
> Caesar not been knifed to death. They are not to be thought
> away. Time has branded them and fettered they are lodged
> in the room of the infinite possibilities they have ousted.
> But can those have been possible seeing that they never were?
> Or was that only possible which came to pass? Weave, weaver
> of the wind.[48]

These speculative thoughts occur to Stephen while he is teaching a class of boys inclined to rowdiness. They interrupt the train of thought indicated above by the (ironic) demand: 'Tell us a story, sir. [...] A ghoststory.'[49]

Later, the ancient keeper of the cabman's shelter in *Eumaeus*[50] doubts what is, to Bloom and to Stephen, the obvious, indisputable fact of Parnell's death in 1891.

On the other hand, the drinkers in Barney Kiernan's pub in

Green Street are quite certain that they 'know' something which is not in fact true at all, that Bloom has had a great betting coup on 'Throwaway', the winner of that day's Ascot Gold Cup race, and is escaping without so much as buying them a drink.

In his works, Joyce discusses or mentions several cases of unnatural death, notorious or obscure, all of which illustrate the difficulties and uncertainties I have just mentioned. He appreciated and approved the legal distinctions between proved and unproved assertions, and the legal insistence that the onus of proof lies on the person who asserts that something is the case. Though these principles can seem technical and tedious, Joyce prefers them to the jumping to conclusions based on prejudice that he illustrates so brilliantly in *Cyclops*. He asserts the moral viability of, and indeed the moral imperative for, philosophical and judicial doubt.

The short article written in Trieste is Joyce's first literary engagement with these crimes and trials and the issues they raise. The impact the Great Wyrley case made upon him is obvious. His reference to it is laconic, but this is quite typical of his other legal references. His approach in the article casts important light on his treatment of the other cases mentioned in his fiction and indeed on the underestimated role of facts – real, verifiable, historical 'hard' facts – in his writings. The more these facts are examined, and their context elucidated, the more significant they appear to me to be in themselves. By this I mean that they are significant when considered as historical facts, in a historical context, and should not be subordinated to some theory of 'fictionality', as that term is used, for example by Margot Norris in *Virgin and Veteran Readings of Ulysses*. Norris quotes another critic, Ruth Ronen, as saying: 'Within the fictional universe of discourse, truth is not determined relative to an extra textual universe, but relative to a fictional world in which only some of the textual assertions can establish facts.' Norris continues: 'In other words, "facts" in the fictional world of [*Ulysses*] are not determined by "facts" in the historical space of 1904 Dublin but only by the semantic or meaning-producing operation of the text.' Rather than 'truth' or 'error', fictional texts produce what Ronen calls 'warranted assertibility'.[51]

Norris and the author she quotes are reputable academic critics and her book is well worth reading. But the language she and her source use is typical of a sort of scholarly language which conveys no specific meaning at all. If one analyses it painstakingly she appears to be arguing for a world of factual references quite outside that of the hard historical facts which were the basis of *Ulysses*. The passages just cited come from Norris's article titled 'Possible Worlds Theory and the Fantasy Universe of *Finnegans Wake*'.[52] The 'possible world' to which Norris refers scorns the very notion of 'truth' or 'error' in favour of something that transcends these categories, or at least exists outside them, 'warranted assertibility'. With every respect to Margot Norris, this phrase is devoid of connotation outside the (barely) possible world of the academy. Though Norris herself is clearly a person who reveres Joyce, the kind of language I have quoted is a major disincentive to his works being widely read outside academia. It is also greatly at variance with what Joyce himself asserted, in the simplest of language, to be the basis of *Ulysses*, namely that he stuck close to the facts. He should be taken at his word.

The hard facts of the Maamtrasna and Great Wyrley cases are complex but entirely comprehensible. My premise is that if the actual, historical, facts of Joyce's references are teased out, they help to clarify Joyce's work and his intent. The process whereby this can be done is a historical and not a theoretical one. The history clarifies; the theory too often obscures and repels.

By the time *Ulysses* was published in book form in 1922, or even in serial form some years earlier, very few readers (and surely only Irish ones) would have preserved a memory of the Childs case of 1899 or the Flower case of 1900. But the details of these cases, when recovered, recall so strongly the themes of Joyce's 1907 article that it is hard to believe that he did not expect them to be appreciated in a similar way. The Edalji case is much better known and remembered, as is illustrated by the fairly recent republication of Conan Doyle's book and Julian Barnes's still more recent novel. This is perhaps accounted for by the fact of its being an English case.

The Edalji case and others like it reflect the gradual appreciation by the English public that its criminal justice system was not infallible and that prejudice and unjustified faith in police evidence had led to miscarriages of justice. This process was almost incredibly protracted. Some of Joyce's treatment of those themes directly reflects the social and intellectual changes that led to the creation of a Court of Criminal Appeal in England. This was in itself a recognition of the possibility of judicial error and the necessity of doubt.

The Court of Criminal Appeal for England and Wales sat for the first time on 15 May 1908, having been created by the Criminal Appeal Act 1907, 7 Edw. 7 c. 23. The Act was conceded in the Free State in 1924 and in Northern Ireland in 1930.[53]

For over fifty years prior to 1908, thoughtful opinion both within and outside the legal profession considered the lack of a Court of Criminal Appeal a serious defect in the British legal system. But the judiciary and Parliament had in general been firmly opposed to such a development on the ground that it would tend to undermine the reputation of the administration of criminal justice in England and Wales. In 1848 the Act for the Further Amendment of the Administration of the Criminal Law, 1848, 11 and 12 Vict. c. 78, had provided for a 'Court of Crown Cases reserved'. This was a court, composed on an *ad hoc* basis, to which a trial judge could, at his sole discretion, 'state a case', that is ask a question on a point of law only. This measure provided no real relief to a defendant unless the trial judge felt inclined to ask a question about the correctness of a decision he himself had made in the course of the trial.

Between 1844 and 1906 the question of providing a fuller appeal as of right was raised in the British Parliament on many occasions. Parliament considered thirty-one bills on the subject in those years but all of them were either withdrawn, defeated, or perished for lack of sufficient support in the preliminary stages of legislation – 'died on the order paper', as the parliamentary phrase went.

Predictably, much of the demand for a Court of Criminal Appeal arose out of capital cases where there was a risk of a wrongful execution. The Crown had always had a prerogative of mercy, that is, a power to commute the death sentence. After 1837, when the teenage Princess Victoria ascended the throne, it was arranged that this power should be exercised instead by the Home Secretary. Opponents of a Court of Criminal Appeal considered that this was a sufficient safeguard against wrongful executions. But a convict saved from the noose would still be subjected to penal servitude for life and there was nothing whatever that could be done about the conviction itself, however disturbing the circumstances of that decision might be. Pressure to establish a permanent Court of Criminal Appeal, to which there would be appeals as of right, continued throughout the nineteenth century, peaking at times when there had been a surprising conviction in a capital case.

On 13 November 1847 an editorial in *The Times* endorsed the campaign for a court of appeal, 'in the interest of that numerous class of persons who have been condemned contrary to law and justice, and who are left to languish out the best years of their life in imprisonment or banishment for want of such power of appeal'. The reference to banishment is to transportation to colonial penal colonies, a fate to which Irish political prisoners were subjected in 1848 and again after the Fenian uprisings of the 1860s.

A decisive role in the campaign for the establishment of a Court of Criminal Appeal was played by Sir James Fitzjames Stephen, a very distinguished public servant, and later a High Court judge. He was a brother of Leslie Stephen, founder and first editor of the *Dictionary of National Biography*, and an uncle of the novelist Virginia Woolf. Fitzjames Stephen was a man of commanding intellect, a distinguished academic lawyer at an early age, subsequently a member of the legislative council of India and parliamentary draftsman. In the latter capacity he drafted the Criminal Code (Indictable Offences) Bill, 1878, which would have created a Criminal Appeal Court. The bill was withdrawn but Stephen was created a High Court judge in part as recognition of his work on it.

Most unfortunately and ironically, it was the bias, confusion and growing mental incapacity of Stephen himself as a High Court judge in two notorious murder cases that gave real impetus to the campaign for a Court of Criminal Appeal.[54] Legal scholarship has identified four cases in particular, including the two presided over by Stephen, as having destroyed faith in the infallibility of the

English criminal process and led to the establishment of a Court of Criminal Appeal.[55]

These cases, accordingly, put Joyce's work into the context of contemporary legal thought in the time of his youth and early manhood. The changes in legal thought at that time, however, reflect the intellectual crisis of the end of the Victorian era generally. These included the undermining of religious certainty by developments in geology and biology, and, significantly, the erosion of belief in the literal truth of the Bible, specifically the age of the earth suggested there; crises within the Christian religion and in particular disputes between Anglicans and Roman Catholics, especially in England; and a consequential loss of belief in the necessary correctness of the pronouncements of authority, including legal authority. At the same time developments in philosophy questioned the nature of certainty itself, and raised the issue of whether truth was not a relative, as opposed to an absolute, conception.

Joyce never entered into these discussions of an abstract basis. But he recognized that great shifts were taking place in politics, science and law and he chronicled them creatively by focusing on the way in which these changes were manifested in the speech and patterns of thought of ordinary people. When the fictional characters living in Dublin in June 1904 discuss famous law cases, it is natural for them to focus on Irish cases of which they have direct experience, but the then new Yellow Press has made them aware of English ones as well. It is natural enough for Molly Bloom to think of the real or alleged crimes of Mrs Maybrick, whose sentence had been commuted only a few months previously. But if notorious English cases were well known in Ireland, there is no evidence that Irish cases, even notorious ones, were familiar in England or had any effect on the imperial legislature in introducing the Court of Criminal Appeal. The hanging of Myles Joyce for the Maamtrasna murders of 1882 was still felt as a scandal and political grievance in Ireland twenty-five years later, but it had ceased to excite any attention at all in the larger island. By contrast, the less serious (because non-capital) case of George Edalji commanded Joyce's attention when he lived in faraway Trieste precisely because it was a case of the sort (cattle-maiming) which the English Yellow Press used to discredit Irish people generally.

The Childs and the Great Wyrley cases are obviously seminal to Joyce's consideration of disputed allegations. The Childs case proceeded in the way that many cases did in Joyce's time and still do today: by the careful marshalling of material gathered on a one-sided basis, and the assiduous cultivation of prejudice against the accused, in the hope that this will cause the jury to overlook the fact that there is no logical, probative evidence at all for guilt. In some cases, like that of the unfortunate Mrs Maybrick mentioned by Molly Bloom, this technique worked. In others it failed, usually because of the skilful conduct of the defence.

The Childs case accustomed Joyce to think like a lawyer, that is to think in a rigorous way about what is, and what is not, logically probative evidence, and what is required before a chain of circumstantial evidence can convict a person beyond reasonable doubt. Various Irish cases in Joyce's youth, and in particular the Maamtrasna trial, demonstrate how short cuts were taken with the law of evidence and even show a government prepared to execute an innocent man and to keep various others in custody for decades rather than undermine confidence in the legal system. Many in Ireland believed that these things were the result of a cruder and more one-sided application of the law to Irish political defendants than to others. But the English Great Wyrley case confronted Joyce with the fact that this was not the whole story.

In literature, history and other academic subjects, no great harm is done when the received view of a particular event changes over the course of a couple of generations. But in law, decisions do not exist in the abstract: they have immediate and often devastating consequences for individuals. Joyce never lost sight of this, never lost what Andrew Gibson calls the 'will to justice' that is so evident in *Ulysses*.

Part II

3. Law, Crime and Punishment in Bloomsday Dublin

*U*lysses, famously, is rooted in time and place – Dublin, 16 June 1904 – while nonetheless aspiring to and achieving universality. The legal themes reflected in the novel are part of the techniques of that achievement.

This chapter offers a survey of most – not all – of Joyce's legal themes and cases, and of the lawyers who were, mostly, real-life contemporaries of James Joyce. It discusses Joyce's handling of these themes for his literary purposes and the light that legal and historical knowledge can sometimes throw on this. The richness of legal reference is paralleled by references to other subjects: medicine, music, politics and religion, to mention only the most obvious.

Amongst the criminal cases he mentions, Joyce had a marked partiality for doubtful cases where guilt and innocence seemed difficult to discern. He was also and independently interested in the public perceptions of notorious cases, especially the received view of them which the man or woman in the street gathered from the popular press. The civil cases cited may also be notorious, like the O'Shea divorce,[1] or reflect contemporary controversies such as bequests for the saying of Masses.[2] But most of them in one way or another relate to the strategies and misfortunes of people clinging to respectability in financially precarious positions: decrees for some small sums of money,[3] 'writs and garnishee orders',[4] bills of exchange requiring a backer,[5] and life insurance policies mortgaged or pledged.[6] The DMP and the Royal Irish Constabulary also feature: they are treated warily, with some respect but little affection.[7] Numerous barristers and solicitors appear in the book, from the wealthy and successful like Seymour Bushe, QC[8] and John Henry Menton,[9] the hard-headed solicitor, to the penniless J. J. O'Molloy[10] with his ruined career at the Bar and the struck-off solicitor O'Callaghan begging in the streets.[11] There are unexpectedly copious references to the judges of the day, seen generally as a caste apart, privileged and insulated, but respected and sometimes admirable.[12]

Criminal trials

As has been noted, eighteen of the thirty-two cases mentioned in *Ulysses* are criminal trials. All but a few of the cases in *Ulysses* and *Finnegans Wake* are real ones, ranging from *causes célèbres* well known to general history, Irish or otherwise, to others known principally to aficionados of the 'golden age of English murder' – like the 1912 trial of Frederick Seddon for the murder of his lodger

Miss Barrow[13] and the 1889 trial of Mrs Florence Maybrick for that of her husband.[14] As the mention of Seddon shows, some of the references are to events that took place during the writing of *Ulysses* (1914–22), rather than in and around 1904.

Mrs Maybrick

The case of Mrs Maybrick was hugely notorious in late-Victorian and Edwardian society. She was a respectable married woman who was accused of poisoning her husband, a Liverpool cotton broker, with arsenic. Whether she did so or not (the husband was addicted to patent medicines containing arsenic), it was certainly proved against her that she had taken a lover. It was exactly the sort of case Joyce loved: guilt or innocence probable but not certain. But Molly Bloom's reflections on the case reveal no doubts and are probably not untypical of their time:

> take that Mrs Maybrick that poisoned her husband for what I wonder in love with some other man yes it was found out on her wasnt she the downright villain to go and do a thing like that of course some men can be dreadfully aggravating drive you mad [...] white Arsenic she put in his tea off flypaper wasnt it I wonder why they call it that if I asked him hed say its from the Greek leave us as wise as we were before she must have been madly in love with the other fellow to run the chance of being hanged O she didnt care if that was her nature what could she do besides theyre not brutes enough to go and hang a woman surely are they.[15]

Mrs Maybrick was defended by Sir Charles Russell, QC, a Newry man, who later, as Lord Russell of Killowen,[16] became the first Catholic since the Reformation to hold the office of Lord Chief Justice of England. He also, famously, represented Parnell at the Special Commission, discredited *The Times*, which had set out to destroy Parnell, and uncovered the forger Piggott in an extraordinary cross-examination of which there are many echoes in *Finnegans Wake*. Russell never accepted Mrs Maybrick's guilt, believing that she had been convicted because of prejudice against her arising from her lax morals. He campaigned ceaselessly for her release, even as Chief Justice. She was in fact freed on 25 January 1904, a few months before the original Bloomsday.

Two Dublin murders

Less accessible to present-day readers are two Dublin murder cases which caused great excitement in the contemporary city but are now utterly obscure. The first was the Childs case, which, because of its importance, is discussed in some detail in the following chapter.[17]

The other contemporary case was the abortive trial of DMP Constable Henry Flower for the murder of Bridget Gannon, a 'slavey' working in Baggot Street, in August 1900.[18] The Flower case is deeply rooted in the texture of *Ulysses*: Bloom conducts a highly suggestive correspondence with the typist Martha Clifford under the pseudonym Henry Flower; his father's original name, Virag, means flower. Wordplay with these names and Bloom's own recurs in the novel. The story 'Two Gallants' in *Dubliners* also appears to reflect the Henry Flower case. The police had an unfortunate reputation. 'Was she in the habit of walking with policemen?', a friend of the dead woman was asked at the inquest.

Bridget Gannon's body was found in the River Dodder on 23 August 1900. The place is still clearly identifiable today from the descriptions at the police court hearings: it is opposite the south-east corner of Lansdowne Road rugby ground. The body was removed from the river by a sergeant and two constables of the DMP, one of whom was Henry Flower. The sergeant asked the constables and bystanders whether anyone knew her: Flower said he did not. At a rapidly convened inquest a verdict of accidental drowning was found. But almost immediately another housemaid called Margaret Clowry came forward and described an outing she and the deceased woman had had with Constable Flower and a Constable Dockery some ten days previously. More pointedly, she described how she, the deceased and Constable Flower met and went for a walk on the night previous to the finding of the body; at a hint from Flower she had left the deceased woman and the constable less than a quarter-mile from the fatal spot at Londonbridge Road. The gatekeeper at the Lansdowne Road junction then came forward to say that he had seen the constable and the deceased crossing the railway junction, two or three minutes' walk from Londonbridge road, late on that evening.[19]

On the basis of this information a second inquest was convened. Flower's counsel objected to this, invoking the verdict at the first inquest. Proceedings were adjourned and on 5 September 1900 Mr Justice Barton made a conditional order of *certiorari* quashing the verdict of the first inquest, and an absolute order two days later. Barton himself, as we shall see, is independently mentioned in *Ulysses* in his capacity as a Shakespearian scholar. On 11 September 1900, Flower was arrested and charged with the murder of Bridget

Gannon. Three days later there was a major sensation in Dublin when Sergeant Hanily, the man in charge of the party that had removed the body from the river, committed suicide by cutting his throat in the sergeants' mess of Irishtown Police Station. After five days of evidence, Flower was returned for trial for the murder of Bridget Gannon. But he was never tried, for reasons I will mention in a moment.

Apart from literary considerations, the historical interest of these cases is considerable. The leading counsel in each case – Tim Healy ('that brilliant calamity') and Timothy Harrington,[20] three times Lord Mayor of Dublin, who features in *Ulysses* in that connection also – displayed a coat-trailing anti-establishment effrontery in the successful defences of their respective clients. Healy's co-counsel and technical senior, much praised by Joyce in the *Aeolus* episode of *Ulysses*, was Seymour Bushe. Bushe was a descendant of Lord Chancellor William Conyngham Plunket and 'the silver-tongued' Chief Justice, Charles Kendal Bushe. But he is in decline: his promotion is impossible because of his dalliance with the 'beast with two backs'[21] and he is also a symbol of a liberal caste destined for eclipse, crushed between the Unionist and nationalist masses. An example of Bushe's eloquence, in the High Victorian style, is given in the *Aelous* episode of *Ulysses*, where the Childs case is also discussed.

The cryptic reference to the reasons why Bushe had not become a judge is historically well founded and is explained in a note of October 1970 by the late Colum Gavan Duffy, Librarian of the Incorporated Law Society of Ireland:

It seems that a certain Sir [name omitted] Brook and his wife were rather estranged, and that on a certain occasion the husband followed his wife to Dublin. He eventually found his wife in the room of Mr Bushe and threatened to take proceedings against him. As there was no divorce in Ireland these proceedings would consist in the tort of criminal conversation, whereby the husband would sue the alleged co-respondent for damages for adultery. It is for this reason that I understand Mr Bushe left... he also drank heavily.[22]

In 1886 Gerald Brooke, a wealthy Dubliner, obtained a parliamentary divorce from his wife, formerly the Honourable Kathleen Maude, daughter of Viscount Hawarden, on the grounds that on 2 October 1885 she did 'elope with Seymour Bushe, of Ely Place, Dublin, Barrister-at-Law, with whom she had since lived and cohabited in a state of adultery'. The private Divorce Bill, which became Brooks Divorce Act 1886,[23] chronicles the extraordinary rapidity with which between October 1885 and the following June Mr Brooke obtained a divorce from his wife, a decree for £1,000 damages for criminal conversation against Bushe the very next day, and subsequently the parliamentary divorce. Bushe left Ireland in 1904 and took silk – became a Queen's Counsel – in London with a view to practising at the parliamentary Bar. He seems to have abandoned the practice after a short time and died in 1921, leaving an estate of just over £12,000. He is spoken of very kindly by legal memoirists of the day[24] and by the historian of the Dublin University Club and the Kildare Street Club, Professor R. B. McDowell.[25]

Timothy Harrington is an interesting figure in his own right, and in terms of his Joycean connections. An MP from 1883 until his death in 1910, he was known for his expertise in financial policy and Land Law and for his prowess in party organization, rather than as a platform or parliamentary orator. He practised as a barrister from 1882. He did not take silk, and his practice is said to have suffered by reason of his political commitments. He was present in Green Street Court House for the opening of the Dublin City Commission in the winter of 1900, when Flower was brought up, even though it was polling day in the general election of that year. He was a close friend of John Stanislaus Joyce,[26] and was apparently instrumental in getting him several jobs, including the post in the rate collector's office that provided Joyce senior with the only steady employment of his life until he lost it in 1891. In November 1902, as Lord Mayor of Dublin, he gave James Joyce a reference or testimonial on the occasion of his departure for Paris. It may be that it was his involvement in the Flower case that drew Joyce's attention to it. In the same year Harrington hosted at the Mansion House a Land Conference which led to the Land Act 1903 – the Wyndham Act, which made it easier for tenants to purchase their holdings from landlords and effectively subsidized the transfer of farms to tenants. This was seen by extreme nationalists as 'conciliationism' and distanced him from the leadership of the Irish Party under John Redmond, who maintained (at least publicly) an attitude of non-co-operation with the government. At his death he left an estate of just £1,500.

Each of these cases has features of considerable legal historical interest. Central to the result in the Childs case was the fact that the Criminal Evidence Act 1898, permitting a defendant or his spouse to give evidence in a criminal trial, was deliberately not applied to Ireland, a decision very controversial at the time. During the debates on the measure, two Irish legal members who usually found themselves opposed combined to exclude Ireland from the effect of the Act. These were Edward Carson and Tim Healy. The latter envisaged a peasant woman on trial and counsel 'plying her with question after question, knowing that the time must come when her answer will take her to the gallows'.[27] The legal case in favour of the measure was principally put by Sir Edward Clarke, who had of course been Carson's opponent when he defended the Marquis of Queensbury against the prosecution for criminal libel taken by Oscar Wilde. Interestingly, it appears that in view of the united Irish opposition the government decided that it was unconstitutional to force the measure on Ireland. At the Childs trial, each side went to great lengths to hint that the wife, if only she could speak, would prove its case beyond doubt. But her body language in sitting beside the dock, accompanied by a clergyman who gave character evidence for the prisoner, clearly indicated that she favoured the defence.

In Flower's case, the constable successfully claimed privilege in refusing to answer even basic questions, such as whether he had known the deceased woman, at the coroner's inquest. He was duly returned for trial on a murder charge with an apparently strong case against him. But the judge, Mr Justice Gibson, a brother of the Lord Chancellor of Ireland, Lord Ashbourne, strongly urged the grand jury to refuse to return a 'True Bill' of Indictment. They obliged, thereby ending the case without a trial.

In his address to the grand jury, Gibson emphasized the possibility that a person walking along the path by the River Dodder might accidentally have fallen in, especially since the body was found near a point where the low wall was somewhat broken down. He said he had visited the spot himself. He also considered the possibility that her companion, especially if he was indeed a policeman, might have thought it wise to make himself scarce after such an event rather than draw attention to his presence with the lady in this secluded location. Such conduct, he said, would be disgraceful but not criminal.

Flower may have been innocent after all. The distinguished if maverick Joycean scholar (and leading Dublin civil servant) John Garvin records that in the 1940s a gravely ill woman in a Dublin tenement, on the advice of a priest attending her, sent for a solicitor to whom she made a 'dying declaration' in relation to the death of Bridget Gannon. She was Margaret Clowry, the woman who first drew suspicion on Flower. She said that she had met Bridget Gannon after Flower had left her and quarrelled with her about money which was in her possession, perhaps as a *douceur* from Flower. She said she had purloined her cash and pushed the woman into the river.[28] As it happens, the solicitor to whom the dying woman made this declaration was John Cusack, a son of Michael Cusack, a prominent late-nineteenth-century nationalist and founder of the GAA who is the prototype for the Citizen in the *Cyclops* episode of *Ulysses*. This character, an object of ridicule, is a cruelly effective parody of a bombastic nationalist.[29]

The police

The evocation of the DMP by the mention of Constable Flower is of a piece with Joyce's cautious attitude to the force in general. They feature throughout the book. He sees them as a shrewd, earthy, sensual body of men, always on the lookout for the main chance in police work or in their personal affairs, or preferably both at once. They are 'prepared to swear a hole through a ten gallon pot';[30] 'always courting slaveys';[31] 'Peeping Tom through the keyhole'.[32] A squad of constables are seen on College Street after their lunch in the barracks:

Foodheated faces, sweating helmets, patting their truncheons. After their feed with a good load of fat soup under their belts. Policeman's lot is oft a happy one. They split up in groups and scattered, saluting, towards their beats. Let out to graze. Best moment to attack one in pudding time. A punch in his dinner. A squad of others, marching irregularly, round Trinity railings making for the station. Bound for their troughs. Prepare to receive cavalry. Prepare to receive soup. [...]

He gazed after the last broad tunic. Nasty customers to tackle. Jack Power could a tale unfold: father a G man. If a fellow gave them trouble being lagged they let him have it hot and heavy in the bridewell. Can't blame them after all with the job they have especially the young hornies.[33]

At a higher level Assistant Commissioner John Mallon, the self-described 'great Irish detective',[34] credited with the solving of the Phoenix Park murders, is portrayed giving 'a strong hint to a blind horse'[35] about a fortunately placed member of society who was then spirited away 'so as not to be made amenable under section two of the criminal law amendment act, certain names of those subpoenaed being handed in but not divulged'.[36] The Act is that under which Oscar Wilde was prosecuted for 'gross indecency' with another man, though under section 11, not section 2. It has been speculated that the numeral 11 was mistaken by Joyce or his printers for the Roman numeral II. The network of informants controlled by Mallon and his like is portrayed as notorious and a reason for not getting involved in subversion, 'there always being the offchance of a Dannyman coming forward and turning queen's evidence or king's now like Denis or Peter Carey',[37] thinks Bloom, remembering the Invincible approver of that surname: 'Quite apart from that he disliked those careers of wrongdoing and crime on principle.'[38]

Less notorious cases feature too, often with just a phrase, throughout the text: 'Jack Fleming embezzling to gamble';[39] 'Bags Comisky [...] fined ten bob for a drunk and disorderly and refusing to go with the constable'.[40] In *Cyclops* we read about a certain Michael Geraghty, plumber, decreed to pay three shillings a week off his debt to Moses Herzog – the plaintiff said the action was for goods sold and delivered but the defendant said it was a dressed-up moneylending transaction and that Herzog had no moneylenders' licence[41] (the court accepted the plaintiff's account); the 'Canada swindle case' when 'James Wought alias Saphiro alias Spark and Spiro, put an ad in the papers saying he'd give a passage to Canada for twenty bob' and 'Swindled them all, skivvies and badhachs from the county Meath, ay, and his own kidney too';[42] hawkers up before the recorder for selling memorial cards for the Invincible Joe Brady,[43] and many other petty cases.

Civil actions

Another episode, *Wandering Rocks*, follows many Dublin citizens going about their business in Dublin on 16 June 1904. One of the places visited is the Four Courts, the Round Hall of which was then festooned with statues of former luminaries of the legal profession:

> Lawyers of the past, haughty, pleading, beheld pass from the consolidated taxing office to Nisi Prius court Richie Goulding carrying the costbag of Goulding, Collis and Ward and heard rustling from the admiralty division of king's bench to the court of appeal an elderly female with false teeth smiling incredulously and a black silk skirt of great amplitude.[44]

These 'lawyers of the past' were Lord Chancellor Plunket, Sir Michael O'Loughlen, Master of the Rolls, Chief Baron Joy, Chief Justice Whiteside, Richard Lalor Sheil and Lord Chancellor O'Hagan. All the statues were erected between 1851 and 1887. The appetite of the profession and the judges for statuary seemed to have become sated in that year because two niches left vacant were still unfilled when the rest were destroyed by the bombardment of the Four Courts by Free State forces in 1922, when the buildings were occupied by the IRA faction opposed to the Anglo-Irish Treaty. There is another, seated, statue of Chief Justice Whiteside by the same sculptor in St Patrick's Cathedral.[45]

This lady's exit from the courts is described a few pages later:

> An elderly female, no more young, left the building of the courts of chancery, king's bench, exchequer and common pleas, having heard in the lord chancellor's court the case in lunacy of Potterton, in the admiralty division the summons, exparte motion, of the owners of the Lady Cairns versus the owners of the barque Mona, in the court of appeal reservation

of judgment in the case of Harvey versus the Ocean Accident and Guarantee Corporation.[46]

The Admiralty case was a simple marine collision. Shipping cases interested Joyce, especially the series of unexplained collisions and wreckings which destroyed the plan to develop Galway as a transatlantic port. These are referred to several times, notably in the discourse of the old sailor in the cabman's shelter in *Eumaeus*: 'What he wanted to ascertain was why that ship ran bang against the only rock in Galway bay when the Galway harbour scheme was mooted [...] Ask the then captain, he advised them, how much palmoil the British government gave him for that day's work, Captain John Lever of the Lever Line.'[47]

The judge in the case of the *Lady Cairns* would have been Mr Justice Johnson, Admiralty judge between 1897 and 1910. The physical appearance of the Admiralty Court during a collision case is described in an anonymous pamphlet, *Our Judges*, published under the pen name 'Rhadamantus' in 1890:

Like a Court scene in private theatricals. Everything seems to be out of proportion. The nautical assessors are cooped up in one corner of the Bench [...] there is a little black table with white lines and figures, showing the points of the compass; and on the Registrar's desk stands a model of a ship, for all the world like a toy in Lawrence's window, but intended to illustrate to the unskilled advocate the important distinction between the port and starboard sides of a vessel.[48]

The *Mona* was a German vessel which collided with the *Lady*

Cairns off the Kish Bank outside Dublin Port on 20 March 1904, in 'muggyish' weather. The *Lady Cairns* was lost with all hands. The case was resolved in favour of the *Mona* in June 1904, on the basis that the other vessel was on a port tack and not keeping a proper lookout, being obliged to give right of way to the *Mona* on a starboard tack. There was apparently some feeling against the *Mona* in Dublin at the time and a later reference in *Eumaeus* records: 'No aid was given. Her master, the *Mona*'s, said he was afraid his collision bulkhead would give way. She had no water, it appears, in her hold.'[49] However, the evidence in court was that the *Mona* was disabled and had to be towed into Dublin Port.

Joyce was also very interested in insurance cases, as we will see in Chapter 5. The boozers in the *Cyclops* episode debate about whether Paddy Dignam's widow will benefit from his life insurance policy, which Dignam had mortgaged, without notice to the insurer. Bloom opines that, as Dignam did not serve notice of the assignment, the mortgagee cannot recover on the policy.[50] The Act in question is the Policies of Assurance Act 1867.[51] This provides that an assignment of a policy of life assurance did not confer on the assignee any right to sue on the policy until a written notice of the assignment had been given to the insurance company which had issued the policy at their principal place of business. The consequences of failing to give this notice are illustrated in the Irish case, In the Matter of R. F. Young, a bankrupt (see pp. 158–9).[52] The third case mentioned is *Harvey v The Ocean Accident and Guarantee Corporation*, for a detailed discussion of which see pp. 172–3.[53] The technical point raised relates to the onus of proof in an action on a life insurance policy which excludes payment in the event of suicide; the case is a fascinating one as a social document.

The case has striking similarities to that of Constable Flower, though I do not think the correspondence has previously been noticed. Both cases deal with a type of uncertainty that fascinated Joyce. The episode in *Ulysses* in which the case is mentioned was drafted perhaps a decade and a half after the case, and this may indicate that Joyce used the Irish Reports as a source; if so, he is likely to have been attracted by the detailed account of the financial strategies and shifts of poor Harvey as he lived from hand to mouth, just as he was by those of Paddy Dignam mortgaging his policy and J. J. O'Molloy looking for someone to back his bills of exchange, and pawning his watch. These and other strategies of those who lead lives of quiet desperation are a staple of the book and are ridiculed in *Circe*, when Nosey Flynn asks: 'Can I raise a mortgage on my fire insurance?'[54]

Libel and publication

The law of libel is represented in *Ulysses* by the demented Denis Breen going from one solicitor to another wanting to sue for libel the sender of a very obscure postcard with the letters U. P. on it. He hopes, his wife says, for £10,000 damages. Strange as it seems, this episode leads to one of the two citations of a reported case in the book. The broken-down barrister J. J. O'Molloy construes the letters as meaning that Breen is not *compos mentis*, and cites *Sadgrove v Hole*[55] about the circumstances in which one can sue for libel in respect of a message on an open postcard. And he solemnly warns the boozers who point out that Breen is indeed quite mad, that 'the truth of a libel is no defence to an indictment for publishing it in the eyes of the law',[56] thus confusing civil and criminal libel. Truth is a full defence to a civil action for defamation.

Breach of promise

Another case tried in the Irish courts in June 1904 makes several appearances in the book. This is *Delaney* v *Burke*, an action for breach of promise of marriage against a Revenue official. The facts are bizarre, since the parties met in the Gaelic League and part of their relationship seems to have been conducted in Irish. 'Lovemaking in Irish,' declared the *Evening Telegraph* headline, '£200 damages.'[57] However, what impressed Joyce was the defendant's shaming experience of having private letters with pet names and lovey-dovey language read out in open court to general amusement; this occurs to Bloom in the *Sirens* episode, especially when he tries to get some privacy to reply in suitably salacious terms to Martha Clifford, under his pen name of Henry Flower, as he sits in the bar of the Ormond Hotel on Dublin's Quays: 'Blot over the other so he can't read. [...] Something detective read off blottingpad. [...] Letters read out for breach of promise. From Chickabiddy's owny Mumpsypum. Laughter in court. Henry. I never signed it.'[58]

Bloom's (and presumably Joyce's) fear of detection in this clandestine correspondence is dramatically mirrored in *The King* v *Bloom* in the *Circe* episode.[59] This is a crazy, nightmarish, Kafkaesque case in which Bloom, drunk in Nightown (the Dublin red-light district in an area near Amiens Street railway station) imagines himself the hapless defendant, accused of all sorts of sexual peccadilloes, most of which he has committed (if at all) only in his head. All Bloom's insecurities are exposed in this piece, but an alibi is eventually provided for him by his spectral defence counsel, an amalgam of the characters of J. J. O'Molloy, Seymour Bushe, QC and John F. Taylor, QC.

The O'Shea divorce

The fate of Charles Stewart Parnell preoccupied Joyce and features again and again in his writings, most famously in the bitter family row which breaks out over Christmas dinner in the house in Bray, Co. Wicklow, in *A Portrait of the Artist as a Young Man*.[60] A poem he wrote on the topic as a child, addressed to Parnell's chief tormentor under the title *Et Tu, Healy*, became his first published work when his proud father had it privately printed; unfortunately no copies of the poem survive.[61]

In the *Eumaeus* episode of *Ulysses* the Parnell case comes up in conversation in the cabman's shelter where Bloom takes Stephen Dedalus to sober up after their trip to Nighttown. A cabman there expresses the view that Parnell is not dead but simply living abroad and will return. Bloom dismisses this canard in his own mind, though reflecting that Parnell's undoubted habit of disappearing for long periods and adopting aliases had given some colour to the story. He reflects in a tolerant way on Parnell's affair with Katherine O'Shea. It was: 'First it was strictly Platonic till nature intervened and an attachment sprang up between them till bit by bit matters came to a climax and the matter became the talk of the town [...] it

was simply a case of the husband not being up to the scratch [...]
and then a real man arriving on the scene'.[62]

Bloom rejects the shelter proprietor's theory that: 'That bitch,
that English whore, did for him [...] She put the first nail in his
coffin.'[63] But he cannot understand why the unhappy couple let the
matter proceed as far as the divorce court:

> Since their names were coupled, though, since he was her
> declared favourite, where was the particular necessity to
> proclaim it to the rank and file from the housetops, the fact,
> namely, that he had shared her bedroom which came out in
> the witnessbox on oath when a thrill went through the packed
> court literally electrifying everybody in the shape of witnesses
> swearing to having witnessed him on such and such a particular
> date in the act of scrambling out of an upstairs apartment
> with the assistance of a ladder in night apparel, having
> gained admittance in the same fashion, a fact the weeklies,
> addicted to the lubric a little, simply coined shoals of money
> out of.[64]

Then he reflects that 'the matter became the talk of the town till
the staggering blow came as a welcome intelligence to not a few
evildisposed, however, who were resolved upon encompassing
his downfall'.[65] Bloom ruefully recalls the famous meeting of the
Irish Parliamentary Party after the divorce court proceedings 'then
seventytwo of his trusty henchmen rounding on him with mutual
mudslinging'.[66] He also blames 'the priests and ministers of the
gospel as a whole, his erstwhile staunch adherents, and his beloved
evicted tenants [...] very effectually cooked his matrimonial goose,

thereby heaping coals of fire on his head'.[67] But the topic is an uncomfortable one for Bloom, who that very day is playing the cuckolded Captain O'Shea to Blazes Boylan's Parnell and Molly Bloom's Katherine O'Shea.

Bloom's bewilderment about how the case went as far as the divorce court was of course shared by many contemporaries. The affair was an open secret to large sections of the leadership of the Liberal Party and the Irish Party for years before the divorce proceedings were issued at the end of 1889, but they were not called upon to take a public stance on the relationship until after the divorce hearing.[68] The tragic Mrs O'Shea asked Parnell in 1890, 'Why does it matter more now – they have all known about it for years?'[69] But the divorce case, as Joyce put it, proclaimed the affair from the house tops, and not merely the affair but the sordid details of backstairs escapes, the subornation of servants and the like. Yet many English statesmen behaved with great reserve. Gladstone denied that being the leader of a party 'constitutes a man a judge and accuser of faith and morals'. There was another reason for this restraint: as a clerical correspondent pointed out to Gladstone, 'It would be unfortunate if the Irish were to retort [to any condemnation of Parnell] with the case of Lord Hartington,' a Cabinet member who like at least one other (John Morley) was believed to reside with his mistress.[70] There is an echo of this in the *Circe* episode when Bloom, who had claimed to be English, is defended by J. J. O'Molloy on a charge of indecently assaulting his maid on the grounds that 'such familiarities as the alleged guilty occurrence being quite permitted in my client's native place'.[71]

Bequests for Masses

When Bloom steps into the Catholic church in Westland Row with his letter from Martha Clifford,[72] his thoughts turn to one of the longest-running legal disputes of the nineteenth and early twentieth centuries. Catholics often left money in their wills for the celebration of Masses for the salvation of their own or other people's souls. At the time there was a lively legal issue about whether a bequest of this sort was 'merely [i.e. entirely, purely] charitable' within the meaning of section 8 of the Stamp Duties (Ireland) Act 1842. If so the legacy was exempt from duty. The question gave rise to a good deal of litigation and various forms of bequest were used. Two of these – an alternative legacy to a clergyman to be used at his own discretion in the event of the testator dying within three months of the will, and a bequest for Masses to be said in public – were frequently adopted. Bloom thinks:

> Squareheaded chaps those must be in Rome: they work the whole show. And don't they rake in the money too? Bequests also: to the P. P. for the time being in his absolute discretion. Masses for the repose of my soul to be said publicly with open doors. Monasteries and convents. The priest in that Fermanagh will case in the witnessbox. No browbeating him. He had his answer pat for everything. Liberty and exaltation of our holy mother the church. The doctors of the church: they mapped out the whole theology of it.[73]

Three of the judges mentioned in *Ulysses*, Christopher Palles (the grandly titled Lord Chief Baron of the Exchequer), Hedges Eyre

Chatterton, Vice-Chancellor of Ireland for nearly forty years until 1904, and Lord Justice Gerald Fitzgibbon considered some of these issues. *Attorney General* v *Delaney*[74] was a claim by the Attorney General to legacy duty on sums left for Masses on the basis that these bequests were 'pious' but not charitable. Palles thought that 'It is said in some of the cases that religious purposes are charitable but that can only be true as to religious services tending directly or indirectly towards the instruction or edification of the public.' He therefore concluded that charitable status could only attach to Mass bequests which required that the Masses be celebrated in public. This was a somewhat restrictive decision, delivered by a man who was a Clongowes-educated Catholic. Twenty years later, in *Attorney General* v *Hall and Byrne*,[75] a much less restrictive view was taken by Fitzgibbon (a high-ranking Freemason) who concluded that bequests for Masses were valid charitable requests whether the Masses were said in public or in private. Moreover, he did not think it proper for the civil courts to second-guess the views of the church concerned: 'I cannot think that the temporal courts are to compare or to contrast the public benefit involved in the ministration of clergy of different denominations where the ministrations, according to the creed and ritual of the church concerned, edify and benefit those who participate in them.'

Fitzgibbon's colleagues at this time did not consider it necessary to go as far as that, but the issue was conclusively resolved in favour of Fitzgibbon's view in *O'Hanlon* v *Logue*.[76] Unusually, both Palles and Fitzgibbon were on the court in this case and Palles executed a remarkable and elaborately reasoned volte-face. Bequests for Masses were thenceforth regarded as charitable whether their celebration took place in public or private.

Judges and lawyers

Some nineteen Irish judges of the day are involved in one way or another in the action of *Ulysses*, ranging from the Dublin Police Magistrate Mr Thomas Wall, KC[77] to the Lord Chancellor of Ireland, Lord Ashbourne.[78] By far the most favourably treated is Sir Frederick Falkiner, QC, Recorder of Dublin from 1876 to 1905. Joyce admires this judge because he is reluctant to give decrees to moneylenders and because he tries to keep the police in order: in the *Lestrygonians* episode, the eighth, Bloom sees him going into Freemasons Hall in Molesworth Street, after he himself has enjoyed a glass of Burgundy in Davy Byrne's 'moral pub':

> Sir Frederick Falkiner going into the freemason's hall. Solemn as Troy. After his good lunch in Earlsfort terrace. Old legal cronies cracking a magnum. Tales of the bench and assizes and annals of the bluecoat school. I sentenced him to ten years. I suppose he'd turn up his nose at that stuff I drank. Vintage wine for them, the year marked on a dusty bottle. Has his own ideas of justice in the recorder's court. Wellmeaning old man. Police chargesheets crammed with cases get their percentage manufacturing crime. Sends them to the rightabout. The devil on moneylenders. Gave Reuben J. a great strawcalling. Now he's really what they call a dirty jew. Power those judges have. Crusty old topers in wigs. Bear with a sore paw. And may the Lord have mercy on your soul.[79]

The circumstances of Sir Frederick's attack on the money-lender Reuben J. Dodd are given in the *Cyclops* episode, where Sir

Frederick receives a typically backhanded Dublin compliment from the late-afternoon boozers, in which a shrewd appreciation of his weakness is combined with an acknowledgement of his fundamental decency:

—Who tried the case? says Joe.

—Recorder, says Ned.

—Poor old sir Frederick, says Alf, you can cod him up to the two eyes.

—Heart as big as a lion, says Ned. Tell him a tale of woe about arrears of rent and a sick wife and a squad of kids and, faith, he'll dissolve in tears on the bench.

—Ay, says Alf. Reuben J was bloody lucky he didn't clap him in the dock the other day for suing poor little Gumley that's minding stones, for the corporation there near Butt bridge.

And he starts taking off the old recorder letting on to cry:

—A most scandalous thing! This poor hardworking man! How many children? Ten, did you say?

—Yes, your worship. And my wife has the typhoid.

—And the wife with typhoid fever! Scandalous! Leave the court immediately, sir. No, sir, I'll make no order for payment. How dare you, sir, come up before me and ask me to make an order! A poor hardworking industrious man! I dismiss the case.[80]

Falkiner, who wrote several books and was the subject of affectionate reminiscences after he died, narrowly escaped death in 1882, the year of the Invincible murders. A man came into Green Street Court House, where he was sitting, and discharged a pistol at him at point-blank range. The weapon misfired twice and the man was captured. Falkiner did not mention the event to his family, who were bemused when they read of it in the newspaper.[81] In the same year, Mr Justice Lawson was the subject of an attempted shooting in Nassau Street as he walked from his house in Merrion Square to a dinner in King's Inns. He overcame his assailant with the aid of his detective and stepped in to regale the drinkers in the bar of the adjacent Kildare Street Club with the episode, 'where the occurrence produced considerable excitement',[82] according to the club's history.

The other judicial characters vary widely. The greatest of all Irish judges of the nineteenth and early twentieth centuries, Chief Baron Palles, merits only two lines of a never-completed anecdote.[83] His colleague Lord Justice Fitzgibbon, a brilliant Unionist apologist as well as a judge, is more extensively but more coldly portrayed speaking against the Irish language revival movement. Professor MacHugh takes up the narrative in the *Aeolus* episode:

—[...] Mr Justice Fitzgibbon, the present lord justice of appeal, had spoken and the paper under debate was an essay (new for those days) advocating the revival of the Irish tongue.

He [Professor MacHugh] turned towards Myles Crawford and said:

—You know Gerald Fitzgibbon. Then you can imagine the style of his discourse. [...] It was the speech, mark you, the professor said, of a finished orator, full of courteous haughtiness and pouring in chastened diction I will not say the vials of his wrath but pouring the proud man's contumely upon the new movement. It was then a new movement. We were weak, therefore worthless.[84]

Lord Justice Fitzgibbon was himself the son of a Master in Chancery, also Gerald Fitzgibbon. He was a brilliant man of High Tory politics, one of a select circle who were intimates of Lord Randolph Churchill when the latter was Private Secretary to his father, the Chief Secretary, in the 1870s. He was much concerned with educational and other charities and is also mentioned in *Ulysses* as sitting with Tim Healy, MP on the Trinity College Estates Commission.[85]

His son, the third Gerald Fitzgibbon, was appointed by the Cosgrave government to the Irish Free State Supreme Court in 1924, where he served until 1938. This Fitzgibbon had previously been successively MP and TD for Trinity College. Those with a taste for judicial *arcana* will enjoy his judgment in *O'Conghaile* v *Wallace*.[86] The passage from pages 560–66 of the report is perhaps the most savage rebuke by one member of an appellate court to another member to be found outside the United States. The victim was Mr Justice Creed Meredith, ironically another non-Catholic member of the court.

Having quoted 'Professor' MacHugh's somewhat prejudicial description of Lord Justice Fitzgibbon, it seems fair to record a more human, though still somewhat disapproving, impression of him by John Morley, sometime Chief Secretary for Ireland. He describes Fitzgibbon's annual house party at his residence in Howth, at which the guests were all male:

> They dined in shooting coats and slippers, or anyhow provided it is not clean, at seven, ate and drank 'til about eight-thirty, played cards 'til twelve, then a supper of oysters and snipe, then cards 'til any hour [...] no woman was allowed in

the house and in the morning at ten Lord Justice Fitzgibbon, unshorn and untoothed, brought them each a cup of tea. They breakfasted at eleven; they again began to play cards and this went on for a week.[87]

Sir Andrew Porter, the Master of the Rolls and prosecutor of the Invincibles in 1883, is noted in *Ulysses* only for a culinary reason: 'Spread I saw down in the Master of the Rolls' kitchen area. Whitehatted *chef* like a rabbi. Combustible duck. Curly cabbage *à la duchesse de Parme*. Just as well to write it on the bill of fare so you can know what you've eaten.'[88] This feast was glimpsed by Bloom as he passed Porter's residence at 42 Merrion Square East. There is still a plaque to Porter inside the main gateway of Queen's University, Belfast.

Sir Dunbar Plunket Barton[89] of the Chancery Division and the Honourable Dodgson Hamilton Madden[90] of the Queen's Bench both feature during the long discussion of Shakespeare in the National Library in the *Scylla and Charybdis* episode; both were Shakespearian scholars. Madden wrote *The Diary of Master William Silence*,[91] a Shakespearian study very well known in its day, and Barton wrote *Links between Shakespeare and the Law*, and *Links between Ireland and Shakespeare*.[92] He also wrote an affectionate memoir of Tim Healy.[93] He was a cousin of Seymour Bushe, QC. Barton was a wealthy man who on appointment to the bench resigned as a director of the Guinness brewery, and from several bank and other boards.

The Childs murder case which interested Joyce so much was tried by Mr Justice William Kenny,[94] reputed to be an impartial judge by most members of the Bar but a Castle Catholic of so deep a dye that, as Healy recalls, 'He would have given anything except his immortal soul to be a Protestant.'[95] From a very different political background was Richard Adams, sometime county court judge of Limerick, who features in *Eumaeus* as the 'legal luminary [who] saved the skin' of James 'Skin-the-Goat' Fitzharris, the getaway driver for the killers during the Invincible trials.[96] In *Aeolus* he is praised by Myles Crawford, the overbearing editor of the *Evening Telegraph*. He was appointed to the county court bench in 1892 (see p. 218). As a judge, however, Adams was sometimes capable of broad, not to say gross, humour on the bench. According to Serjeant Sullivan, a particularly bad outburst of this sort led the Bishop of Limerick to warn his flock against unnecessary attendance in Judge Adams's court.[97]

Solicitors and barristers

References to solicitors and barristers abound in *Ulysses*. There are also many allusions to medical practitioners, and these have been ably explored by Dr J. B. Lyons.[98] (As has been noted, Joyce, like his father before him, spent two very brief periods as a medical student, and he also attended law lectures for a short time; he was very seriously urged by his father to become a barrister.)[99] In each case, there are also references to the less distinguished members of the professions, Dr O'Gargle, the 'whiskey breathed doctor',[100] having his counterpart in the struck-off solicitor O'Callaghan.

Joyce enormously – I believe excessively – admired the liberal and progressive Seymour Bushe. He is portrayed as the only Irish lawyer of the day fit to compare for eloquence with John Philpot Curran.

His speech in the Childs case is lauded to the skies (see pp. 133–5). But a perusal of the trial reports shows that the brunt of the defence was borne by Healy, not Bushe.

In *Aeolus* Stephen Dedalus is deeply impressed by an extract from Bushe's speech declaimed by an admirer in the editor's office of the *Evening Telegraph* and by another extract from a speech by the nationalist barrister John F. Taylor, QC, also quoted at great length there. This was in response to the oration of Lord Justice Fitzgibbon mentioned above. Stephen, impressed anew, wonders whether he could try his hand at law himself,[101] briefly flirting with the idea of a legal or political career and perhaps reflecting Joyce's own roads not taken. In the *Ithaca* episode there is a list of a number of careers which might have been open to Bloom. Amongst them is the Bar and the exemplars given are again Seymour Bushe, QC and Rufus Isaacs, KC.[102] Isaacs was a flamboyantly successful English Jewish barrister who as Attorney General prosecuted Frederick Seddon, and then became Lord Chief Justice and wartime Ambassador to the United States. He later resigned judicial office and became Viceroy of India and Foreign Secretary. The comparison is hugely flattering to Bushe.

Social and economic perceptions of lawyers

Joyce, famously, was brought up in stifling and worsening poverty, the son of a man who started life both well provided for and well connected, and dissipated both his fortune and his chances.[103] Like many people with this background, Joyce was almost morbidly sensitive to the penumbra of poverty and decline, especially amongst those who, like his father, were precariously clinging to the lower slopes of the lower-middle class. In the *Proteus* episode, the third, he reflects on the decline of his father and his uncle, and the shame he experienced on that account as a schoolboy and his compensating boasts: 'Houses of decay, mine, his and all. You told the Clongowes gentry you had an uncle a judge and an uncle a general in the army.'[104]

Later, while James was at school in Belvedere, Joyce's father's remaining properties were sold to satisfy a creditor, the money-lender Reuben J. Dodd, who was the father of a classmate. This presumably explains his praise of Sir Frederick Falkiner's condemnation of Dodd for rapacity in *Ulysses*. Most of the lawyers in the novel are portrayed as enjoying the prosperous professional lifestyle to which Joyce, as a youth, had aspired.

It may amuse a much later generation of lawyers and judges to discover that in *Ulysses* it is judges rather than practitioners who are perceived as obviously wealthy. The accuracy of this is confirmed by Maurice Healy's early-twentieth-century legal memoir *The Old Munster Circuit*. Healy thought there were few barristers who did not improve their income by going on the bench.[105] In the *Aeolus* episode, Hedges Eyre Chatterton, Vice-Chancellor of Ireland, enters Bloom's thoughts when he sees the old man's great-nephew, Ned Lambert:

Old Chatterton, the vicechancellor, is his granduncle or his greatgranduncle. Close on ninety they say. Subleader for his death written this long time perhaps. Living to spite them. Might go first himself. Johnny, make room for your uncle. The right honourable Hedges Eyre Chatterton. Daresay he writes him an odd shaky cheque or two on gale days. Windfall when he kicks out. Alleluia.[106]

Chatterton (1819–1910) had been on the bench, and in the same judicial office, since 1867. He retired from the bench in 1904 at the age of eighty-five and celebrated the event by marrying for a second time, his first wife having died some years previously. He left a manuscript autobiography in the library of Trinity College.[107]

Later, in the long Shakespearian discussion in the National Library in the *Scylla and Charybdis* episode, the income of the Lord Chancellor of Ireland, Edward Gibson (Lord Ashbourne) is held up as an example of great prosperity. The glimpses afforded of the diet, liquid and solid, of Sir Frederick Falkiner, Recorder of Dublin and Sir Andrew Porter, Master of the Rolls, suggest a quietly lavish lifestyle.

Incomes at the top of the legal profession were indeed very generous for the time. The Lord Chancellor had £6,000 a year, recently reduced from £8,000. A puisne judge of the High Court was paid £3,500 and the Recorder of Dublin £2,400. By contrast the country's senior civil servant, the Under-Secretary, was on a salary of £2,000. The senior partner of Craig Gardner, Dublin's leading accountancy firm, earned about £2,700 a year in 1907 and the five executive directors of Bolands Biscuits averaged £1,400. A well-informed source, R. Barry O'Brien, estimated that the few top barristers could earn as much as £5,000 a year, though the average of those in active practice was nearer to £800 or £1,000 – this in an era when an Eason's bookshop executive on £9.00 per week was one of the founder members of the Dublin Bay Sailing Club and kept a modest yacht.[108]

Joyce balances this picture with two rather chilling portrayals of poverty and failure amongst lawyers. In the *Hades* episode O'Callaghan, the struck-off solicitor, is glimpsed in Sackville Street by the gentlemen passing in their carriage in Paddy Dignam's funeral procession:

> Oot: a dullgarbed old man from the curbstone tendered his wares, his mouth opening: oot.
> —Four bootlaces for a penny.
> Wonder why he was struck off the rolls. Had his office in Hume street. Same house as Molly's namesake, Tweedy, crown solicitor for Waterford. Has that silk hat ever since. Relics of old decency. Mourning too. Terrible comedown, poor wretch! Kicked about like snuff at a wake. O'Callaghan on his last legs.[109]

J. J. O'Molloy, Barrister-at-Law, is first seen trying to get one of the men congregated in the editor's office in *Aeolus* to back a bill for him. Bloom reflects: 'Cleverest fellow at the junior bar he used to be. Decline, poor chap. That hectic flush spells finis for a man. Touch and go with him. What's in the wind, I wonder. Money worry. [...] Practice dwindling. A mighthavebeen. Losing heart. Gambling. Debts of honour. Reaping the whirlwind. Used to get good retainers from D. and T. Fitzgerald.'[110]

Later, J. J. O'Molloy turns up in the *Cyclops* episode, when he enters the public house in Green Street (opposite the recorder's court) with Ned Lambert. The anonymous Dublin narrator of the episode muses:

> Now what were those two at? J. J. getting him off the grand jury list and the other give him a leg over the stile. With his

name in Stubbs's. Playing cards, hobnobbing with flash toffs with a swank glass in their eye, adrinking fizz and he half smothered in writs and garnishee orders. Pawning his gold watch in Cummins of Francis street where no-one would know him in the private office when I was there with Pisser releasing his boots out of the pop. What's your name, sir? Dunne, says he. Ay, and done says I. Gob, he'll come home by weeping cross one of these days, I'm thinking. [111]

Punishments

Ulysses pays great attention, from several standpoints, to the pains and punishments attaching to breaching the law, extending to capital and corporal sanctions as well as imprisonment.

There are several execution scenes in *Ulysses* and it is fair to say that a considerable interest is taken in the gory details. Mr Kernan, returning from making a good sale up in St James's Gate in the *Wandering Rocks* episode, looks down Thomas Street and thinks: 'Down there Emmet was hanged, drawn and quartered. Greasy black rope. Dogs licking the blood off the street when the lord lieutenant's wife drove by in her noddy.'[112]

A little later in the day, in *Cyclops*, which is set in Barney Kiernan's public house in Green Street, a discussion about a real-life Dublin hanging leads to a very graphic discussion of the priapic effects of hanging on the victim,[113] a remarkably gung-ho letter from an aspirant hangman,[114] and then to a sustained parody of a patriotic execution.[115] It is a mordant send-up of the loving descriptions of the executions of patriots by nationalist historians of the school of Dr Richard Robert Madden, author of a highly influential book in the 1840s, *The United Irishmen: Their Lives and Times*.[116] The execution is plainly modelled on that of Robert Emmet and anachronistically features two of Stephen's boon companions mingling with a crowd. The whole episode is elaborately embroidered with what Joyce disrespectfully called 'The Tommy Moore touch'.[117] There are two near-hangings, a hangman and an interrupted flogging in *Circe* and incidental reflections on hanging and the penal policy generally in Molly's long soliloquy in *Penelope*, the last episode in the novel.

Floggings and canings feature quite prominently in Joyce's work, notably in the *Cyclops* and *Circe* episodes of *Ulysses*. This, together with certain aspects of *Ulysses* and other works in the Joyce canon, have led some literary commentators to speculate on sado-masochistic tendencies in the author. There is some support for that view,[118] but it is fair to point out that the discussion of naval discipline in *Cyclops* reflects a lively correspondence in the London *Times* on the topic in the early part of 1904.[119] This was initiated by no less a person than George Bernard Shaw, who pointed out that though flogging in the navy had been outlawed by statute for almost half a century, certain of the still-permitted punishments were very nearly as severe. In this he was ably seconded by an Irish parliamentarian, J. G. Swift McNeill, MP, and the practice was eventually abolished.

Joyce seems to have thought of a fondness for corporal punishment, whether in a carnal or a judicial context, as a peculiarly English predilection. After listening to a graphic description of naval disciplinary practices, Bloom mentally parodies English attitudes in a new version of the Creed, beginning:

They believe in rod, the scourger almighty, creator of hell upon earth, and in Jacky Tar, the son of a gun, who was conceived of unholy boast, born of the fighting navy, suffered under rump and dozen, was scarified, flayed and curried, yelled like bloody hell, the third day he arose again from the bed, steered into haven, sitteth on his beamend till further orders whence he shall come to drudge for a living and be paid.[120]

Despite Bloom's liberalism, and the labours of people like Shaw and McNeill, corporal punishment continued to be provided for in statute law, both in the United Kingdom and in the Free State, for many years after the original Bloomsday.[121]

4. 'A Gruesome Case'

HORRIBLE MURDER IN DUBLIN
—AN AGED MAN BEATEN TO DEATH IN HIS OWN HOUSE
—BODY DISCOVERED BY HIS BROTHER
THE DEED SHROUDED IN MYSTERY

THE FREEMAN'S JOURNAL announces a murder,
Monday, 4 September 1899

The Childs trial is by far the most talked-about case in *Ulysses*. It exemplifies Joyce's belief that 'the universal [was] contained in the particular' and illustrates his statement that 'in *Ulysses* I have tried to forge literature out of my own experience, and not out of a conceived idea or a temporary emotion'. He added, in a phrase disregarded at the reader's peril and as quoted as the epigraph to Chapter 1, that he tried to keep close to facts and reality.

On 3 September 1899, when James Joyce was seventeen years

old, Thomas Childs, a wealthy old man of impeccable background, was found bludgeoned to death in his house beside Glasnevin Cemetery, Dublin. He lived in No. 5 Bengal Terrace, a sombre place then and now, whose dinginess belies its exotic name. Joyce knew the area well: a relative lived next door and he had accompanied his father, who was an assiduous funeral-goer in the Dublin tradition, to Glasnevin, the great urban cemetery favoured by the Catholics of the city, from the time he was eleven years old. Both the crime and the subsequent trial for murder of the dead man's brother, Samuel Childs, an accountant retired from Brooks Thomas (a big firm of builders' providers, still trading), fascinated the writer for years. Like other episodes of his youth, it is refracted frequently and unpredictably in *Ulysses*, that most prismatic of novels.

Joyce's treatment of the case is very typical of his interest in law cases, and indeed in contemporary historical events more generally. They often crop up in the conversation or the thoughts of his characters. No detailed background or synopsis of the facts of the cases is given, because the characters already know all about them. Their conversation focuses on the aspects of those legal dramas that dominate the minds of the speakers, and not on the objective legal or historical significance of the individual case.

The events are refracted through the prejudices and the often limited understandings of fictional characters. Joyce is very good at this and it allows him to express a variety of views on any particular topic. Perspectives on the case vary: for the medical students in the *Oxen of the Sun* episode Childs is 'the wrongfully accused';[1] others attribute his acquittal to the fact that the Crown had no conclusive evidence, but all are united in giving the credit for obtaining the acquittal to his brilliant but flawed advocate, Seymour Bushe, who got him acquitted.[2] We know Bushe is flawed because 'He would have been on the bench long ago, the professor said, only for… But no matter.'[3] Only amongst the medical students is it positively stated that Childs was innocent. In *Oxen of the Sun*, Haines, the eccentric visiting Anglo-Irishman, declares that *he* is the murderer of *Samuel* Childs.[4] All are agreed, however, that there was not sufficient evidence to support a case of murder against the man charged. The Dublin newspaper of record, the *Irish Times*, agreed: 'The evidence in no way justified the charge'.

At 11 a.m. on the original Bloomsday, 16 June 1904, five years after the killing, Joyce has Mr Leopold Bloom with three other solid citizens of Dublin sitting in a horse-drawn carriage making its way, as part of Patrick Dignam's funeral procession, from 9 Newbridge Avenue, Sandymount to Glasnevin Cemetery. The mood is melancholy, as befits the occasion. As the carriage app-roaches the burial ground, it passes on the right-hand side a row of six wide but decayed houses of dirty red brick, Bengal Terrace. 'Gloomy gardens then went by: one by one: gloomy houses.'

One of the gentlemen, Mr Power, a Dublin Castle official, points out one of the houses:

—That is where Childs was murdered, he said. The last house.
—So it is, Mr Dedalus said. A gruesome case. Seymour Bushe got him off. Murdered his brother. Or so they said.
—The crown had no evidence, Mr Power said.
—Only circumstantial, Martin Cunningham added. That's the maxim of the law. Better for ninetynine guilty to escape than for one innocent person to be wrongfully condemned.[5]

This conversation supplies the main features of the case as it lodged in the minds of Dubliners five years after it occurred.

Bloom's interior monologue then takes over:

> They looked. Murderer's ground. It passed darkly. Shuttered, tenantless, unweeded garden. Whole place gone to hell. Wrongfully condemned. Murder. The murderer's image in the eye of the murdered. They love reading about it. Man's head found in a garden. Her clothing consisted of. How she met her death. Recent outrage. The weapon used. Murderer is still at large. Clues. A shoelace. The body to be exhumed. Murder will out.[6]

This is the first mention in *Ulysses* of the Childs murder case. In one way or another the case or its protagonists are referred to more than twenty times in the text, sometimes very plainly, at other times obscurely. The case thus emerges as just one of the numerous threads, often submerged but constantly recurring, that form the fabric of the novel.

All the speakers are men – women did not then attend burials, although quite small boys did: the deceased's son was there. Two of the speakers in the funeral coach conversation, Mr Power and Mr Cunningham, have already been introduced in *Dubliners* as civil servants in the Dublin Castle headquarters of the Royal Irish Constabulary. Martin Cunningham, the senior figure, is there described as a man of 'natural astuteness particularised by long association with cases in the police courts'.[7] It is related that his friends deferred to his opinions because 'it was known that [he] had secret sources of information'.[8] They are in a position to know about the Childs case and it is notable that, despite their police connections, they do not quibble with the jury's verdict.

A classic murder

The well-off Thomas Childs had, so the Crown witnesses later said, the reputation of a miser. He lived alone and very modestly in the unprepossessing six-room, two-storey, over-basement house beside Glasnevin Cemetery; Mr Serjeant Dodd, QC for the Crown pointed to the unusual feature that he 'transacted his own domestic business'. The crime was a brutal one: the dead man had been cold-bloodedly battered to death with his own fire irons in his front parlour on the night of 2–3 September 1899, a Saturday/ Sunday. The room and the rest of his house were filled with books, 'the ancient classics and the fine old classics of English literature', according to prosecuting counsel, as well as religious ones. The books had mostly been inherited from the deceased's brother, the Rev. Edmund Childs, a clergyman in the Church of Ireland. But the murdered man, too, had been a reader and Dodd emphasized as 'somewhat pathetic' the fact that on his table was *The History of the Bible* with the dead man's spectacles resting on two heavily bloodstained pages, 1316 and 1317. There were two pools of blood near the victim's chair, a leg of which was broken off, and several splatters elsewhere. There was a kettle of water on the burnt-out fire and glasses and a decanter of whiskey elsewhere in the room. The fire irons – poker, hammer and tongs – were scattered around; the hammer was broken and the knob of the tongs was found on the floor. These were the murder weapons, said the Crown.

The body, however, was not in the room. It had apparently been dragged from the parlour to another room across the hall. When examined, the dead man was found to be fully dressed and to have grievous wounds to the head, one overlying a depressed fracture, and a wound to the left forearm, suggesting an attempt to ward off a blow to the head.

Perception of the case

The murder of Thomas Childs caused horror in contemporary Dublin. Apart from times of political unrest, murders were very rare in late-nineteenth-century Ireland, perhaps two or three a year. The *Irish Times* was the newspaper favoured, in the main, by Protestant and Unionist opinion. Speaking of the death of Thomas Childs it said: 'Not since, many years ago, the cashier of the Midland Railway was somewhat similarly murdered in his office at the Broadstone has there been a crime in our midst so horrible as the slaughter of THOMAS CHILDS at Glasnevin.'[9]

The paper went on to praise his 'good Dublin family'. It said that Thomas 'was a solitary man – eccentric but kindly – his sympathies with the poor and struggling were shown in the founding of a loan society for their benefit, which he started with his own money'. The loan society was of course a commercial venture and the paper made no mention of his moneylending activities nor of the fact that he was stated by his neighbour to have been penny-pinching.

Suspicion forms

Two features of the scene drew suspicion on to Samuel Childs, the dead man's brother. Samuel Childs lived at 51 St Patrick's Road, Drumcondra, about a mile from Bengal Terrace. He had retired after many years with Brooks Thomas in February 1899, a year previously, as a result of a 'scheme of re-organization'. His pension was £1 per week. Samuel was the only keyholder apart from the dead man and the house, the DMP concluded, had not been entered forcibly. It was in fact (they said) virtually sealed against anyone but a keyholder, or someone the occupant might admit. There was a back door but it was double-bolted and so badly cobwebbed, the DMP thought, that it could not have been opened for months. Furthermore, Samuel Childs had met one of the constables investigating the case by chance on Tuesday afternoon, 5 September, at Dunphy's Corner and had said to him in some distress: 'Suspicion points to me. O, that unfortunate latch key.'

Samuel said that he had found the body when he called to the house just after noon on Sunday, 3 September when he had let himself in after getting no reply to a knock. He had alerted the neighbours and set off for Mountjoy DMP station. The previous night, he said, he had been home from 6 p.m. except for a few minutes around 8 p.m. when he had gone around to Cotter's, a local grocers, for a pint of whiskey to make punch.

If the latch key showed that Samuel had the *opportunity* to commit the crime, the second discovery the DMP made seemed to indicate motive. In the parlour where Thomas Childs died, his business papers were found on a table and on several chairs. They demonstrated him to be an active and methodical businessman even though he was in his seventy-seventh year. There was a cash box, open, three account books, dividend warrants, bank books, share certificates and deposit receipts. The accounts showed numerous small advances to Samuel Childs since 23 February 1899, about the time he had left Brooks Thomas's employment. Two-thirds of these had been repaid. There were also papers which revealed that Thomas Childs had just capitalized the New Century Loan Society, with offices in Bachelors Walk, of which Samuel Childs was the secretary and a neighbour of Thomas's, Mr Hilferty, was treasurer. But most tellingly of all, under 'The History of the Bible' was the dead man's will, naming Samuel Childs as the principal beneficiary. It also, rather pathetically, required his executor to have printed five volumes of poetry which he had composed 'in the heyday of my intellectual powers' and to present copies to Trinity College and to the National Library.

The police concluded on the basis of these facts that Samuel Childs was a newly poor man, with a wife and three children aged from twelve to three to support and in need of constant small loans. He had only one source of financial expectation, from his brother's estate, and he possessed the only key to the virtually sealed house where the murder took place.

Over the next few days, evidence was gathered showing that he had spent the afternoon preceding the crime in and out of various public houses, and had been seen opposite Hedigan's Brian Boru House at Cross Guns Bridge, a few hundred yards from Bengal Terrace, at 8.30 p.m. on that day. When, a few weeks later, a grave-digger and retired soldier called Norton came forward to identify Samuel as a man he had seen entering the house at 11.30 p.m. on the Saturday night, the noose tightened – literally and metaphorically.

Samuel was arrested and charged with the murder and lodged in Mountjoy Prison to await his trial. This trial was, as his counsel Seymour Bushe was to point out in a fine Victorian flourish, 'to be determined for this mortal the aye or nay of that appalling alternative, whether he went hence [...] to the home where wife and children awaited him, or on the other hand, whether from the cell in which the prisoner awaited his trial he merely passed to that other cell in which the convict awaited his doom – the vestibule of the grave'.[10]

Joyce's interest

The Childs trial was a great sensation in the Dublin of the day, the *Daily Express* pointing out that the courtroom was so crowded that it was almost impossible to get in or out. But why did it interest James Joyce? Interest him it certainly did: he attended all three days of the trial and described a particular piece of evidence to his school and college friend Eugene Sheehy (later a circuit judge under the Irish Free State) so vividly that the latter recalled it clearly fifty-four years later when Joyce's biographer Richard Ellmann asked him about the case.[11]

The reason for this lies partly in Joyce's interest in murders and other *causes célèbres* generally, and partly in an extraordinary series of coincidences linking Joyce and his father, the Simon Dedalus of the novel, to the Childs trial.

Joyce's interest in these and other cases seems to be (at least) twofold. Firstly, there was simply the notoriety of the cases, the way people talked about them, accurately or otherwise, and the phrases beloved of the Yellow Press which they attracted. At another level,

Joyce uses the cases to illustrate one of his recurring concerns: to question what can be truly known about any past event, or about the human motivation that lay behind it. From each perspective, Joyce was focused not on the actual facts but on the 'felt history', the way in which past events were 'narrativized', whether in the popular imagination or by writers: in Joyce's view, perhaps the only way the past survives.

This way of seeing things, applied to major crimes, led Joyce to acknowledge factual events but to doubt if the full truth of them often, or ever, emerged. This induced him, at one level, to focus on doubtful cases, of innocence convicted or guilt unpunished. When, in the *Circe* episode, Bloom himself is arraigned by spectral accusers, he mutters: 'No no [...]. Mistaken identity. The Lyons mail. Lesurques and Dubosc. You remember the Childs fratricide case. We medical men. By striking him dead with a hatchet. I am wrongfully accused. Better one guilty escape than ninetynine wrongfully condemned.'[12] The French names refer to an infamous case of the 1790s where an innocent man was executed by mistake instead of an infamous notorious criminal who subsequently turned up alive.

In the third episode of *Ulysses*, *Proteus*, Stephen Dedalus recalls his time in Paris, which paralleled Joyce's own first sojourn there in 1902. He thinks:

> My Latin quarter hat. God, we simply must dress the character. I want puce gloves. You were a student, weren't you? Of what in the other devil's name? Paysayenn. P.C.N., you know: *physiques, chimiques et naturelles*. Aha. Eating your groatsworth of *mou en civet*, fleshpots of Egypt, elbowed by

belching cabmen. Just say in the most natural tone: when I was in Paris, *boul'Mich'*, I used to. Yes used to carry punched tickets to prove an alibi if they arrested you for murder somewhere. Justice. On the night of the seventeenth of February 1904 the prisoner was seen by two witnesses. Other fellow did it: other me. Hat, tie, overcoat, nose. *Lui, c'est moi.* You seem to have enjoyed yourself.'[13]

Added to this interest in crime in general and the doubtful business of proving it in particular, Joyce was fascinated, in *Finnegans Wake* almost to the point of obsession, by fratricide. He saw it as an unnatural crime, a radical form of betrayal and a metaphor for the destruction by the conscious mind of unconscious aspects of itself or of the id by the ego, or vice versa. This is manifest in his constant references to Shakespeare's *Hamlet* and the archetypal fratricide of Hamlet's father by his brother, notably in *Hades* and *Scylla and Charybdis*. Mention of the Childs murder case leads Stephen Dedalus, alter ego of the young Joyce, immediately to brood on the murder of King Hamlet by his brother Claudius, as related in the play by the father's ghost.

The Crown's circumstantial evidence

Samuel Childs was arraigned on the capital charge, with a case against him which, though circumstantial, seemed very strong. The trial took place between Thursday and Saturday, 19 to 21 October 1899, in Green Street Court House on the north side of Dublin, not far from the Four Courts.

The courtroom at Green Street is typical of an eighteenth-century legal edifice, its densely packed wooden furniture built *in situ*, and even today needing only the addition of wigs, quills, ink pots and candlelight to bring out its somewhat grim patina. By 1899 it had, for upwards of a century, accommodated the trials of many tragic Irish heroes, from the Sheares brothers and other rebels of 1798, the impossibly romantic Robert Emmet in 1803 (see Appendix), John Mitchell and his Young Ireland colleagues in 1848, to the Irish National Invincibles in 1883. Many of these people were condemned at the Bar of Green Street to die by the ancient ritual of hanging, drawing and quartering.

The building, no less than those tried there, had become part of Dublin history, or at least of the history of British rule in Dublin. It later housed Ireland's own non-jury Special Criminal Court, used principally for the trial of subversive cases from 1972 down to 2012. Independent Ireland had little sense of irony.

By the time of the Childs trial, the letters VR (for *Victoria Regina*) had surmounted the canopy above the judge's bench for sixty-two years; now their place is taken by a harp, symbol of the Irish State.

R v *Childs*: a trial in its time

The trial which Joyce attended was not one of the great state trials which the grim building had often hosted, with theatrically staged public hangings and beheadings to follow. But it *was* a classic Victorian murder trial. The case involved (so the Crown asserted) a fratricidal slaying in Dublin's professional and commercial elite, committed for Orwell's classic middle-class motives of money and status, not lust or anger. There was on the face of it a very strong, if largely circumstantial, case against the defendant, Samuel Childs. Childs's own death at the end of a greasy rope in the 'hanghouse' of Mountjoy Prison was confidently expected by the large throng who sought admission to the trial.

Joyce attended each of the three days which the trial occupied, viewed as 'rather prolonged' by the presiding judge. He saw, to his surprise, the elaborate edifice of the Crown case crumble to less than nothing. It not only failed to convince; it was revealed as deeply flawed, and, worse, flawed in ways that must surely have been known in advance to the Crown and police. But this did not prevent them from seeking the judicial hanging of the defendant. This, in turn, left Joyce deeply if humanely sceptical, imbued with an apprehensive sense of what Marcuse has more recently called 'the myth of the benevolent State', and the sometimes mixed motives of society's enforcers.

A notorious trial presents epistemological issues in an acute, concrete and accessible form. It exhibits the classic dramatic unities, of place, time and action. Every trial is, or involves, an inquiry into past events. Nearly all trials are locally rooted and reveal the texture of the society which gave rise to them very accurately, often precisely because they do so randomly. This is very much of a piece with Joyce's literary technique in *Ulysses*. He makes no assertions, proclaims no theories; he chronicles the varied events and episodes of a single day, in such number and variety as to baffle a casual reader. He allows his characters to react to them, comment on them and most of all to live through them. He approaches the universal through the local and the specific.

The Victorian era in the old United Kingdom was one of supreme intellectual and material confidence. Such was the trust reposed in the English legal system that, at the time of the Childs case, there was as we have seen no Court of Criminal Appeal even for capital cases. The Roman Catholic Church was not the only polity in late-Victorian times to feel itself infallible.

Joyce's preoccupations with the four very disturbing cases in the period 1889–1905 that led to the introduction of an appeal court in 1907 mirrored the legal thought of the day. They approached, hesitantly, reluctantly and obliquely, both a belief in the necessity of philosophical and judicial doubt, resistant to reliance on flawed or inadequate evidence, and the need for an awareness of prejudice, one's own or other people's.

The trial begins

The Childs case caused a great deal of excitement in contemporary Dublin. The newspapers recorded that it was almost impossible to get a seat at the trial due to the throngs seeking admission. But Joyce got one through the good graces of his father's friend 'Long John' Clancy, Sub-Sheriff of Dublin. In that capacity Clancy was in charge of the administration of the trial. If the defendant were convicted, Clancy would then be responsible for making the logistical arrangements for his hanging, a matter of some complexity, discussed at length in the *Cyclops* episode.

In any event, we must imagine the seventeen-year-old Joyce walking confidently through the throng to take his privileged seat in the tightly packed courtroom. We know there were ladies present in some numbers because the newspapers commented somewhat pointedly upon the fact. Nearly thirty years later, in the last Irish murder trial that Joyce noted in his work, that of Honor Bright, the Dublin papers continued to disapprove of ladies attending capital cases.

The Childs case attracted public attention for a number of reasons. As we have seen, the Childses were a respectable, Protestant, professional and business family – Samuel an accountant, Thomas a financier and company director, their late brother Edmund a minister in the Church of Ireland, up to 1869 the Established Church. Earlier in the century their father, Alexander Childs of Arran Quay, had been, by viceregal appointment, Carver and Gilder to the Lord Lieutenant. The Protestant community generally tended to be wealthier than the Roman Catholics who composed the bulk of the population. They also tended (with notable exceptions) to support the existing British connection as opposed to the Catholics, who generally favoured Home Rule or outright independence. It was most unusual for a Protestant business or professional man to appear in the dock at Green Street Court House.

Quite apart from the strength or weakness of the allegation of murder, then, the Childs case held great interest for the Dublin citizenry generally and for Joyce in particular. The two leading defence counsel, Seymour Bushe, QC and Timothy Healy, QC, were public figures in Dublin. As has been noted, Healy, a constitutional nationalist MP, was hated by Joyce and his family because he had led the persecution of their hero, the Parliamentary Nationalist leader Charles Stewart Parnell, after the O'Shea scandal.

The Childs case, then, met all of Orwell's criteria for a great murder case: highly respectable protagonists from the business or professional classes, a crime at odds with the professed principles of the parties (both the Childs brothers were churchgoers) and a 'respectable' motive of money or social standing. And the standing of the Childs family in the city's business and professional, not to mention religious, elite added a *frisson* of shame for their co-religionists and a powerful incentive to voyeurism for the majority Catholic community.

On the morning when the young Joyce took his reserved seat in Green Street, public feeling amongst the ladies and gentlemen clamouring for entry was strongly against Samuel Childs. The medical evidence, heard early in the trial, must have strengthened the distaste for the defendant. But the Crown's doctor, having dilated upon the savagery of the attack, was then forced to concede in cross-examination that the assailant in so savage an attack must have been covered in blood, and this turned out to be a very significant concession. Samuel was known to have had a key to his brother's premises and it was not clear who else could have entered and killed the old man. As has been noted, Samuel Childs was a poor man and had no financial prospects except from his brother, whose heir he was. And the Crown and police obviously believed him guilty, in an era when that counted for a great deal. Yet when, three days later, the case ended in Samuel Childs's acquittal, not even the strongest proponents of the Crown and police had any complaint.

James Joyce never forgot the experience of hearing the case against the accused proclaimed with total confidence and in considerable detail, only to see it collapse completely over the next three days.

In opening the Crown's case Serjeant Dodd said that:

the surrounding circumstances, [the defendant's] own conduct on the Saturday, his own motive for the crime, his own relationship to his brother and *the fact that nobody else could*

have been in a position to commit the murder that night save the
prisoner at the bar – all pointed irresistibly to the conclusion,
that the hand that caused the death of Thomas Childs was
the hand of Samuel Childs, the prisoner at the Bar, and that
it was caused by the instruments ready to his hands while he
was a guest in his brother's house. *It was a case, as they saw it,*
largely of circumstantial evidence, the only evidence directly
affecting the prisoner being that of the witness Norton [...]
In a case of murder no human eye as a rule saw the deed
committed, but there were circumstances surrounding the
case that sometimes gave a clue to the perpetrator, and very
often those circumstances were more powerful witnesses than
would be the evidence of a person who had actually seen it
committed.[14] [Emphasis added.]

On the physical circumstances he said: 'The front door was not
burst open, and the person who got in must have done so by the
door opened to him by the deceased or must have made his way in
by a latch key. Every other theory was excluded by the situation of
the house.'[15]

He referred to the sighting of the prisoner at the nearby Cross
Guns Bridge at about six o'clock and said that it was 'a matter of
reasonable probability that the place he was going to was to see his
brother and that he had made an appointment to see his brother
later on that night'.[16] He emphasized that robbery was not the
motive since nothing was missing. He went on to suggest:

Apparently a discussion had been going on over the papers,
and that Samuel Childs was in need of money was obviously

true. What happened between the two men before the first blow was struck no human being could tell as there was nobody there but that something occurred that ended in the prisoner taking those three instruments, the poker tongs and hammer, which lay ready to his hand and caused the death of his brother by means of these instruments, the Crown suggested there could be no reasonable or probable doubt [...] It is no wonder that the prisoner should have said 'O that unfortunate latch key'. It was an unfortunate latch key and [the Crown] suggested that *all the accumulated evidence excluded any person but the accused*.[17] [Emphasis added.]

In the last phrase, counsel was describing precisely what is required before a conviction on circumstantial evidence can take place: it must exclude any reasonable hypothesis other than the guilt of the accused. This was the position in the Childs case, Serjeant Dodd claimed. He did anticipate that 'one of the strong points which the prisoner might rely upon was the fact that there was no blood found on his clothes'.[18] Counsel, however, suggested that 'it was not usual that there would be much blood in such cases'.[19]

This proposition was shortly to be destroyed by one of the Crown's own witnesses, the doctor. The prosecution case later unravelled further and Samuel Childs was acquitted. How did that happen? The answer Joyce gives is a simple one: he was acquitted by reason of the brilliant oratory of his leading defence counsel, Seymour Bushe. In the *Aeolus* episode, which immediately follows the *Hades* one in which the case is first discussed, the Childs trial comes up for discussion during an argument between some gentlemen (including Stephen Dedalus) assembled in the offices of the *Evening Telegraph,* as to whether there are any contemporaries who could rival the great figures of the eighteenth and nineteenth centuries in polemical writing or in parliamentary or forensic oratory. The editor thinks not, but the broken-down barrister J. J. O'Molloy takes him on:

LINKS WITH BYGONE DAYS OF YORE

—Grattan and Flood wrote for this very paper, the editor cried in his face. Irish volunteers. Where are you now? Established 1763. Dr Lucas. Who have you now like John Philpot Curran? Psha!

—Well, J. J. O'Molloy said, Bushe K.C., for example.

—Bushe? the editor said. Well, yes: Bushe, yes. He has a strain of it in his blood. Kendal Bushe or I mean Seymour Bushe.

—He would have been on the bench long ago, the professor said, only for... But no matter.

J. J. O'Molloy turned to Stephen and said quietly and slowly:

—One of the most polished periods I think I ever listened to in my life fell from the lips of Seymour Bushe. It was in that case of fratricide, the Childs murder case. Bushe defended him.[20]

Stephen's interior narrative then takes over. The reference to fratricide makes him think of *Hamlet*:

And in the porches of mine ear did pour.
By the way how did he find that out? He died in his sleep.
Or the other story, beast with two backs?
—What was that? the professor asked.

ITALIA, MAGISTRA ARTIUM

—He spoke on the law of evidence, J. J. O'Molloy said, of Roman justice as contrasted with the earlier Mosaic code, the *lex talionis*. And he cited the Moses of Michaelangelo in the vatican.

—Ha.

—A few wellchosen words, Lenehan prefaced. Silence! Pause. J. J. O'Molloy took out his cigarettecase. [...]

A POLISHED PERIOD

J. J. O'Molloy resumed, moulding his words.

—He said of it: *that stony effigy in frozen music, horned and terrible, of the human form divine, that eternal symbol of wisdom and of prophecy which, if aught that the imagination or the hand of sculptor has wrought in marble of soultransfigured and of soultransfiguring deserves to live, deserves to live.*

His slim hand with a wave graced echo and fall.

—Fine! Myles Crawford said at once.

—The divine afflatus, Mr O'Madden Burke said.

—You like it? J. J. O'Molloy asked Stephen.

Stephen, his blood wooed by grace of language and gesture, blushed. He took a cigarette from the case. J. J. O'Molloy offered his case to Myles Crawford. Lenehan lit their cigarettes as before and took his trophy, saying:

—Muchibus thankibus.[21]

Joyce's view that the Childs case had been won by the sublime eloquence of Seymour Bushe is repeated on several occasions in *Ulysses*. In the *Oxen of the Sun* episode the medical students attached to Holles Street Maternity Hospital discuss, somewhat less than soberly, various aspects of their profession and thoughts suggested by them. It is recounted that:

> Every phase of the situation was successively eviscerated: the prenatal repugnance of uterine brothers, the Caesarean section, posthumity with respect to the father and, that rarer form, with respect to the mother, the fratricidal case known as the Childs Murder and rendered memorable by the impassioned plea of Mr Advocate Bushe which secured the acquittal of the wrongfully accused.[22]

Firstly, the house was not hermetically sealed as the Crown claimed to believe. This was revealed when the Crown called a small boy called Richard Corcoran who lived next door to the deceased to say that he had seen him alive in his front garden at about six o'clock on the Saturday evening. The defence, however, cross-examined him in the police court about whether or not there was running water in the houses in Bengal Terrace. The Crown's desperate objection to this very simple question suggests that they could see their theory unravelling. He said there was no running water in the houses but that each had a tap in the back yard. Each had a water closet there as well, and an ash pit. He, the boy, often went into the deceased's garden to play with Samuel Childs's children when they were on their weekly visit to the deceased with their father. He had personally seen the back door open not long before the crime. His father gave similar evidence.

This effectively ended the 'hermetically sealed house theory' but, like the Austrian cavalry defeated by Napoleon, the Crown were unable to change front. The police witnesses at the trial continued to insist that the back door could not have been opened for a long time. Healy pointed to the fact that, on the Crown case, the deceased had been boiling a kettle on the fire in his parlour when attacked. He asked where the water came from and a stolid sergeant of the DMP replied that he did not know but that the back door had not been opened. The Crown case then went from bad to worse. A scale model of the house which they had prepared for the trial had to be withdrawn in humiliating circumstances because it was incomplete. It did not show the rear of the house. It was admitted that the defendant had borrowed small sums from the deceased but it transpired that the deceased owed him a much larger sum. It turned out that when their clerical brother died about twelve years previously he had left his estate to his three surviving brothers in equal parts; Samuel Childs had, however, allowed his brother to take his share, about £580, asking only that the sum be a first call on Thomas's property. Samuel's generosity in this was acknowledged in Thomas's will.

Then the identification evidence collapsed. Firstly, the witness, Norton, had not come forward for weeks after the alleged sighting; he said that his wife did not want him to. Secondly, he could not identify the defendant at an identification parade but picked him out only when the men on the parade were asked to walk; he said that he identified him because he 'walked like a tailor'. He gave an elaborate description of the man's features in court but had to admit that he had not been able to give any such description to the police. Finally, when challenged by Healy to say, knowing the consequences of his evidence, whether he was sure the prisoner was the man he had seen he said he could not: he was not sure.

The man claiming to have seen Samuel at 8.30 p.m. was, manifestly, a drunk.

The DMP suffered a further blow during the evidence of a Superintendent Dempsey. The defence produced a letter from the Commissioner of the Force, addressed to the deceased and written in reply to a complaint Thomas had made in July 1898 about 'corner boys' hanging around the area and breaking glass in windows. Although Thomas's letter was addressed to Superintendent, D Division, which was himself, Dempsey said he had never seen it. He had, however, been told of it some days after the murder by an inspector, but its existence had not been disclosed to the defence. The letter, when produced, turned out to contain a request for police protection because of the congregation of 'corner boys' around his house and in the lane behind, which put him, Thomas said, in fear of his life.

This presented the prosecution with a serious problem in the form of the possibility of an opportunist small-time criminal hanging around the area. Their difficulty was worsened by a cross-examination of their engineer. Perhaps shaken by having to admit the inaccuracy of the model and plans, he conceded that if one were in the laneway at the back of the garden there would be no difficulty in getting into the garden. Still worse, he agreed that if anyone said the back door to the garden had not been opened for a long period, that would be 'nonsense'.

All of this raised the possibility that the deceased might have left the house through the back door to visit the water closet, or to get water from the tap, allowing a casual intruder entry. There was no evidence that this had occurred and it is of course unlikely that such an intruder would have left cash or valuables, including the deceased's watch, untouched. But the prosecution had committed themselves to the theory that the house was physically sealed against intrusion. Not only had that theory been exploded, but the deceased's request for police protection, never mentioned by them until the defence produced the Commissioner's reply, created the possibility at any rate of a lurking intruder. Why else would the Crown have concealed the letters?

The dramatic speech attributed to Seymour Bushe, KC in *Ulysses* is not reflected in the contemporary records at all. He did make the opening speech for the defence, and made it very well. In addition to the points mentioned above he emphasized that the Crown's doctor conceded that the killer must have had a lot of blood on him, but none had been found on the accused or his clothing. He was able to call highly respectable Protestant businessmen, doctors and clergymen to testify to the caring and affectionate relationship which existed between the Childs brothers. Indeed, a prosecution witness, Mr Hilferty who lived in 6 Bengal Terrace, positively stated that Thomas Childs had set up the New Century Loan Society in order to give employment to Samuel.

In this way, the Crown's theory both as to Samuel's allegedly exclusive opportunity to commit the crime, and as to his motive for doing so, were very gravely damaged in the course of the hearings. Most of the work of destruction was achieved by hard, pointed and continuous cross-examination, nearly all of which was done by Healy. It appears also that it was Healy who directed the proofs for the defence, that is, directed the steps to be taken by the defendant's solicitor by way of investigating the case and securing evidence. There were, for example, photographs taken on behalf of the defendant which led the judge to disallow the prosecution's scale model of the house.

Why then did Joyce give the credit of the acquittal to Seymour Bushe? The reasons appear to be both political and literary. Given Joyce's lifelong hatred of Healy for his role in Parnell's downfall, he was most unlikely to give Healy any credit for anything. The Childs acquittal was very popular with the public and the *Daily Express* account shows that the not guilty verdict was greeted with cheers for 'Tim Healy', but Joyce allowed him no credit at all. Though Healy is mentioned in *Ulysses*, unfavourably, it is not in connection with the Childs case.[23] Yet Joyce must have been aware of his leading role.

The literary reason for downplaying Healy's role relates to the nature of that role itself. As we have seen, it was one of painstaking preparation and dogged cross-examination. Joyce was not interested in that aspect of the case at all and the one detail he has Mr Power give of the case, other than that it was one of fratricide, is wrong: the Childs house was the second-last and not the last house in Bengal Terrace. Joyce was interested in quite different, and disparate, features of the case: firstly in the abstract question of how one could ever know what really happened and secondly in the crime of fratricide. Separately, he was interested in the public perception of the case, how it was spoken of in Dublin five years after it happened, how it had entered the public consciousness. Part of that consciousness was a recollection of the case as a 'gruesome' one, as Mr Dedalus said; but another part was the linkage of the trial in the public mind with the kindly, louche, liberal and histrionic character of Seymour Bushe. As we have seen, long before 1904 Bushe had become the subject of his own quite separate scandalous notoriety.

Seymour Bushe was the epitome of a well-connected Protestant Irishman of the late nineteenth century. He was descended from the early-nineteenth-century lawyer Charles Kendal Bushe, who became Chief Justice of the King's Bench. Charles's daughter married a son of Lord Plunket, who had a similar (but still more successful) career to that of Kendal Bushe. As a young man Plunket had been an anti-Union lawyer and parliamentarian who dramatically signalled his conversion to the government side by prosecuting Robert Emmet in 1803. He went on to become Lord Chancellor and the greatest nepotist in nineteenth-century Ireland. By the late nineteenth century prominent descendants of these men included William, 5th Lord Plunket, Archbishop of Dublin and David Plunket, Lord Rathmore, the Tory Party's principal Irish organizer. Bushe's other grandfather, Charles Kendal Bushe, was known as 'the incorruptible' for his probity as a very young MP in 1799, in refusing government bribes to vote for the Act of Union in the old Irish House of Commons. The government manager's list of MPs, with the bribes they were offered or demanded set against their names, featured Bushe's name with the note 'incorruptible' opposite it. It was a dramatic acknowledgement from a hostile source of his integrity, unusual in that time and place. Of this distinguished lineage, it would have to be conceded that Seymour Bushe was to be found away on its left fringe. He was a liberal, a supporter of causes such as women's suffrage and a man about town. He had the reputation, confirmed by many contemporary sources, for exalted forensic eloquence.

The defence's principal point on the law of evidence, which Bushe urged with great vehemence and eloquence, related to the inadmissibility of the testimony of Mrs Samuel Childs. It will be recalled that Samuel told the DMP that he had spent the evening at home, apart from a brief trip to an off-licence at about 8 p.m.

Police witnesses made a point of saying that they had taken a statement from Mrs Childs; the suggestion was that it did not support the alibi. Mrs Childs, however, was not a competent witness for the prosecution as she was the defendant's wife; but neither was she for the defence, because under the law of evidence then prevailing in Ireland neither the defendant nor his or her spouse was competent to give evidence. The law in this respect had been altered in England only the previous year, by the Criminal Evidence Act 1898. After the passing of that measure the defendant or his spouse could give evidence in a criminal trial in England, but the Act did not apply to Ireland, where the law was not altered until the Irish Free State enacted the Criminal Justice (Evidence) Act 1924. Bushe complained eloquently and bitterly about the absence of the wife's evidence and the irrationality, in the context of the then United Kingdom of Great Britain and Ireland, of holding the wife's evidence admissible in part of the kingdom and inadmissible in another. He may possibly have referred to ancient legal codes by way of contrasting them with the law then applied in Ireland.

The defence also arranged for Mrs Childs to sit in court throughout the trial, as near the dock as possible. She was accompanied by her brother and by the Rev. Mr Gibson, Chaplain to the McGeogh Home in Cowper Road, Dublin. The clergyman gave character evidence for the defence and then ostentatiously returned to his place beside Mrs Childs. All this, combined with Bushe's complaints about the law which kept her out of the witness box, was intended to suggest that she knew him to be innocent, and could have said so but for the silly prohibition against receiving her evidence, or his.

Whether Bushe referred to Moses and to Roman law or not, there is no doubt that his eloquence made an enormous impression on the young James Joyce. A photograph of Bushe survives in *Five Years in Ireland 1895-1900* by Michael McCarthy,[24] an Anglo-Irish journalist, and a line drawing in A. M. Sullivan's *Old Ireland*. In both he appears as something of a dandy, with a wide, tapering moustache, and is distinguished by a very large nose. These features also claim Joyce's attention when, in the *Circe* episode, Bloom is arraigned in a surreal court on charges of concupiscence on the complaint of Mrs Yelverton Barry, Mrs Bellingham and other ladies. J. J. O'Molloy appears to defend him and is described as assuming 'the avine head, foxy moustache, and proboscidal eloquence of Seymour Bushe'.[25] He delivers a much shorter reprise of the speech attributed to him in the Childs trial and Bloom then proceeds shamelessly and suggestively to drop names, saying: 'I have moved in the charmed circle of the highest... Queens of Dublin society.'[26]

Joyce on the police

The Dublin Metropolitan Police do not come out especially well from a scrutiny of the Childs trial, in particular because they stolidly and repeatedly stuck to their theory that the back door could not have been opened for months, even when it was contradicted by the obvious necessity to open the door to get water and for other domestic purposes, and at least one Crown witness said he had seen it recently opened. This was consistent with Mr Bloom's view of the police: in *Eumaeus*, when Stephen and Mr Bloom leave the cabman's shelter near Butt Bridge, Bloom gives his young companion some fatherly advice about the need to avoid getting involved in fights and thereby ending up in the Bridewell:

The reason he mentioned the fact was that a lot of those policemen, whom he cordially disliked, were admittedly unscrupulous in the service of the Crown and, as Mr Bloom put it, recalling a case or two in the A division in Clanbrassil street, prepared to swear a hole through a ten gallon pot. Never on the spot when wanted but in quiet parts of the city, Pembroke road for example, the guardians of the law were well in evidence, the obvious reason being they were paid to protect the upper classes.[27]

Joyce's connections with the Childs case

Many of Joyce's characters are modelled on friends or acquaintances of his parents acquired during the happy and relatively prosperous time when they lived in Emorville Avenue, off Dublin's South Circular Road. His maternal grandfather lived nearby in Clanbrassil Street with his two sons John and William Murray, who feature in *Ulysses*. William was married to Josephine Murray, née Giltrap. This lady was a very beloved aunt to the entire Joyce family, both before and after the death of Joyce's mother in 1903. He remained in correspondence with her until her death in the 1920s.

Josephine's father, James Giltrap, a legal cost accountant, provides the first coincidental link between the Joyces and the Childs murder. On 1 September 1899, the day before Thomas Childs was killed, old James died in No. 6 Bengal Terrace. His funeral left the house on the Monday and the preparations for it must have taken place there over the weekend. The comings and goings of policemen, doctors, relatives and undertakers at No. 5 Bengal Terrace cannot have escaped the attention of the mourners for Mr Giltrap, very probably including James Joyce. The inquest on Thomas Childs was opened in 5 Bengal Terrace on the day of Mr Giltrap's funeral (where the jury viewed the body of Thomas Childs) and actually moved into number 6 to take the evidence of a bedridden lady there.

An equally odd coincidence emerged once the jury was empanelled for the trial of Samuel Childs. It was a county jury, most of whose members seem to have been gentlemen of some substance. One of them was Alexander Keyes, proprietor of the Ballsbridge Luncheon Company and formerly a publican at No. 128 Capel Street. Keyes is referred to frequently in *Ulysses* under his own name, particularly in the *Aeolus* episode. In the book, his successor in Capel Street, Cassidy, is anxious to place an advertisement in the *Evening Telegraph* through the agency of Leopold Bloom. Bloom negotiates, not without difficulty, between him and the newspaper for an editorial 'puff' in return for continuing the ad for three months. Bloom then has to go to the National Library to get a back number of another paper for the artwork of the advertisement. This features two enormous crossed keys. The pub was called 'The House of Keys', with (Bloom says) its echoes of the Manx Parliament, and thus of Home Rule. He comments explicitly on this symbolism.

In 1892 John Stanilaus Joyce had lost his pleasant and undemanding job in the Rates Office and was eking out a living as an advertising canvasser. One of his customers was Captain Thomas Cunniam, a Yankee publican, whose name could until recently be seen above the Lord Edward pub in Christchurch Place, Dublin. He took a regular advertisement in the *Evening Telegraph* through the agency of John Joyce. In the spring of 1896 a man called James Cassidy left his employment with Captain

Cunniam and took over Alexander Keyes's Capel Street business when the latter moved to Ballsbridge. An advertisement for this change of ownership, featuring precisely the artwork described in *Ulysses*, appeared in the newspaper on 21 March 1896. The symbol of the keys occurs constantly in *Ulysses*, including a reference in Molly Bloom's soliloquy at the end of the book, and may have been part of Joyce family lore. The coincidence must have been very striking for James when he attended the trial in 1899. However, he draws no explicit connection in the book between the Childs trial and Alexander Keyes, probably because Keyes would have been unknown to the various characters who speak about the case, other than Simon Dedalus.

Whodunit?

Though Samuel Childs was acquitted, quite justifiably as most people thought, the question of whether he actually killed his brother is a quite different one. Several of the references in *Ulysses* suggest, correctly, that the acquittal was due to lack of evidence, a chain of circumstances that did not quite close, and was not equivalent to a finding of innocence. But there is no legal provision for a finding of innocence, simply a verdict of 'not guilty', which does not distinguish between innocence positively established and an insufficiency of evidence. After the passing of a century, however, the reason for the acquittal is plain enough to anyone who reads the contemporary accounts with experience of trials. The police and the Crown thought Samuel had to be the culprit: no one else had the opportunity; Samuel was in desperate need of money and was drinking far too much. In particular, he was in and out of public houses throughout the Saturday. No doubt they thought that he was either steeling himself for the deed or at least drinking himself into a state where he could be easily inflamed.

Like many a litigant before and since, the Crown and their representatives saw only what they wanted to see and failed to step back from their own case and examine it for weaknesses. The DMP thought that the back door couldn't have been opened for months. Neither they nor the Crown's solicitor ever thought to ask neighbours about this vital plank of their case. Thus they were confounded when young Richard Corcoran unknowingly but effectively destroyed their theory in cross-examination. Equally, they were so preoccupied with the accounts showing constant small borrowings by Samuel that they never paused to examine the documents available to them which showed that Samuel was actually a creditor of his brother in a much larger sum, and had indeed repaid most of the advances to him.

The Crown lost these points conclusively and humiliatingly in front of the jury. Neither of them meant, of course, that Samuel did not kill Thomas but they did mean that the Crown's theory and its credibility were grievously undermined. Most advocates with experience of jury trials will confirm that if a jury loses faith in the prosecution theory as expounded to them, or in a prosecution witness, it is very hard to regain it. Here, the Crown were made to look as if they had simply jumped at conclusions and hidden any evidence that did not suit those conclusions.

The case is in some ways reminiscent of the famous trial of Lizzy Borden for the murder of her father and stepmother in Fall River, Massachusetts, in 1893. Here Lizzy had virtually exclusive access to the house at the relevant time but the chain of circumstantial evidence did not absolutely exclude the possibility of an intruder. A combination of some highly favourable rulings on evidence and a reluctance to believe that a woman could bludgeon two elderly people to death led to Lizzy's acquittal. Almost immediately afterwards, however, there was a great and lasting reaction against her on the basis that, whether it could be proved affirmatively or not, it was in practice extremely unlikely that anyone other than Lizzy committed the crime.

This is the position with Samuel Childs as well, though contemporary public opinion did not think so. The evidence was that Thomas usually went to bed about 8 or 9 p.m., and he would be very unlikely to stay up later unless he were expecting a guest; realistically the only remotely likely guest was his brother. The Crown's failure to notice the fact that Thomas owed Samuel a considerable sum of money destroyed their first theory but did not exclude the view that the brothers fought about money on the night of the crime, though not in quite the same way that the Crown originally believed. But the Crown stuck rigidly to their original theory and did not suggest an alternative narrative that might be consistent with the new evidence.

As it happens, we have available the views of Samuel's most active defence barrister: he thought his client guilty, but of manslaughter only and not of murder. In the first volume of his memoirs, *Letters and Leaders of My Day*,[28] Tim Healy had this to say:

An old man was found dead in his parlour near Glasnevin Cemetery, Dublin, with his skull battered in, and the Crown asserted that his brother committed the murder. The chief witness was a grave digger from Glasnevin, who swore before the magistrate that he saw the accused leaving the house on the night of the crime. Unless this story could be shaken it meant that the accused would hang. I believed the accused did not intend to kill, but that in a moment of passion, having been refused money, he struck his brother without premeditation.

So I cross-examined the grave digger at the magisterial inquiry as to the darkness of the night, the shadows cast by the trees, and the doubtfulness of identification by one who had never seen the prisoner before. Then suddenly I asked, 'Do you realise that your evidence if true will put the rope around the prisoner's neck?'

'I do' came the husky answer.

'Then', I said, 'Will you swear positively that he was the man you saw leaving the house?'

The witness hesitated, and falteringly answered 'No, I will not. I am not sure.'

This reply, appearing on the depositions, was fatal to the Crown Case.

At the trial, the jury found the accused not guilty. He then took out probate to his brother's estate and became the sole inheritor of his means.

The Crown could often have got verdicts of manslaughter in Ireland from juries which shrank from convicting prisoners on capital charges, but its counsel pressed for 'the rigour of the game'.

It may be true that the Crown could have got a verdict of manslaughter if they had prosecuted the defendant for that offence, and not for murder, in the first place. At the trial before Mr Justice William Kenny, he told the jury that manslaughter was open to them but, having regard to the nature of the case for the prosecution, and the fact that 'the case of the prisoner was that he was never there at all that night: it really seemed that this was not a case of manslaughter'. Whatever Tim Healy's views (and the propriety of his expressing them in print thirty years after the case), there is no doubt that Samuel Childs was correctly acquitted on the case as presented.

Most unusually, the acquittal of Samuel Childs was celebrated in an *Irish Times* editorial:

> The anguish of the fell deed was vastly worse when suspicion pointed to his brother, and the police took up the idea that his was the guilt of an unexampled atrocity [...] On Saturday evening, at five minutes to eight o'clock, after twenty-five minutes consideration, the jury acquitted the prisoner. This is a verdict in which the public will universally concur, and we rejoice to record it. The evidence in no way justified the charge.[29]

The *Irish Times* – the 'old lady of Westmoreland Street' – went on to praise the barristers involved in the case: 'The speech of Mr Bushe, and certainly not less that of Mr Timothy Healy, were worthy of the Irish Bar's best days.'[30]

The Ireland of Joyce's youth in the last twenty years of the nineteenth century and the very early twentieth century is the seedbed of his works, the unfailing source of his themes and of the events and narratives that are reflected in the books. Those decades are, as time passes, increasingly inaccessible even to historically aware people. History, like landscape, has its folds and hidden places. The twenty-five years after the fall of Parnell in 1891 is such a place, obscured between that dominating event on the one hand and the First World War and the 1916 insurrection on the other. The period evokes for most people no immediate picture or sense of social texture. In Constantine Curran's phrase, those years are passing 'under the receding wave' of time which leaves only the great prominences clearly visible.[31] The Childs case, saved from utter obscurity only by Joyce's mention of it, is like a time capsule preserving accurately, because incidentally, some of the texture and details of life in the years 1899 and 1904.

5. The Mortgaged Life

T his chapter takes up the related issues of death by natural causes and suicide and the legal and financial, as well as the social and historical contexts of the role of life insurance. Joyce's Bloomsday – 16 June 1904 – begins as the news of Patrick Dignam's death is spreading through the network of his friends and acquaintances. All, like him, are men of self-conscious respectability but of little property. Mr Bloom hears the news when his wife points out the death notice in the morning paper,[1] in time for him to attend the funeral at Glasnevin cemetery. This involves making his way to the Dignam house in Newbridge Avenue, Sandymount, to join the funeral procession northwards across the city from there.[2] As we read in the *Lotus Eaters* episode, Bloom has a busy morning planned. After breakfast at 7 Eccles Street he goes to Westland Row Post Office to collect a *poste restante* letter from Martha Clifford, the fourth in a series of such rather salacious letters.[3] Then he plans to collect a lotion specially made up for his wife Molly in Sweny's Chemists, Lincoln Place. After that he intends to have a bath at Leinster Street Turkish and Warm Baths, before making the short tram journey to Sandymount. The visit to the Leinster Street Baths reflects the fact that there is no bathroom in his home in Eccles Street.

The need to attend the funeral is an intrusion in Bloom's schedule. He thinks, as he walks down Westland Row, 'Bore this funeral affair. O well, poor fellow, its not his fault.'[4] According to *Ulysses*, the *Evening Telegraph* that day declares that: *'The deceased gentleman was a most popular and genial personality in city life and his demise after a brief illness came as a great shock to citizens of all classes by whom he is deeply regretted.'*[5]

In the *Circe* episode we learn that Dignam was certified dead by Dr Finucane,[6] his death being due to natural causes, with 'the wall of the heart hypertrophied'.[7]

Dignam's funeral is the centrepiece of the *Hades* episode, the sixth in the book. The funeral is interesting from many points of view. The procession crosses the River Dodder, the Grand Canal, the River Liffey and the Royal Canal, corresponding to the four rivers of Hades in Homer's *Odyssey*. The reaction of Dignam's associates to his death, and the details and liturgical significance of the funeral service itself, are minutely described. Dignam was a poor man who had lost his employment as a law clerk before dying of the effects of drink, fates dreaded by all the men who attend his funeral. And this aspect dominates their conversation at the funeral and their plans to assist the bereaved family, which they instinctively want to do.[8]

Financial insecurity, the stratagems and ploys of those struggling to maintain a foothold in the lower-middle classes, were a preoccupation of Joyce's. He had ample experience of these things from growing up the son of a famously improvident man. The family had very little income and moved house twenty-two times in as many years, always just ahead of the bailiffs. This led to a preoccupation with the need for a safety net, perhaps in the form of life insurance, a subject in which he took a great interest.

In view of Dignam's poor circumstances, it is no surprise that, in the cemetery, his friends discuss the financial position of the Dignam family, evidently a bad one. Ned Lambert tells Simon Dedalus: 'Martin is going to get up a whip for the youngsters [...]. A few bob a skull. Just to keep them going till the insurance is cleared up.'[9]

The financial position of the family is acute because Dignam had recently lost his job as a clerk in the office of John Henry Menton, solicitor. That gentleman has put his name down for the large sum of £1 (Bloom gives five shillings) in Mr Cunningham's whip-round. Simon Dedalus reflects:

—[...] I often told poor Paddy he ought to mind that job. John Henry is not the worst in the world.
—How did he lose it? Ned Lambert asked. Liquor, what?
—Many a good man's fault, Mr Dedalus said with a sigh.[10]

In this situation, Mr Bloom asks what seems to him the salient question:

—Was he insured? Mr Bloom asked.
—I believe so, Mr Kernan answered. But the policy was heavily mortgaged.[11]

In the Dublin of the early twentieth century married men of modest and often insecure income were acutely conscious of the need for life insurance. Only in that way could many husbands make some provision for a widow and family in the event of the breadwinner's death at a time when widows' pensions were rare. In the *Ithaca* episode towards the end of the book we learn of Mr Bloom's own far-seeing and far from negligible provision in this regard.[12] So long as the insurance premiums were kept up there ought to be a capital sum of some sort available for the widow and dependent children, in Bloom's case quite a comfortable one.

But the existence of this sum, slowly accumulating over the life of the insured man, also provided a temptation. If the man who was servicing the policy fell into financial difficulty, an all too common occurrence, he might be inclined to offer the policy itself as security for a desperately needed loan. This is what is referred to in the alarming tidings that Paddy Dignam's policy was 'heavily mortgaged'. In principle, the effect of this 'mortgaging' of the policy was to transfer the rights of the 'life assured', or of his estate, to the person or company who took the policy by way of security, thus reducing or perhaps extinguishing the rights of the dependants of the estate. In many cases, the insurance policy would be the only asset of the estate of a man of modest means and its loss could be catastrophic, not only to his dependants but equally to the creditors of the estate.

The risk represented by the opportunity to mortgage or pledge the policy was very well known. In an attempt to prevent unpleasant surprises for the dependants and creditors of insured men, and to protect an insurer who had paid the relatives in ignorance of the assignment, the Westminster Parliament enacted the Policies of Insurance Act 1867. The effect of this was to prohibit a person who took such a policy as security from suing on it unless notice of the assignment had been given to the insurance company. As we shall see, Mr Bloom was fully aware of this technicality and he was determined, if possible, to use it for the benefit of Mrs Dignam. This lady herself makes a spectral appearance in *Circe*, where the stage directions emphasize the importance of the insurance to her:

Mrs Dignam, widow woman, her snubnose and cheeks flushed with deathtalk, tears, and Tunney's tawny sherry, hurries by in her weeds, her bonnet awry, rouging and powdering her cheeks, lips and nose, a pen chivvying her brood of signets. Beneath her skirt appear her late husband's everyday trousers and turnedup boots, large eights. She holds a Scottish Widows' insurance policy and a large marquee umbrella under which her brood run with her[13]

The position of Mrs Dignam and her five dependent children will be a very difficult one if the insurance policy turns out to be heavily mortgaged. Molly Bloom is no admirer of Paddy Dignam or of his wife, but she sympathizes with the family in that acute situation:

poor Paddy Dignam all the same Im sorry in a way for him what are his wife and 5 children going to do unless he was insured comical little teetotum always stuck up in some pub corner and her or her son waiting Bill Bailey wont you please come home her widows weeds wont improve her appearance[14]

Mrs Dignam's most trusted adviser is Martin Cunningham, the man who is getting up the whip-round for her children.

Cunningham has already been introduced in *Dubliners* as a civil servant of some significance in the Dublin Castle office of the Royal Irish Constabulary and has the reputation of being a shrewd man of much worldly wisdom:

> He was a thoroughly sensible man, influential and intelligent. His blade of human knowledge, natural astuteness partic- ularised by the long association with case in the police courts, had been tempered by brief immersions in the waters of general philosophy. He was well informed. His friends bowed to his opinions and considered that his faith was like Shakespeare's.[15]

At about 5 p.m. on 16 June 1904 in the *Cyclops* episode, Mr Bloom turns up in Barney Kiernan's pub in Little Britain Street. He refuses a proffered drink.

> —Thank you, no, says Bloom. As a matter of fact I just wanted to meet Martin Cunningham, don't you see, about this insurance of poor Dignam's. Martin asked me to go to the house. You see, he, Dignam, I mean, didn't serve any notice of the assignment on the company at the time and nominally under the act the mortgagee can't recover on the policy.
> —Holy Wars, says Joe, laughing, that's a good one if old Shylock is landed. So the wife comes out top dog, what?
> —Well, that's a point, says Bloom, for the wife's admirers.
> —Whose admirers? says Joe.
> —The wife's advisers, I mean, says Bloom.
> Then he starts all confused mucking it up about mortgagor

under the act like the lord chancellor giving it out on the bench and for the benefit of the wife and that a trust is created but on the other hand that Dignam owed Bridgeman the money and if now the wife or the widow contested the mortgagee's right till he near had the head of me addled with his mortgagor under the act.[16]

Bloom returns to this theme in the *Nausicaa* episode, as he leaves Sandymount Strand at about 8 p.m. on the same day. The beach is situated close to the Dignam house in Newbridge Avenue, from which he is presumably coming. He reflects:

But Dignam's put the boots on it. Houses of mourning so depressing because you never know. Anyhow she wants the money. Must call to those Scottish Widows as I promised. Strange name. Takes it for granted we're going to pop off first. That widow on Monday was it outside Cramer's that looked at me. Buried the poor husband but progressing favourably on the premium. Her widow's mite. Well? What do you expect her to do? Must wheedle her way along.[17]

From these passages it is possible to deduce quite a lot about the details of how exactly Paddy Dignam's estate is encumbered. The policy of life insurance is with Scottish Widows, more formally known as the Scottish Widows Fund (Mutual) Life Assurance Society. The company was based in Edinburgh and had five agents in Dublin in 1904.[18]

It appears that Dignam had pledged his life insurance policy to a person called Bridgeman, who had advanced him money on it.

But Bridgeman had not served notice of the assignment on the Scottish Widows who therefore, by reason of the Act mentioned above, cannot be sued by Bridgeman. If the company pay the widow before getting notice of the assignment, Bridgeman cannot complain at law of that payment, even though it defeats his security.

Section 3 of the Policies of Assurance Act 1867 provides as follows:

No assignment made after the passing of this Act of a policy of life assurance shall confer on the assignee [...] any right to sue for the amount of such policy, or the monies assured or secured thereby, until a written notice of the date and purport of such assignment shall have been given to the assurance company liable under the policy at their principal place of business [...] and the date on which such notice shall be received shall regulate the priority of all claims under any assignment; *and a payment bona fide made in respect of any such policy by any assurance company before the date on which notice shall have been received shall be valid as against the assignee giving such notice as if this Act had not been passed.*

This, of course, may not be the end of Mrs Dignam's difficulties. Her husband's estate is still indebted to Bridgeman for the money he loaned Dignam and he will be able to sue for what he is owed. It appears from the 'Shylock' jibe that Bridgeman is a Jewish moneylender. It is never made quite clear what proposal exactly Bloom is going to put to the Scottish Widows; presumably he is going to invite them to pay the widow the amount of the policy on the basis that Bridgeman will not be able to sue them on the policy. It will then be for Mrs Dignam's advisers to see what they can do by way of defending any action by Bridgeman and preserving the fund for the dependants. But Bloom seems to have hit on a technicality which provides a good prospect of resisting Bridgeman's claim, which had been secured on the policy but is now unsecured.

Section 3 was strictly construed by the Irish courts: in In The Matter of R. F. Young, a bankrupt,[19] Sir George Moyers, a former Lord Mayor of Dublin, guaranteed the borrowings of his brother-in-law, R. F. Young, with the Munster and Leinster Bank. Young assigned to Moyers a policy of insurance on his own life for £500 by way of security. This happened in 1888. The policy was with the General Life Insurance Company and R. F. Young was that company's manager in Dublin. Moyers did not wish to damage Young in the eyes of the company and accordingly gave no written notice of the assignment. He did, however, enquire orally if the policy was still in force and the company told him that it was. Subsequently, in July 1889, Young went bankrupt and the issue was as to whether or not the policy was lawfully in Moyers' possession at that time. It was held that it was not, by reason of the lack of written notice, and that Young's assignee in bankruptcy was entitled to immediate possession of it. So strict an interpretation of the law would tend to support the widow's position, if she could persuade the company to pay the estate before the moneylender gave notice of the assignment.

The fear of sudden death

It is clear from several of the references in the novel that Dignam's death was entirely unexpected. In *Lotus Eaters*, Mr McCoy hails Bloom:

— [...] I couldn't believe it when I heard it. I was with him no later than Friday last or Thursday was it in the Arch. *Yes*, he said. *He's gone. He died on Monday poor fellow.* [...]

—Yes, yes, Mr Bloom said after a dull sigh. Another gone.

—One of the best, M'Coy said.[20]

The Arch was a public house in Henry Street in North Central Dublin, run by 'Molloy and O'Reilly, Grocers and Spirit Merchants'.[21]

In Dignam's funeral procession, Mr Power says: 'He had a sudden death, poor fellow', to which Bloom replies, 'The best death'.[22] But his fellow mourners cannot agree. To a Catholic a sudden death means the possibility of dying unconfessed and unshriven, risking eternal damnation.

On the afternoon of 16 June Mr Alf Bergin joins the drinkers in Barney Kiernan's pub in Little Britain Street. He has not heard of Dignam's death and believes that he saw him a short while previously in Capel Street. A somewhat grim conversation ensues:

—Dead! says Alf. He's no more dead than you are.

—Maybe so, says Joe. They took the liberty of burying him this morning anyhow.

—Paddy? Says Alf.

—Ay, says Joe. He paid the debt of nature, God be merciful to him.

—Good Christ! says Alf.[23]

A number of the day's events – Dignam's death; the sinking of the *General Slocum* in New York Harbor, with hundreds of casualties;

the assassination on the morning of 16 June 1904 of Count Bobrikoff, the Russian Governor of Finland;[24] thoughts of his father's suicide; and Bloom's own narrow escape from being run down by a huge 'sandstrewer' – all remind Bloom, throughout the day, of the risks of sudden death. His reaction to his own narrow escape from the sand-spreading vehicle is to think of insurance as he jumps out of the way: 'Close shave that but cured the stitch. [...] Insure against street accident too. The Providential.'[25]

This preoccupation with insurance was, it seems, typical of Bloom's generation. At the end of the *Calypso* episode, we see Bloom reading *Tit-Bits* in his outdoor water closet in Eccles Street.[26] This publication, published since 1881, had the full title *Tit-Bits from All the Most Interesting Books, Periodicals and Newspapers in the World*. It was a sixteen-page penny weekly, published on Thursdays but dated Saturday. Its title included the slogan '*Tit-Bits* has paid £15,200 insurance money'.[27] This penny paper's principal selling point was the 'Tit-Bit system of life insurance', which offered £100 to the nearest relative of anyone who died in a railway accident while a subscriber to the magazine, or was who found to be bearing the current edition of it on his or her person when killed. As it had paid £15,200 since the scheme's inception in 1888, it followed that 152 people had died in train accidents and could meet the condition of being a subscriber or at least possessed the current edition. It published an account of its insurance scheme in most editions of the paper.

The 11 June 1904 edition of *Tit-Bits* carried, opposite the advertisement for its own insurance scheme, a large notice about the inaugural edition of another 'Penny Home Paper'. This was *Horner's Weekly*, which also offered a dramatic insurance scheme:

There is an old saying that 'accidents will happen' and
every man who buys Horner's Weekly will be able to secure
to his widow a pension of ten shillings a week. It does not
matter whether the reader is killed by train, bus, tram, boat,
street accidents of all kinds, in the workshop, the factory or
any place whatever, the widow will receive the pension just
the same.[28]

In exactly the same way, certain English newspapers even today
offer relatively small sums payable on death and require no medical
examination, medical questions or anything in the way of pre-
conditions. It thus appears that the preoccupation with insurance
of Mr Bloom and his contemporaries is by no means unusual, or
even peculiar to Ireland.

The insurance industry was a huge one by the end of the nineteenth century. Large-scale commercial insurance seems to have
begun with maritime and fire insurance. Life insurance can trace
a history back to the late sixteenth century, but before the development of scientific mortality tables it was really a form of gambling.
There is ample evidence in the eighteenth century of persons
insuring the lives of other people with whom they had no connection,
such as the heir to the throne, or a prominent soldier, politician or
nobleman. Private arrangements such as tontines involved a group
of friends or acquaintances who all subscribed a regular sum, the
total with interest being payable to the last survivor. This was
obviously also in the nature of a gamble. Daniel Defoe wrote that
in his time, 'wagering had become a Branch of Assurances'.[29] The
Westminster Parliament passed the Act for Regulating Insurances
on Lives in 1774. This required that an individual wishing to take

out a policy on the life of another had to demonstrate a bona fide financial interest in that life.

It is instructive that the 1774 Act was commonly known as 'the Gambling Act' because, of course, to insure the life of a person in whom one has no financial interest is neither more nor less than gambling. A wife or a child has an obvious financial interest in the life of an earning father. In more recent times, insurance companies have advertised on the basis that a husband has a financial interest in the life of a wife, even one who works exclusively in the home, measured by the amount it would cost to replace her services, but an attempt to insure the life of a person in whom one has no material interest at all is seen as a suspicious transaction. The Act of 1774 was aimed at stamping out such speculations.

As the nineteenth century went on, the profession of actuary emerged to place the life insurance industry on a scientific basis.[30] There is a good deal of evidence that English and Scottish companies were reluctant to cover Irish lives. In the late nineteenth century the Royal Exchange Assurance was the largest operator in the Irish market and considered something of a 'specialist in the region'.[31] The Pelican Insurance Company, the life insurance subsidiary of the Phoenix Fire Office, was 'seriously worried about Ireland' as early as the 1820s. According to the history of the Phoenix, 'the rejection rate for loan proposals from the West of Ireland approached 100 per cent'. The Pelican placed an additional premium of £1 per £100 for the 'State of Ireland' and the Phoenix insisted on an exclusion of liability in life policies for Irish landowners, if death occurred by 'assassination'.[32]

From about 1840 onwards, another feature of the insurance trade was that companies might decline proposals on the lives of heavy drinkers or, on the other hand, might offer cheaper insurance to total abstainers. Roderick Moore, the actuary of the United Kingdom Temperance and General Provident Institution, conducted a study, published in 1904 which concluded that:

> The abstainers showed a marked superiority to the non-abstainers throughout the entire working years of life, for every class of policy, and for both sexes, however tested. In our daily experience we know that of all the points to be considered in connection with a proposal for life assurance, by far the most important, in the majority of cases, is the question of 'habits' by which the general term 'habits' in this connection will nearly refer to the use, moderately or otherwise, of alcoholic beverages.[33]

This was indeed bad news for many men seeking life insurance. For someone like Paddy Dignam, it would have been difficult to secure insurance if he had answered the insurer's questions truthfully. As early as 1826, according to the history of the Phoenix, a company was compelled to contest liability to pay on the death of an Irish gentleman because his medical reports 'stated the gentleman to be extremely sober and temperate; whereas the Board have the best possible testimony that he was for the last twenty years of his life a most notorious drunkard and that he occasionally continued in a state of intoxication for three days together'.[34]

In the case of poor Dignam, it seems likely that his fondness for 'John Barleycorn' was both the cause of his death and the reason for his mortgaging of his life insurance.[35] But it does not appear that

Scottish Widows raised any questions about alcohol consumption when he sought insurance cover.

Stratagems and safety nets

The suddenness of Paddy Dignam's death would have created difficulty for his dependants even if he had been in employment and there had been no problem with the insurance policy. On the credit side, he lived at a 'good' address in inner suburban Newbridge Avenue, near Sandymount, a solid Victorian red-brick house, almost certainly rented. But he had lost his employment and was a heavy drinker. Both Molly Bloom in her soliloquy and Dignam's friends at his funeral acknowledged this. He may have been doing some freelance law clerking since parting company with John Henry Menton.

Having got a whip-round going for Dignam's family,[36] his friends' next reaction is to seek to lessen the widow's immediate problems by placing the older children in some form of training or employment. The savvy Martin Cunningham takes the lead in this:

—Martin is trying to get the youngster into Artane.
—How many children did he leave?
—Five. Ned Lambert says he'll try to get one of the girls into Todd's.[37]

Artane was then a small rural village three miles north of Dublin. It was the location of the O'Brien Institute for Destitute Children, a reformatory and industrial school run by the Irish Christian

Brothers, a lay order of unordained religious celibates – 'brothers'. In June 1904 the institute was administered by the Rev. Brother William Swan. In later years the school was to acquire a most unfortunate reputation for physical and sexual abuse of some of its inmates. Christian Brothers' schools were conducted, by present-day standards, along somewhat brutal lines. But for that matter, so were many expensive 'private' schools of the time, both in Ireland and in England.

'Todd's' is a reference to Todd Burns & Company, Silk Mercers, Linen and Woollen Drapers, Tailors, Boot, Shoe and Furnishing Merchandisers, a large department store in Dublin. One of Joyce's sisters, May Joyce, at one stage worked there as a sales assistant. This is the genteel employment envisaged for the Dignam girl.

From other references in *Ulysses* we know that Mr Cunningham's approach to his task of getting Dignam's son into Artane was to make use of his clerical contacts. Mr Cunningham first appears in the short story 'Grace' in *Dubliners*. There he is one of a group who encourage the backsliding Tom Kernan to attend a spiritual 'retreat' or 'mission' in the Jesuit Church in Gardiner Street; Cunningham is associated with the Sodality or Religious Confraternity which the Jesuits run there.

Other references in *Ulysses* tell us precisely how Mr Cunningham approached his self-imposed task. In *Wandering Rocks* we hear him tell his companions:

—The youngster will be all right, Martin Cunningham said, as they passed out of the Castleyard gate. [...]
—Yes, Martin Cunningham said, fingering his beard. I wrote to Father Conmee and laid the whole case before him.[38]

The result of this intervention is seen as Father Conmee leaves the Jesuit house in Gardiner Street to walk to Artane:

The superior, the very reverend John Conmee S.J. reset his smooth watch in his interior pocket as he came down the presbytery steps. Five to three. Just nice time to walk to Artane. What was that boy's name again? Dignam. Yes. *Vere dignum et iustum est.* Brother Swan was the person to see. Mr Cunningham's letter. Yes. Oblige him, if possible. Good practical catholic: useful at mission time.[39]

The Latin phrase is from the Canon of the Mass, meaning 'It is indeed right and just', the Latin word *dignum* reminding the priest of the boy's name.

The Dignam family, accordingly, find themselves assisted by a private network of Catholic charity. As a member of the Jesuit Sodality, Mr Cunningham helps organize the annual mission in their church. Father Conmee is thus disposed 'to oblige him if possible' and is setting out to walk to Artane with a view to doing so. Brother Swan will then have done a favour to Father Conmee, an ordained Church dignitary of higher rank, and he will no doubt expect Conmee's assistance or support on some future occasion in return.

The object of placing young Patrick Dignam in Artane is so that he can learn a useful trade, a number of which were taught in the O'Brien Institute, to increase the boy's future earning capacity. Obtaining employment for one of the girls would lessen the financial pressure on the widow in the shorter term. The family's support network is not exclusively Catholic: Ned Lambert is a Protestant, a nephew of the ardent Protestant Vice-Chancellor Chatterton, and thus a suitable person to approach Todd Burns, a Protestant firm.[40]

Freemasonry

Mr Cunningham has also taken it upon himself to see if he can expedite the payment of Dignam's insurance policy. In this regard he has enlisted the assistance of Mr Bloom, a move which is interesting from a number of points of view. Bloom is the only Jewish member of the late Paddy Dignam's overwhelmingly Christian circle of friends, acquaintances and drinking companions. But Mr Cunningham thinks it worthwhile to enlist this outsider's assistance. In *Lestrygonians*, the sapient publican Davy Byrne, speaking of Bloom, asks Nosey Flynn:

—What is this he is? Isn't he in the insurance line?
—He's out of that long ago, Nosey Flynn said. He does canvassing for the *Freeman*.[41]

A little later Nosey Flynn provides the additional information:

—He's in the craft, he said.
—Do you tell me so? Davy Byrne said.
—Very much so, Nosey Flynn said. Ancient free and accepted order. He's an excellent brother. Light, life and love, by God. They give him a leg up. I was told that by a – well, I won't say who.
—Is that a fact?

James Joyce, 1882–1941. The great Argentinian writer Jorge Luis Borges described Joyce as being 'less a man of letters than a literature'.

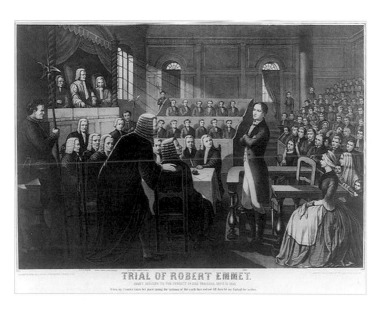

TRIAL OF ROBERT EMMET.

Robert Emmet, executed in 1803 for rebellion. Here he replies to the court's verdict. After a century during which Emmet had become a cult figure, indeed a secular saint as W. B. Yeats called him, it was generally believed that he had in fact been hanged, drawn and quartered.

John Philpot Curran 'in a terse and frigid letter, withdrew as Emmet's counsel'. The government had made him fully aware of his daughter Sarah's compromised position.

The fate of Charles Stewart Parnell preoccupied Joyce and features again and again in his writings. A poem he wrote on the topic as a child, addressed to Parnell's chief tormentor under the title *Et Tu, Healy*, became his first published work when his proud father had it privately printed; unfortunately no copies of the poem survive.

The Maamtrasna murders of 1882, which led to the execution of
Myles Joyce and two other men, universally believed (and now proven)
to have been innocent, is a significant theme in *Finnegans Wake*.
Here one of the boys who survived the murders gives evidence in court.

The Invincibles' murder
of Lord Cavendish and
Thomas Burke occurred
in Dublin just three
months after Joyce's birth
in 1882 and is a recurring
theme in *Ulysses*.

Sir William Joynson-Hicks, 1st Viscount Brentford and scourge of obscenity. 'There cannot have been a more enthusiastic book-burner since the High Victorian era.'

Timothy Michael Healey, 1885–1931, who was mainly responsible for the acquittal of Samuel Childs in the 'gruesome case' of his brother's murder. The dramatic speech attributed to Seymour Bushe, KC, in *Ulysses* is not reflected in the contemporary records at all. Joyce's lifelong hatred of Healy stemmed from the latter's role in Parnell's downfall.

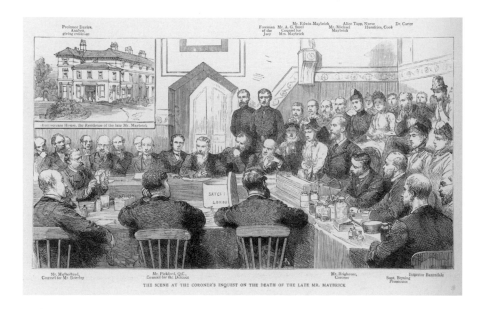

THE SCENE AT THE CORONER'S INQUEST ON THE DEATH OF THE LATE MR. MAYBRICK

One of the cases that Molly Bloom thinks of in her long soliloquy is that of Mrs Maybrick. In 1889 she was convicted of poisoning her husband. The evidence against her was extremely thin and she was reprieved from hanging. She was eventually released in 1904.

The half-Indian solicitor, George Eldaji, jailed for seven years for cattle-maiming in 1903 on the basis of flawed evidence and a huge fund of prejudice. One of the cases that convinced Joyce of the moral necessity of doubt.

THE LITTLE REVIEW

Vol. V.   MARCH, 1918   No. 11

ULYSSES

JAMES JOYCE

Episode 1

STATELY, plump Buck Mulligan came from the stairhead, bearing a bowl of lather on which a mirror and a razor
lay crossed. A yellow dressing gown, ungirdled, was sustained gent-
ly behind him on the mild morning air. He held the bowl aloft and
intoned:

—*Introibo ad altare Dei.*

Halted, he peered down the dark winding stairs and called up
coarsely:
—Come up, Kinch. Come up, you fearful jesuit.
Solemnly he came forward and mounted the round gunrest.
He faced about and blessed gravely thrice the tower, the surrounding country and the awaking mountains. Then, catching sight of
Stephen Dedalus, he bent towards him and made rapid crosses in
the air, gurgling in his throat and shaking his head. Stephen
Dedalus, displeased and sleepy, leaned his arms on the top of the
staircase and looked coldly at the shaking gurgling face that blessed
him, equine in its length, and at the light untonsured hair, grained
and hued like pale oak.
Buck Mulligan peeped an instant under the mirror and then
covered the bowl smartly.
—Back to barracks, he said sternly.
He added in a preacher's tone:
—For this, O dearly beloved, is the genuine christine: body
and soul and blood and ouns. Slow music, please. Shut your eyes,
gents. One moment. A little trouble about those white corpuscles.
Silence, all:

Margaret Anderson, editor of the *Little Review*, said on reading the opening of the *Proteus* episode: 'This is the most beautiful thing we'll ever have. We'll print it if it's the last effort of our lives.' She was prosecuted for obscenity.

John S. Sumner, Secretary of the New York Society for the Prevention of Vice, whose complaint about *Ulysses* led eventually to a trial in the New York City police court and the conviction of Margaret Anderson and Jane Heap on obscenity charges.

The United States Circuit Court of Appeals for the Second Circuit was dominated by the personality and legal genius of Judge Learned Hand, the most distinguished American judge never to have been appointed to the Supreme Court.

By the early 1930s Morris Ernst was incontestably the leading legal expert on obscenity in the United States. He was an archetypal New York liberal Jew and subsequently became President of the American Civil Liberties Union (ACLU).

Judge John M. Woolsey was at the time of the Ulysses trial 'a plump, dapper, sharply dressed man aged fifty-six. His record in censorship cases had been uniformly liberal; he had authorized the importation into the United States of Dr Marie Stopes' book.'

Bennett Cerf, Publisher of Random House. 'In March 1932 I had lunch with Ernst and I said 'If I can get Joyce to do an edition of *Ulysses* for America, would you fight the case for us in court?' I added 'We haven't got the money to pay your fancy prices' – he was a very high powered lawyer – 'but if you win the case you will get a royalty on *Ulysses* for the rest of your life.'

—O, it's a fine order, Nosey Flynn said. They stick to you when you're down. I know a fellow was trying to get into it. But they're as close as damn it. By God they did right to keep the women out of it.[42]

This is by no means the only hint in the text that Bloom is a member of, or connected with, the Freemasons and has benefited from this association. The insurance industry, like other aspects of financial services at that time, was largely the preserve of Ireland's non-Catholic minority, many of whom, especially in the higher echelons, were believed to be Freemasons. It seems likely that it was for this reason that Mr Cunningham asked Bloom to deal with the Scottish Widows about Dignam's policy rather than doing so himself or asking an influential Catholic, such as Father Conmee, to do so.

In the twelfth episode, *Cyclops*, Mr Bloom gives the explanation of the Policies of Insurance Act 1867. He somewhat annoys the afternoon boozers by his know-all tone. The anonymous narrator, tired of hearing Bloom going on about the position of the 'mortgagor under the act', thinks to himself:

He was bloody safe he wasn't run in himself under the act that time as a rogue and vagabond only he had a friend in court. Selling bazaar tickets or what do you call it royal Hungarian privileged lottery. True as you are there. O, commend me to an israelite! Royal and privileged Hungarian robbery.[43]

This is a suggestion that Bloom himself might have been prosecuted for illegally selling foreign lottery tickets, were it not for the fact that he was friendly with someone in court. That this friend was a Freemason or group of Freemasons seems implied in Molly Bloom's reflections on the same topic in *Penelope*:

> every time were just getting on right something happens or he puts his big foot in it Thoms and Helys and Mr Cuffes and Drimmies either hes going to be run into prison over his old lottery tickets that was to be all our salvations or he goes and gives impudence well have him coming home with the sack soon out of the Freeman too like the rest on account of those Sinner Fein or the freemasons.[44]

'Drimmies' was David Drimmie & Sons, 41 Lower Sackville Street, agents in Dublin for English and Scottish Law, Life and the Phoenix Fire Office. Bloom was once employed there and it may be where he gained his knowledge of insurance law.

Bloom himself reflects on the same topic in *Lestrygonians*: 'Windy night that was I went to fetch her there was that lodge meeting on about those lottery tickets after Goodwin's concert in the supperroom or oakroom of the Mansion house.'[45]

From these references it seems safe to conclude that Bloom had some more or less nefarious dealings with lottery tickets from which, however, he escapes scot-free. The subject was discussed at a lodge – that is, a Freemason lodge – meeting, which may suggest that Bloom himself was present and that he was a member, as Nosey Flynn claims.

This rather obscure topic of foreign lottery tickets was referred to in the illustrated *Irish Weekly Independent and Nation* of 16 June 1904. There it was reported that:

From a prosecution which took place at the Clerkenwell Police Court [London] the other day it would appear that the authorities have decided on the adoption of strong measures for the purpose of putting a stop to the circulation of announcements relating to foreign lotteries. A printer was summoned by the treasury for publishing a certain proposal and scheme for the sale of tickets and chances and shares in certain tickets in a lottery called 'The Privileged Royal Hungarian Lottery' authorised by the government of the State of Hungary.

It seems likely that this is the contemporary basis for the reference to the Hungarian lottery in *Ulysses*.

Bloom seems to confirm his Masonic associations in *Circe* when the 'First Watch' demands that he accompany them to the station:

(*scared, hats himself, steps back, then, plucking at his heart and lifting his right forearm on the square, he gives the sign and dueguard of fellowcraft*)
No, no, worshipful master, light of love. Mistaken idendity.[46]

In other words, he gives a Freemason sign, hoping to be recognized by the policeman as a fellow member of the Masonic 'craft'.

There thus seems little doubt that Bloom is a member of the Freemasons or, at least, is willing to be taken for a Mason. This is explicitly stated by Molly when she refers to Bloom trying to insinuate them both into Catholic musical circles 'till the jesuits found out he was a freemason'.[47]

The demon drink

It is clear that everyone who knew Dignam was aware of his propensity to drink far too much. This was how he came to lose his job in John Henry Menton's legal practice and how his wife and eldest son were reduced to waiting for him outside public houses, as Mrs Bloom relates. It is clear from her account that Dignam had a bad reputation for failing to maintain his family through drink, a failing which Mrs Bloom attributes to his (and Bloom's) circle of drinking companions:

> and they all with their wives and families at home more especially Jack Power keeping that barmaid he does of course his wife is always sick or going to be sick or just getting better of it and hes a goodlooking man still though hes getting a bit grey over the ears theyre all a nice lot all of them well theyre not going to get my husband again into their clutches if I can help it making fun of him then behind his back I know well when he goes on with his idiotics because he has sense enough not to squander every penny piece he earns down their gullets and looks after his wife and family goodfornothings[48]

It is plain that, though Molly sees various foolish or furtive aspects of her husband, she credits him with being a better breadwinner than most of his associates. Similarly, a little later on she appears to credit Bloom with being a better prospect in the long term than her lover, Blazes Boylan, with whom, however, she had dallied in the matrimonial bed only a few hours previously, and not without some satisfaction. Bloom's principal advantage as a breadwinner is vividly expressed: he won't squander every penny on drink, and will look after his wife and family.

Insurance and suicide

The social and economic importance of life insurance and other forms of insurance designed to guarantee a payment on death meant that disputes over policies of insurance were quite common. A surprisingly broad swathe of the community had some knowledge of the technicalities of insurance law. Joyce demonstrates this by his familiarity, which he attributes to Bloom, with the Policies of Insurance Act 1867 and Bloom's consequent ability to explain the technical issue affecting the estate of Paddy Dignam to his companions in Kiernan's public house. This understanding was not limited to the fact that, by reason of the Act, the assignee of the policy, the moneylender Bridgeman, could not himself sue on the policy. It extended to the very practical insight that this did not cancel out the moneylender's claim to the money that Dignam owed him, but merely prevented him recovering what was due in one particular way.

This was an important restriction, however. Because of section 3 of the Act, the assignee of the policy would not be entitled to recover directly under the policy itself, thereby getting instant priority over other creditors. Now, Bridgeman would have to compete with the other creditors, and with the dependants. If the wife was successful in obtaining a rapid payout, without publicity, of the sums due under the policy, Bridgeman might have considerable difficulty in recovering his debt from that fund.

In *Wandering Rocks*, when the unnamed 'elderly female, no more young'[49] 'rustled' from the Admiralty Division to the Court of Appeal (see pp. 96–7), she was coming from the case of the Barque Mona to that of *Harvey* v *The Ocean Accident and Guarantee Corporation*. This Harvey case had been at hearing by a divisional court (three judges instead of the usual one) of the King's Bench Division of the High Court on 22, 25 and 27 January 1904. The High Court gave its judgment on 14 May. The executor of the deceased man's estate appealed and the appeal was heard on 14 and 15 June 1904, leading to the reservation of judgment on the latter day. Judgment in the Court of Appeal was given on 30 June.

Harvey v *The Ocean Accident and Guarantee Corporation*, briefly mentioned though it is, is one of the most significant legal cases in the entire Joyce canon. In the first place it illustrates perfectly and simply Joyce's lasting preoccupation with epistemology, the science of how, precisely, we 'know' what we know, or at least what we think we know. Harvey died by drowning in the River Lee. In legal terms he was 'found drowned', as the coroner's jury found. There was no dispute about that. However, how he came to drown was a different and highly contentious issue. But this question did not trouble the courts in a spirit of abstract inquiry: it was intensely debated before the High Court and the Court of Appeal in Ireland because the question of whether or not his relations were entitled to the proceeds of his life policy depended on whether he drowned accidentally or by suicide. As often happens, this resolved itself in law into an issue which turned on the question of who bore the onus of proof. This important point has been addressed earlier in *Ulysses*, firstly in *Hades*, where 'the maxim of the law', to the effect that guilt must be proved and not merely asserted, is discussed, and during the Shakespearian passage in the *Scylla and Charybdis* episode when Stephen routs his adversaries with the observation that 'The burden of proof is with you not with me'.[50]

As we shall see later in this chapter, the issue of suicide raised particular questions, social, philosophical as well as legal. In the Ireland of 1904 there was a genuine horror of suicide which manifested itself in the conversation of the men in Dignam's funeral procession. This has a particular personal significance to Bloom because his late father committed suicide in the Queen's Hotel, Ennis, in 1886 (see pp. 185–6). He knows that some at least of his companions are aware of this and is mortally embarrassed when they turn to discussing suicide in general.

This social or religious attitude in Ireland was very strongly manifested in the law as it was at the time, and up until our own time. Suicide was both immoral and illegal and attempted suicide was a crime which, at that time, was regularly prosecuted. A clause in an insurance policy excluding the insurance company's liability for death by suicide was commonplace, and would be upheld by the courts. But the very fact that suicide was unlawful meant that it attracted the presumption against crime, the presumption of innocence, placing the onus of proof of suicide firmly on the party who asserted it. This was a somewhat paradoxical result, since the terms of the policy seemed to give great discretion to the directors of the insurance company. But Joyce loved such subtleties.

It is also easy to see why Joyce, with his knowledge of and interest in insurance cases, was attracted to the Harvey action. Charles Meade Harvey was the steward of the Queenstown Yacht Club based at Queenstown (now Cobh), a transatlantic port in the eastern part of the County of Cork. He was a bachelor with an annual income from the club of £150, together with free accommodation and board as Club Steward. He had a further income of another £100 arising from his position as a consul.

According to *Thom's Directory* for the year 1900, C. M. Harvey was Vice-Consul in Cork for Brazil, Denmark and the then state of 'Sweden and Norway'. Much of a consul's work is to do with the nationals of the state he represents who become sick, get into debt, are arrested for crime or suffer other misfortunes, such as sailors paid off when the ship on which they work is detained for debt under the Admiralty procedures. A man in Charles Harvey's position, already resident in the port of Cork at Queenstown, would be well placed to discharge the duties of Vice-Consul. Moreover, the consular business appeared to run in the family: Harvey's brother (and the plaintiff in the later case about his life insurance) was William W. Harvey, who was Vice-Consul in Cork for the German Empire, Liberia (a famous flag of convenience for merchant shipping) and for Portugal.[51]

Harvey had no significant property beyond a small number of shares in a shipping company worth about £70. At the time of his death he owed about £1200, mostly debts of long standing. There was no evidence of immediate financial pressure except for a dispute about a sum of £16, the price of a cigarette case which he had purchased 'on appro'. But he was in urgent need of about £50 at the time of his death. He was in the habit of receiving club subscriptions and bar money for which he had to account to the Committee of the club. On 1 April 1902 he owed the club £59, and had just written up the accounts which showed this liability. The accounts would, he knew, shortly come before the Committee. This would probably trigger a demand for immediate payment, which he would not be able to meet. Joyce was fascinated by these small but crippling financial difficulties which had pushed many men he knew, including his own father, into poverty or insolvency, and sometimes suicide.

Accordingly, it appears that the bulk of Mr Harvey's debts were of long standing and were not particularly pressing. What was immediately pressing at the start of April 1902 were the relatively small debts of £59 to the club and £16.0.5 to the jewellers who had supplied the silver cigarette case. He had received a threatening letter from a solicitor about this latter debt. The debt to the club carried the intimidating prospect of the loss of his employment, which would have made his position truly acute as he would have lost the bulk of his income and his right to board and lodgings on the club premises.

Harvey had, however, some good friends from whom he appears to have borrowed in the past. On the Saturday preceding 1 April 1902, a Mr Daly gave him £40 'with pleasure' to square his bank account. At the same time Harvey told a Mr O'Grady that he wanted some money urgently and he would have got it 'if Mrs O'Grady had not interfered', as Lord Justice Holmes subsequently put it. Harvey did not press the matter and it was likely that if he had he would have got the money from O'Grady, because the latter was his guarantor to the Yacht Club. Some days before 1 April he wrote to a Mr Brennan in London requesting a loan of £50 and sending as security the certificate for his shares in the shipping company. Mr Brennan replied by return of post, in a letter that reached Cork on 2 April, enclosing a cheque for that sum and returning the share certificates. He was prepared to make the loan without security.

Mr Harvey was last seen alive on the evening of 1 April 1902. At about 7 p.m. on that day Harvey, together with a person who was not named in the law report, entered the refreshment room of the Glanmire Station of the Great Southern and Western Railway in Cork city, and had a single drink.

He asked for an envelope from the attendant and put into it the disputed silver cigarette case and addressed it to the solicitor in Queenstown who had written the threatening letter. He asked the attendant to post the envelope, which she subsequently did.

About twenty-five minutes later he was seen alone in a covered hackney cab which was being driven through King Street from the direction of the station towards the centre of the city. He was not seen alive after that. On the evening of Sunday, 20 April 1902 his dead body was found in the southern branch of the River Lee about a mile 'above' (west of) Cork city. At an inquest two days later a verdict of 'found drowned' was returned.

Mr Harvey had had an insurance policy. It was not a life insurance policy in the ordinary sense, still less an endowment policy which would have provided a fixed sum, or a sum calculated in a pre-determined manner, upon death. In contrast to these more usual types of provision, a claim under the policy only arose 'if the insured sustained any bodily injury *by accident* from an outward, external, and visible means or cause and died solely from the effects of such accident within ninety days'.

As to how these things were to be established, the policy provided that the company was bound to pay 'only after proof, satisfactory to the Directors of the Company for the time being, of the cause of death had been given'. The policy specifically insisted that it would not extend to death by suicide. It also stipulated that in the event of a dispute between the company and any claimant, the conflict should be referred to arbitration.

The policy provided for the payment of £1,000 to the insured person's executors, administrators or assigns upon his *accidental* death while the policy was in force, and contained an exclusion for death by suicide.

In the Harvey case, the policy had not been assigned, as Patrick Dignam's had been. Indeed, it is unlikely that Harvey's policy would have been acceptable as security because of its very narrow scope: both now and then people were much more likely to die of disease than by accident. Correspondingly, a policy covering accident only would have been considerably cheaper to acquire and maintain than a life policy covering death from all causes. The policy had been in force since 1897, five years before Harvey's death, but the clause against suicide was not limited as to time: some policies exclude suicide only within a fixed time of taking out the policy. The topic of suicide may have been embarrassing to Bloom, because of the manner of his father's death, but the stern disapproval of suicide and the harsh condemnation of it by the Irish law of 1904 ironically redounded to the benefit of Harvey's estate.

Suicide in Irish law

The law in relation to suicide, that is the intentional killing of oneself, was remarkably stable for many centuries. In our time, however, it has undergone (internationally as well as in Ireland) dramatic change, more dramatic however in some jurisdictions than in others. In Ireland, suicide was decriminalized in 1993, but the crime of assisting a suicide was re-enacted by the same Act, the Criminal Law (Suicide) Act 1993.

Ireland is, and has been since the Norman invasion of the twelfth century, part of the common-law world and shares a legal inheritance with England and Wales (above all), the United States, Canada, Australia, New Zealand and certain other countries. From this common-law inheritance derives both the traditional law against suicide and the current statute law. Indeed, this Irish Act is directly derived from an English exemplar as, of course, is a goodly portion of Irish statute law in general.

It is impossible to improve on what was said on the status of suicide at common law (which was the Irish law on the subject in 1904) by the United States Supreme Court. There, Chief Justice Rehnquist, giving the Opinion of the Court, wrote:

for over seven hundred years the Anglo-American Common Law tradition has punished or otherwise disapproved of both suicide and assisted suicide. In the 13th century, Henry de Bracton, one of the first legal treatise writers, observed that 'just as a man may commit felony by slaying another so he may do so by slaying himself'. The real and personal property of one who killed himself to avoid conviction and punishment for a crime were forfeit to the King; however, thought Bracton, 'if a man slays himself in weariness of life or because he is unwilling to endure further bodily pain [...] only his movable goods were confiscated'. Thus 'the principle that suicide of a sane person, for whatever reason, was a punishable felony was [...] introduced into English Common Law'. Centuries later, Sir William Blackstone, whose Commentaries on the Laws of England not only provided a definitive summary of the Common Law but was also a primary legal authority for eighteenth and nineteenth century American lawyers, referred to suicide as 'self murder' and 'the pretended heroism, but real cowardice, of the Stoic philosophers, who destroyed themselves to avoid those ills which they had not the fortitude to endure [...]'. Blackstone emphasised that 'the law has [...] ranked suicide among the highest crimes', although, anticipating later developments, he conceded that the harsh and shameful punishments imposed for suicide 'border a little upon severity'[52]

Writing in 1759, Blackstone commented on the reason for criminalization as follows:

The law of England *wisely and religiously considers* that no man hath a power to destroy life but by commission from God – the author of it. And a suicide is guilty of a double offence: one spiritual, *in invading the prerogative of the almighty and rushing into his immediate presence uncalled for*; the other temporal, against the King who hath an interest in the preservation of all his subjects. The law has therefore ranked this amongst the highest crimes, making it a peculiar species of felony, a felony committed on oneself [...]

What punishment can human laws inflict on one who has withdrawn himself from their reach? They can only act upon what he has left behind, his reputation and fortune; on the former by an ignominious burial in the highway with a stake driven through his body; on the latter by forfeiture of all his goods and chattels to the King hoping that his care for either his reputation or the welfare of his family would be some

motive to restrain him from so desperate and wicked an act.
[Emphasis added.]

It is plain, therefore, that the historic criminalization of suicide,
which subsisted in Ireland until 1993, is based on a *religious*
intuition. This explained the evil of 'invading the prerogative of
the almighty and rushing into his immediate presence uncalled for'
and also considered that suicide was derogatory of the interests of
the King, who may be regarded as a symbol of the state or the community. Indeed, the opinion of the United States Supreme Court
placed the origins of the offence back beyond the thirteenth century,
approving what was said by Professor Baker in his *Introduction to
English Legal History*. The court concluded:

> The Common Law is thought to have emerged through the
> expansion of pre-Norman institutions sometime in the 12th
> century. England adopted the ecclesiastical prohibition on
> suicide five centuries earlier, in the year 673, at the Council of
> Hereford, and this prohibition was reaffirmed by King Edgar
> in 967.[53]

The condemnation of suicide, and the somewhat theatrical
treatment of its victims – burial by night in unconsecrated ground,
and the rest – survived into modern times. The full severity of
the laws of forfeiture were mitigated in 1823 and daylight burial
of suicides was permitted from 1882. By the time suicide was
decriminalized in England and Wales in 1961, the proposal to do so
had attracted the support of the Church of England. This measure
appears to have inspired the Irish legislation of 1993.

It thus appears that, whether coincidentally or otherwise, measures to mitigate the traditional condemnation of suicide and to alleviate the macabre penalties attached to it developed with the rise of secularism. In Ireland, this did not occur for many years after 1904.

Mr W. H. Harvey, brother and executor of Charles Harvey, claimed under the policy, relying entirely on the verdict of the coroner's jury 'found drowned'. The company refused to pay, relying on the suicide clause and stating that proof of the accidental nature of the death satisfactory to the directors had not been given. In accordance with the terms of the policy, the dispute was referred to a single arbitrator, Mr George Lawrence, Barrister-at-Law. Mr Lawrence was simply unable to make up his mind, so he stated a 'special case' pursuant to the Common Law Procedure Act 1856, section 8. This provided a consultative procedure whereby he could obtain the opinion of the courts on a point of law.

In this special case he raised questions which he described as questions of law.

The first question was: 'Whether proof that Harvey was found drowned in the River Lee, and that his death resulted solely from drowning, was a sufficient compliance with the terms of conditions of the policy, unless it was proved by the Company that death resulted from one of the excepted causes?' This rather obvious question was answered in the affirmative. The second question was as to whether 'proof satisfactory to the Directors of the Company of the cause of the death of Charles Harvey was given, within the meaning of the policy?'.

These questions purported to express questions of law referred by the arbitrator to the decision of the courts. But in reality they raise questions of fact. The High Court held that, since all the facts had been referred to them, they were of the opinion that the directors had been justified in failing to conclude that death was due to accident rather than suicide, but the Court of Appeal reversed this decision and answered the questions in a manner favourable to the claimant, Harvey's brother. Lord Justice Holmes said:

> So far as the first question is at all intelligible to me as a question of law, I can only understand it as asking this – if a man is found drowned and certainly drowned either by accident or by suicide, and there is no preponderance of evidence as to which of the two caused his death, is there any presumption against suicide which will justify a jury or an arbitrator in finding that the death was accidental and innocent, and not suicidal and criminal. *In my opinion there clearly is such presumption.* I have no jurisdiction to decide the question of whether there is a preponderance of evidence one way or the other in this case. *If I had such jurisdiction, I should have little hesitation in finding that the assured fell by accident into the Lee, from the dangerous path he was following by night.* [Emphasis added.]

With this very broad hint, the matter was referred back to the arbitrator, who no doubt reached the same conclusion that the judges of the Court of Appeal had suggested.

There was virtually no difference on the law between the Court of Appeal and the High Court, but the two courts drew very different inferences of fact.

Over and above that, the judges of the Court of Appeal were

strongly of the opinion that policies payable on the death of an insured person should if possible be validated and allowed to take effect, because of their importance from the point of view of the dead person's relatives and creditors. Quoting an English case, Lord Justice Holmes said:

Cockburn C. J. said in *Trew* v *Railway Passenger Assurance Company* 'We ought not to give to these policies a construction which will defeat the protection of the assured in a large class of cases.' To require affirmative evidence of accident in cases like the present would undoubtedly have that effect.[54]

Secondly, the court was deeply influenced by the fact that, since time immemorial, suicide was criminally unlawful and attempted suicide was a felony at common law. Suicide was therefore a crime and there was a presumption against crime, so that there should be no finding of suicide without overwhelming proof.

Lord Justice Holmes said:

In such a case is there any presumption of law in favour of accident as against any other cause of death? I think there is. The death can only be reasonably accounted for in one of two ways – immersion in the water by accident or design; *and an innocent cause ought to be presumed as against what would prima facie be a crime.* [He cited an American case where] it has been held in a civil action [e.g. in an action on a policy of insurance] that where there is no evidence as to its cause, a death must be presumed to have been natural, and not to have been suicide, since suicide is a felony. [Emphasis added.]

This, then, was 'the maxim of the law' as Mr Cunningham described it in the *Hades* episode: that there should be no finding of a crime, such as suicide, in the absence of very strong proof. The appellate judges were not as impressed as the judges of first instance either by the evidence of Mr Harvey's financial problems, or by the fact that his body was found far from his house 'in the upper waters of the Lee'.

As to the latter point, Lord Justice Holmes said:

> At the inquest no explanation was given of the body being found in the upper waters of the Lee. This circumstance indeed is as difficult to account for on the theory of suicide as of accident. I know no place affording better facilities for drowning than from Queenstown seaward; and why a man residing there should go into the city of Cork, and some distance beyond it, to look for water, is a mystery.

This part of the judgment is very rigorously expressed. The judge went on to find that the fact that the pathway above the river was a short cut to the residence of his sister, Mrs Haynes, who had loaned the deceased money on several occasions in the past, was a sufficient reason to account for Mr Harvey's presence in the area where the body was found without any suicidal intention. Moreover, the day of his disappearance was Mrs Haynes's birthday and he was in the habit of writing to her or visiting her on that day.

The Court of Appeal was wholly unimpressed by the idea that financial difficulty made it likely that Harvey killed himself; the same judge said at p. 33 of the report:

At the time of his death he owed about £1200.0.0 consisting for the most part of debts of longstanding. There is no-one on whom money troubles sit more lightly than on a bachelor, with an income which his creditors cannot touch. This seems to have been the deceased's position and I am not surprised that there was nothing found in his papers or elsewhere indicating pecuniary pressure, except for a sum of £16.0.0, the price of a cigarette case.

Suicide in *Ulysses*

Joyce selected the Harvey case, together with two others reported on 16 June 1904, for mention in *Ulysses*, in the knowledge that it was a case relating to suicide.

The topic of suicide looms quite largely in *Ulysses*. Mr Bloom's father, born Rudolph Virag in Szombathely in the kingdom of Hungary and subsequently of 52 Clanbrassil Street, Dublin, had changed his name to Rudolph Bloom. In later life he became the proprietor of the Queen's Hotel, Ennis, Co. Clare and committed suicide in that hotel, apparently because it was not a commercial success. He was also downcast at the recent death of his wife. When Bloom inspects the contents of the drawer in his home which contained the assurance policies already mentioned, he also found his father's suicide note, addressed 'To My Dear Son, Leopold'.[55]

In light of this, as we have seen, it is a great embarrassment to Mr Bloom when the topic of suicide is raised by one of the gentlemen in Patrick Dignam's funeral procession, Mr Power:

—But the worst of all, Mr Power said, is the man who takes his own life.

Martin Cunningham drew out his watch briskly, coughed and put it back.

—The greatest disgrace to have in the family, Mr Power added.

—Temporary insanity, of course, Martin Cunningham said decisively. We must take a charitable view of it.

—They say a man who does it is a coward, Mr Dedalus said.

—It is not for us to judge, Martin Cunningham said.[56]

Mr Bloom feels considerable gratitude to Martin Cunningham for his attempts to deflect the conversation from the topic of suicide:

Mr Bloom, about to speak, closed his lips again. Martin Cunningham's large eyes. Looking away now. Sympathetic human man he is. Intelligent. Like Shakespeare's face. Always a good word to say. They have no mercy on that [i.e. suicide] here or infanticide. Refuse christian burial. They used to drive a stake of wood through his heart in the grave. As if it wasn't broken already. Yet sometimes they repent too late. Found in the riverbed clutching rushes.[57]

Bloom then thinks of the circumstances of his father's death:

That afternoon of the inquest. The redlabelled bottle on the table. The room in the hotel with hunting pictures. Stuffy it was. Sunlight through the slats of the Venetian blind. The coroner's sunlit ears, big and hairy. Boots giving evidence. Thought he was asleep first. Then saw like yellow streaks on his face. Had slipped down to the foot of the bed. Verdict: overdose. Death by misadventure. The letter. For my son Leopold.[58]

As soon as there is an opportunity, Mr Cunningham reproves Mr Power for what he has said:

—I was in mortal agony with you talking of suicide before Bloom.
—What? Mr Power whispered. How so?
—His father poisoned himself, Martin Cunningham whispered. Had the Queen's hotel in Ennis. You heard him say he was going to Clare. Anniversary.
—O God! Mr Power whispered. First I heard of it. Poisoned himself?[59]

Mr Bloom is not in any way condemnatory of his father's suicide but he is conscious that the attitude to suicide in Ireland was a condemnatory one. The verdict at the inquest into the death of Mr Bloom senior was one of death by misadventure. Verdicts of this sort were often found by coroners, with or without juries, where the evidence permitted any doubt at all as to whether the case was one of suicide. This was done partly out of a deference to the feelings of the survivors and partly to avoid ecclesiastical censures or the invalidation of insurance policies, such as that of Mr Harvey. Accordingly, it was generally believed that suicide was considerably under-reported in Ireland in 1904 and for many years afterwards.

From the internal evidence in the novel, it appears that the suicide of Mr Bloom senior took place in 1886. Bloom's reminiscences of his father are affectionate ones tempered by remorse, principally because he himself has disrespected certain religious beliefs and practices taught to him by his father but which now appear to him 'Not more rational than they had then appeared, not less rational than other beliefs and practices now appeared.'[60] He derives 'partial consolation' for these melancholy reflections from 'The endowment policy, the bank passbook, and the certificate of the possession of scrip'.[61] There is perhaps a suggestion that these assets, or their origins, are attributable to Rudolph Bloom, or at least to his example.

6. Political Violence: Emmet and the Invincibles

I have but one request to ask at my departure from the world: it is the charity of its silence. Let no man write my epitaph; for as no man who knows my motives dares now vindicate them, let not prejudice or ignorance asperse them, let them rest in obscurity and peace: my memory left in oblivion and my tomb remain un-inscribed, until other times, and other men, can do justice to my character. When my country takes her place among the nations of the earth then, and not till then, let my epitaph be written. I have done.

> Conclusion of ROBERT EMMET's speech from the dock after
> being sentenced to be hanged, drawn and quartered.[1]

Yet […] he certainly did feel and no denying it […] a certain kind of admiration for a man who actually brandished a knife,

cold steel, with the courage of his political convictions […]
until it just struck him that Fitz, nickenamed Skin-the-Goat,
merely drove the car for the actual perpetrators of the outrage
and so was not, if he was reliably informed, actually party to
the ambush which, in point of fact, was the plea some legal
luminary saved his skin on. In any case that was very ancient
history by now and as for our friend, the pseudo Skin-the
etcetera, he had transparently outlived his welcome. He ought
to have either died naturally or on the scaffold high.

LEOPOLD BLOOM on the patriotic assassins of Lord Frederick
Cavendish twenty-two years earlier in 1882.[2]

*U*lysses is haunted by political violence, betrayal, and
the law's appalling revenge on the perpetrators. The
violence is almost always political. The most salient
example, which comes frequently into the minds of the protagonists
in *Ulysses* on 16 June 1904, was the glamorous but chaotic and always
hopeless rebellion of 1803 led by Robert Emmet, and that romantic
hero's public execution shortly afterwards.

It is said in many a ballad and nationalist history that Emmet was
'hanged, drawn and quartered', but this was not quite true. It is true
that he was *sentenced* to be hanged, drawn and quartered by the
judge who tried him, Lord Norbury, 'bully, butcher, and buffoon',
as W. J. Fitz-Patrick called him.[3]

To be hanged, drawn and quartered was from 1351 the statutory
penalty in England for anyone convicted of high treason.[4] The
ritual was first recorded during the time of King Henry III, who

reigned from 1216 to 1272. It was later applied to other felonies. The sentence was one of unique barbarity. Here is the judge's death sentence as read to Harrison, one of the regicides of Charles I:

> That you be led to the place from whence you came and from thence be drawn upon a hurdle to the place of execution, and then you shall be hanged by the neck and, being alive, shall be cut down, and your privy members to be cut off, and your entrails to be taken out of your body and, you living, the same to be burnt before your eyes, and your head to be cut off, your body to be divided into four quarters, and head and quarters to be disposed of at the pleasure of the King's majesty.[5]

This, clearly, is an appalling method of execution. It was a sentence of half hanging, followed by ritual castration, the opening of the body and extraction of the main inner organs which were then burned before the still-living prisoner. After that he would be decapitated and dismembered to facilitate the display of his head and limbs in public places.

This sentence ceased to be mandatory in cases of felony after the passage of the Treason Act in 1814. It was not finally abolished until 1870.[6] Long before this, however, it had ceased to be carried out in any literal way, to avoid public revulsion. What in fact happened to Emmet was that he was hanged by the strangulation method outside St Catherine's Church in Thomas Street, Dublin and his dead body was then beheaded on a butcher's block. But this did not prevent ballad writers and nationalist historians from reciting the sentence as it was imposed and omitting the fact that it was not actually carried out in that way. Thus Mr Kernan believes as a fact that Emmet was 'hanged drawn and quartered' and an anonymous ballad also says so: 'Hung drawn and quartered, sure that was his sentence'.

Lord Norbury and the government were of course all fully aware that Emmet would not in fact be hanged, drawn and quartered, but merely hanged and decapitated. But they nevertheless insisted that the ancient sentence with all its horrific detail be publicly pronounced. Presumably, the purpose of this was to terrorize other potential rebels.

Nationalist balladeers and popular historians colluded with the court and government of 1803 in proclaiming that Emmet's treatment had been even more barbaric than it actually was, though for very different reasons. After a century during which Emmet had become a cult figure, indeed a secular saint as W. B. Yeats called him, it was generally believed that he had in fact been hanged, drawn and quartered. This untruth, initiated by the government of 1803 and the trial judge, was seized upon by Thomas Moore,[7] the historian Dr Madden and many others, until it quite displaced the less dramatic reality. Joyce reproduces the popular belief as opposed to the actual fact, as he often did. In the savage pastiche of the nationalist legend of the execution, in the *Cyclops* episode, the provision of vessels for the reception of Emmet's viscera presupposes that the full ritual had been carried out.

The impact of Emmet's execution was very much greater and infinitely more lasting than the government could possibly have anticipated. One hundred and one years later, one of Bloom's cronies, Mr Kernan, Dublin representative of the English tea-importing firm Pullbrook Robertson, is seen in the *Wandering Rocks* episode as he returns along Thomas Street to his office in

Dame Street, having made a sale and partaken of a convivial gin with his customer in St James's Gate in West Dublin.[8]

Kernan admires his own smart appearance in a shop window and relishes the shot of gin: 'Aham! Hot spirit of juniper juice warmed his vitals and his breath. Good drop of gin, that was. His frocktails winked in bright sunshine to his fat strut.'[9] In this self-satisfied state he sees the site of Emmet's execution. He remembers: 'Down there Emmet was hanged, drawn and quartered. Greasy black rope. Dogs licking the blood off the street when the lord lieutenant's wife drove by in her noddy.[10]

That Kernan thinks of the execution in the way that he does, with the graphic detail about the dogs licking Emmet's blood off the street when the Lord Lieutenant's wife is driving by, shows how vivid Emmet's execution and the events that led to it remained after more than a century. This is confirmed by the fifteen other references to Robert Emmet scattered throughout the novel. Marianne Elliott has devoted a book to the proposition that Emmet's main career and significance in Irish history developed after his death,[11] on the basis of the enduring symbolism of his execution at the age of twenty-five, the figure of high romance that he represented and his forced complicity in his own execution procured by threats against his fiancée, Sarah, daughter of the prominent nationalist lawyer and politician John Philpot Curran. Those aspects of his career made Emmet an internationally recognized symbol of idealistic youth struck down in its prime by tyrannical authority and young love cruelly blighted. Some understanding of this cult of Emmet, growing throughout the nineteenth century in Ireland and Irish America, is necessary to understand Joyce's treatment of him.

Joyce himself takes note of this process of creating a legend in the conversation of the men in Kiernan's public house, scene of the *Cyclops* episode. He portrays the patriotic windbag, Citizen, continuing his ultra-nationalist diatribe, invoking the martyred heroes of the nation:

> So of course the citizen was only waiting for the wink of the word and he starts gassing out of him about the invincibles and the old guard and the men of sixtyseven and who fears to speak of ninetyeight and Joe with him about all the fellows that were hanged, drawn and transported for the cause by drumhead courtmartial [...] the brothers Sheares and Wolfe Tone beyond on Arbour Hill and Robert Emmet and die for your country, the Tommy Moore touch about Sara Curran and she's far from the land.[12]

Thomas Moore, whose talents as a poet and song lyricist made him a major celebrity in England and Ireland, was a contemporary of Robert Emmet's at Trinity College, Dublin. But he prudently refrained from actual involvement in Emmet's rebellion and lay low while it was taking place. However his songs, and especially the one invoked by Joyce, 'She is Far from the Land', were almost single-handedly responsible for turning Emmet into a romantic hero and the subject of poems by Robert Southey[13] and Percy Bysshe Shelley.[14] Moore's song, which is still sung in Ireland, pictures Sarah Curran after her lover's death:

> She is far from the land where her young hero sleeps
> And lovers around her are sighing
> But coldly she turns from their gaze and she weeps
> For her heart in his grave is lying.[15]

A good deal of this posthumous *réclame* was due to Emmet's speech from the dock at his trial. According to Patrick Geoghegan: 'His oration would become one of the great set pieces of Irish history, and win fame internationally. It, rather than the failed rebellion, became the greatest part of his legacy and ensured his place in Irish history.'[16] The same author refers to the fact that 'Within three years the speech from the dock was being performed on the American stage.'

Sixty-two years after Emmet's execution a United States Senator, Willard Saulsbury, wrote to President Abraham Lincoln pleading for the life of a young Confederate spy who had been sentenced to death. This was Lieutenant Samuel B. Davis, who had made a heroic speech from the dock after being found guilty. The Senator, 'no friend of either Lincoln or his administration', begged the President to study the speech and to 'compare it with the celebrated defence of Emmet'.[17] Davis was reprieved.

The reason why a United States Senator of the 1860s could assume that the President was acquainted with Emmet's speech was that the speech was included in many collections of celebrated oratory in the early and mid-nineteenth century. This created nothing short of a cult of Emmet. W. B. Yeats was able to describe him as 'the leading Saint of Irish nationality'.[18] Moore also immortalized him in other songs such as 'O Breathe Not His Name' and 'When He Who Adores Thee'. In 1900, perhaps the best-known Emmet ballad was composed by an anonymous poet:

Bold Robert Emmet, the darling of Eirin,
Bold Robert Emmet he died with a smile,
Farewell companions, both loyal and daring,
I lay down my life for the Emerald Isle.

Patrick Pearse, shortly afterwards the principal leader of the 1916 insurrection, gave two orations about Emmet in New York in 1914.[19] There, he said that Emmet had won a victory which was greater than that of Brian Boru at Clontarf or of Owen Roe O'Neill at Benburb and was 'Christ like in its perfection'. It is of course tempting to see this as the work of a man who had already decided that Ireland required a blood sacrifice. Certainly in putting on a magnificent green uniform to read the Proclamation to an indifferent crowd outside the General Post Office in 1916 Pearse was imitating Emmet's example. Yeats thought that Pearse was 'half-cracked and wanting to be hanged. He has Emmet delusions, the same as other lunatics think they are Napoleon or God.'[20]

When Michael Collins, in his capacity as Sinn Féin Minister for Finance, issued war bonds in 1919 they were shown being signed on a butcher's block, allegedly the one on which Emmet had been beheaded.[21]

On the bicentenary of Emmet's death, the Historical Society of Trinity College, Dublin, from which he had been expelled in his lifetime, voted him the 'greatest Irish person of all time'.[22]

But the ambivalence of his reputation, which is a major aspect of his treatment in *Ulysses*, cannot be better expressed than by Professor Geoghegan in his entry on Emmet in the *Dictionary of Irish Biography*, cited above:

Emmet's life and his legacy remain contentious. Despite attempts to recast him as a realistic conspirator, he continues to be seen as an idealistic and somewhat foolish revolutionary who became a romantic hero despite his own failings. An enigmatic figure, his contribution to Irish nationalism and

Irish history remains elusive. Emmet's place in the pantheon of Irish heroes is assured not despite, but rather because of the discordance between his extraordinary aspirations and his dramatic failings. His story – romantic, tragic, pathetic – serves as an apotheosis of the Irish heroic ideal and continues to inspire, infuriate, excite and provoke.[23]

There are two other aspects of Emmet's history which must be understood in order to make Joyce's references comprehensible. The first is the dramatic challenge posed by his speech from the dock. The terms of its conclusion in particular, as interpreted by later generations of Irish nationalists, was a challenge, an inspiration, and the source of a sacred duty well into the twentieth century.

The portion of the speech quoted in the epigraph to this chapter, especially, was learned by heart and declaimed by generations of Irish schoolchildren. A common subject for school and university debates, at least until recent times, was 'That Emmet's epitaph can now be written'. One of the early Irish-American nationalist organizations was known as 'The Emmet Monument Association', a title which looked forward to a time when Emmet's epitaphs could be written,[24] because Ireland had 'taken her place amongst the nations of the earth'.

This aspect of Emmet's legacy was rendered all the more pathetic by a second extraordinary fact: after his execution and decapitation, his head and body disappeared. Immediately after the execution the remains were brought back to Kilmainham Jail, where the artist James Petrie took a plaster cast of the face in order to make a death mask. The remains were then buried in Bullys Acre, a sort of potter's field in the grounds of the Royal Hospital, Kilmainham, where paupers were interred. A little later they were disinterred and presumably reburied.

The action of disinterring a corpse and burying it privately is understandable in the context of the time, the religious sentiments then prevailing, and the fact that the bodies of executed persons often ended up in the hands of the anatomists. A contemporary work on social aspects of execution by hanging in England observes:

> Since the body's integrity mattered for its resurrection, people worried about how it was treated after hanging – anatomised, decapitated, gibbeted as might be. Surgeons were hated, grave-diggers execrated. Felons wanted to be buried *decently* preferably in the home Churchyard; 'decently' was always the word used.[25]

No doubt similar sentiments prevailed in Ireland. In any event, Joyce's first two references to Emmet relate to this question of his missing body. When Mr Bloom is in Glasnevin Cemetery for Paddy Dignam's funeral he sees 'An obese grey rat' making his way under a plinth and wonders: 'Who lives there? Are laid the remains of Robert Emery. Robert Emmet was buried here by torchlight, wasn't he?'[26]

Later, in *Wandering Rocks*, Mr Kernan, having passed the scene of Emmet's execution, speculates on his burial place: 'Let me see. Is he buried in saint Michan's? Or no, there was a midnight burial in Glasnevin. Corpse brought in through a secret door in the wall. Dignam is there now.'[27]

In the absence of a reliable account of Emmet's burial, speculation suggested that he might have been buried in St Michan's, one of the most ancient churches in Dublin, close to the Four Courts, where many of those executed in 1798 were buried, or in St Peter's in Aungier Street where Emmet's father, Dr Thomas Emmet, had been buried not long before, or in the expanding Glasnevin graveyard, about two miles north of the city. During the nineteenth century and in the centenary year, 1903, the descendants of Emmet's elder brother, Thomas Addis Emmet, sometime Attorney General of the State of New York, made several visits to Ireland. This family was prominent for generations in the legal and medical professions in New York City. They expressed interest in finding the whereabouts of their forebear, but the question was never satisfactorily resolved. It is clear, however, that it was still something which might have occupied a corner of the mind of two Dublin salesmen a century later.

Emmet in *Ulysses*

Joyce, then, fully acknowledged the status of Emmet in nationalist ideology, propaganda and iconography. The manner in which the unidentified narrator of the *Cyclops* episode describes the Citizen holding forth in the public house amply demonstrates this, in the final part of the larger passage quoted above. But Joyce himself is no admirer of Emmet and indeed holds him up to ridicule in two of the most savage pieces of satire in the entire novel.

Remembering Emmet's words

At about 4 p.m., Bloom drops into the Ormond Hotel and becomes part of an informal concert performed by such characters as Simon

Dedalus and Ben Dollard.[28] They sing patriotic songs, and Bloom endeavours to compose a reply to Martha Clifford's salacious letter, which he collected earlier. But Bloom quite soon decides that he wants to leave. The presence of his brother-in-law, still more the presence of Blazes Boylan (about to keep his amorous afternoon appointment with his wife, Molly Bloom), the boozy and slightly raucous camaraderie of the men gathered there and in particular a growing feeling of flatulence which he attributes to the wine he has drunk earlier and to the cider he drinks in the Ormond, all induce him to depart while the patriotic singing is still in progress. When he leaves he is still troubled by a tendency to break wind. He stares into the window of the adjacent 'Antique Saleshop', where he sees 'a gallant pictured hero in Lionel Mark's window. Robert Emmet's last words. Seven last words. Of Meyerbeer that is.'[29] The 'seven last words' of Meyerbeer is a reference to Giuseppe Mercadante's *The Seven Last Words of Our Lord* (plainly meant to evoke an appropriately respectful reception), which Bloom confuses with Meyerbeer's opera *Les Huguenots*.

Nearby he hears the clanking noise of the Dublin trams and more faintly hears the chorus of 'The Memory of the Dead' from inside the hotel:

—True men like you men.
—Ay, ay, Ben.
—Will lift your glass with us.
    They lifted.
    Tschink. Tschunk.[30]

As Bloom stands there, hearing those sounds, he stares at the picture of Robert Emmet and mentally recites his last words: 'When my country takes her place among the nations of the earth then, and not till then, let my epitaph be written. I have done.' But he accompanies this recitation with an apparently uncontrollable breaking of wind. The noise of his crepitations mingles with that of the trams on the Quays:

Seabloom, greaseabloom viewed last words. Softly. *When my country take her place among.*
Prrprr.
Must be the bur.
Fff! Oo. Rrpr.
Nations of the earth. No-one behind. She's passed. *Then and not till then.* Tram kran kran kran. Good oppor. Coming. Krandlkrankran. I'm sure it's the burgund. Yes. One, two. *Let my epitaph be.* Kraaaaaa. *Written. I have.*
Pprrpffrrppffff.
Done.[31]

This is manifestly not a respectful meditation on the hero's last words. Not only that, but the company Bloom has just left are united in slightly boozy emotion engendered by patriotic songs such as the 'Croppy Boy', which is often thought to evoke Robert Emmet. The last verse brings the men to a pitch of shameless sentimentality:

At Geneva barracks that young man died
And at the Passage was his body laid,
All you good Christians who do pass by
Breathe a prayer, drop a tear for the Croppy Boy.[32]

There is reason to think that some of the heroes who are the subject of the songs, like Pearse in Yeats's view, 'wanted to be hung'. Bloom, alone in that company, is unmoved.

Emmet's execution 'a genuinely instructive treat'

But there is worse to come. In the *Cyclops* episode an all-male group is again gathered in a bar, this time Kieran's of Little Britain Street, opposite Green Street Court House where Emmet was tried. As we have seen, Emmet's name is invoked by the hysterical patriot, the so-called Citizen, in common with that of other executed patriots, in a litany which ends with a reference to Sarah Curran (see p. 194).

The Citizen then works himself up to such a pitch of patriotic ecstasy that he screams: '*Sinn Fein!* [...] *Sinn fein amhain!* The friends we love are by our side and the foes we hate before us.'[33] This leads to the most sustained piece of satire in the novel.[34] It is manifestly a pastiche, with cruel mockery, of Emmet's execution which pokes fun not only at Emmet but at his sainted and sacred inamorata, Sarah Curran.

Joyce proceeded to mock the huge edifice of history, ballad, iconography and emotion that nationalist poets and writers had built up around Emmet's speech from the dock and his execution. Even worse, he dared to mention that Sarah Curran had married a well-connected British officer in 1805, a couple of years after Emmet's death. This was a flaw in the virginal image created by Thomas Moore of the abandoned girl, ignoring all suitors because 'her heart in his grave is lying'.

This passage demands to be read as a whole, over the five pages it occupies in the Bodley Head edition of *Ulysses* edited by Hans Walter Gabler. It starts in the pretentious style typical of nineteenth-century popular historians:

> The last farewell was affecting in the extreme. From the belfries far and near the funereal deathbell tolled unceasingly while all around the gloomy precincts rolled the ominous warning of a hundred muffled drums punctuated by the hollow booming of pieces of ordnance. The deafening claps of thunder and the dazzling flashes of lightning which lit up the ghastly scene testified that the artillery of heaven had lent its supernatural pomp to the already gruesome spectacle.[35]

The assembled crowd was 'numbered at the lowest computation five hundred thousand persons'.[36] This gathering is entertained by the York Street Brass and Reed Band and by Stephen Dedalus's intimates Lenehan and Mulligan anachronistically, as well as tastelessly singing 'The Night before Larry was Stretched'.[37] Also present are the 'viceregal houseparty which included many wellknown ladies'.[38]

There is also a large and 'picturesque foreign delegation known as the Friends of the Emerald Isle'.[39] These include many diplomats representing foreign potentates including Ali Baba Backsheesh Rahat Lokum Effendi,[40] a name that recalls amongst other things the confectionery known as Turkish Delight.

The executioner Rumbolt is then introduced, apparently with some admiration:

As he awaited the fatal signal he tested the edge of his horrible weapon by honing it upon his brawny forearm or decapitated in rapid succession a flock of sheep which had been provided by the admirers of his fell but necessary office. On a handsome mahogany table near him were neatly arranged the quartering knife, the various finely tempered disembowelling appliances (specially supplied by the worldfamous firm of cutlers, Messrs John Round and Sons, Sheffield), a terra cotta saucepan for the reception of the duodenum, colon, blind intestine and appendix etc when successfully extracted and two commodious milkjugs destined to receive the most precious blood of the most precious victim.[41]

These viscera were destined for a charitable purpose: 'The house-steward of the amalgamated cats' and dogs' home was in attendance to convey these vessels when replenished to that beneficent institution.'[42] Nor was this the end of the charitable aspect of the event:

Quite an excellent repast consisting of rashers and eggs, fried steak and onions, done to a nicety, delicious hot breakfast rolls and invigorating tea had been considerately provided by the authorities for the consumption of the central figure of the tragedy who was in capital spirits when prepared for death and evinced the keenest interest in the proceedings from beginning to end but he, with an abnegation rare in these our times, rose nobly to the occasion and expressed the dying wish (immediately acceded to) that the meal should be divided in aliquot parts among the members of the sick and indigent roomkeepers' association as a token of his regard and esteem.[43]

No wonder, then, that:

> The children of the Male and Female Foundling Hospital who thronged the windows overlooking the scene were delighted with this unexpected addition to the day's entertainment and a word of praise is due to the Little Sisters of the Poor for their excellent idea of affording the poor fatherless and motherless children a genuinely instructive treat.[44]

Perhaps the cruellest touch of all in this rather cinematographic pastiche is the introduction of the hero's inamorata, who immediately seeks to console herself with an alternative suitor: 'The *nec* and *non plus ultra* of emotion were reached when the blushing bride elect burst her way through the serried ranks of the bystanders and flung herself upon the muscular bosom of him who was about to be launched into eternity for her sake.'[45]

This last assertion, that Emmet died for Curran, is truer than Joyce may have known; see the account, in the Appendix, of the blackmail practised on him by the Crown prior to his trial, on the basis that Sarah's letters could be used to make her part of the conspiracy but would be suppressed if Emmet died quietly.

Their fond farewells are touchingly described, but a sense of practicality eventually triumphs:

> A most romantic incident occurred when a handsome young Oxford graduate, noted for his chivalry towards the fair sex,

stepped forward and, presenting his visiting card, bankbook and genealogical tree, solicited the hand of the hapless young lady, requesting her to name the day, and was accepted on the spot. Every lady in the audience was presented with a tasteful souvenir of the occasion in the shape of a skull and crossbones brooch, a timely and generous act which evoked a fresh outburst of emotion: and when the gallant young Oxonian (the bearer, by the way, of one of the most timehonoured names in Albion's history) placed on the finger of his blushing *fiancée* an expensive engagement ring with emeralds set in the form of a fourleaved shamrock the excitement knew no bounds.[46]

Joyce, then, took one of the most sacred events of Irish history, the trial of Robert Emmet, the immortal speech he made on that occasion and his public execution the following day, and mocked them. His hero, Bloom, farts his way through a reading of the final words of the speech; the execution is reduced to a carnival and, worse still, the leading lady of the whole affair, Sarah Curran, is deprived of her tragic status. She hardly threw herself into another suitor's arms, but it is historically true that she married Captain Robert Sturgeon, nephew of the Marquis of Rockingham, in 1805.

The Invincibles

Emmet's rebellion, however farcical its end, was planned as a proper military coup d'état. Its leaders were gorgeously uniformed and a high-sounding Nationalist Proclamation was read out. No such openly staged rebellion of this kind was to take place in Ireland for over a century, until the Easter Rising of April 1916. Joyce himself, in his Italian journalism, summed up the progress of 'the Irish Revolution' during the nineteenth century:

Whoever studies the history of the Irish revolution during the nineteenth century will find himself confronted by a dual struggle: the struggle, that is, of the Irish nation against the English government, and the struggle, perhaps no less fierce, between the modernist nationalists and the so-called physical force party. That party, under its various names: the 'Whiteboys', the 'Men of 98', the 'United Irishmen', the 'Invincibles' and the 'Fenians' has always refused to have any dealings with either the English parties or the Nationalist parliamentarians [...]

Unlike the ridiculous rebellion of Robert Eminet [*sic*] or the fervent Young Ireland movement of 1845, the Fenianism of '67 was not one of those usual outbursts of Celtic temperament that burn brightly for a moment in the darkness, leaving a deeper darkness than before in their wake. [...] Under the command of James Stephens, the country was organised into cells of twenty-five men each, a plan of campaign eminently suited to the Irish character since it minimised the possibility of betrayal.

Joyce then rapidly surveys the collapse of the Fenian plan for a rising in 1867 and the escape of James Stephens and continues:

Why this collapse of such a well organised movement? Simply because in Ireland, just at the crucial moment, an informer appears. Following the disbanding of the Fenians, the traditional doctrine of physical force sporadically reappears in violent acts. The 'Invincibles' [*sic*] blew up Clerkenwell Prison, snatched their comrades out of the hands of the police in Manchester and killed the escort, and stabbed the English Chief Secretary and Under Secretary, Lord Frederick Covendish [*sic*] and Burke, in broad daylight in the Phoenix Park in Dublin.[47]

Joyce chronicles the escape of Stephens himself in the same article:

Stephens was captured and imprisoned, but managed to escape thanks to the loyalty of a Fenian warder. While the agents and spies were lying in wait at every port in the island watching outgoing ships, he left the capital in a gig, disguised (according to legend) as a bridesmaid with a white crepe veil and orange-blossom. He was then conducted on board a small charcoal boat which hastily set sail for France.[48]

Joyce is not commonly credited with much knowledge of or sympathy for the Fenian movement or their belated offshoot, the Invincibles, which he confuses with the parent organization in his essay. *Ulysses*, however, belies this impression. The Invincibles' murder of Lord Cavendish and Thomas Burke occurred in Dublin just three months after Joyce's birth in 1882 and is a recurring theme in *Ulysses*. It is portrayed both as an appalling murder and, paradoxically, as something for which even the generally pacific Leopold Bloom has a sneaking regard. But Joyce's interest in the Fenian movement goes back a great deal further than 1882.

On 1 December 1902 Joyce left Ireland for the first time, bound for Paris. He was three months short of his twenty-first birthday. He had some idea, never fulfilled, of pursuing a medical course in that city. In fact he returned to Dublin in April 1903 when his mother became seriously ill, and later died. On his departure for Paris he brought with him a reference from his father's friend Timothy Harrington, then Lord Mayor of Dublin. He also had an introduction to an old Fenian, Joseph Casey, who appears in *Ulysses* under the name Kevin Egan.[49]

Casey/Egan was a cousin of the Fenian organizer James Stephens. He was imprisoned in England with Colonel Richard O'Sullivan Burke, an Irish Republican Brotherhood arms dealer based in London. He was arrested with Burke while trying to prevent the latter's capture and both were detained in Clerkenwell Prison in November 1867. While they were held there the Fenians breached the prison walls with a large explosion to secure their escape, which caused twelve fatalities. At a subsequent trial, Casey was improbably acquitted and went to France with his family. He was also accompanied by his brother, the Fenian activist Patrick Casey, whose extradition back to Britain was refused. But Patrick later returned to Ireland and took up residence in St Peter's Terrace, Cabra, Dublin in 1891. There he was a neighbour of John Stanislaus Joyce, who advised his son James to contact his neighbour's brother when he went to Paris in 1902, thirty-four years after Joseph Casey had fled there.

There are numerous echoes of these events in the early part of *Ulysses*. Bloom reflects on the looseness of lip and deliberate informing which had ruined many Irish nationalist initiatives:

James Stephens' idea was the best. He knew them. Circles of ten so that a fellow couldn't round on more than his own ring. Sinn Fein. Back out you get the knife. Hidden hand. Stay in. The firing squad. Turnkey's daughter got him out of Richmond, off from Lusk. Putting up in the Buckingham Palace hotel under their very noses. Garibaldi.[50]

Bloom is reflecting, as he does frequently throughout *Ulysses*, on the prevalence of informers as well as of the merely indiscreet, which has allowed the authorities to break numerous nationalist uprisings. He admires James Stephens's plan for preventing this and reflects also on the manner of Stephens's escape after the abortive rebellion of 1867.

In the third episode in the novel, *Proteus*, Stephens is seen walking along Sandymount Strand. There he reflects on his first visit to Paris and in particular on his encounters there with Joseph Casey/Kevin Egan. He recalls:

Noon slumbers. Kevin Egan rolls gunpowder cigarettes through fingers smeared with printer's ink […] Well: *slainte!* Around the slabbed tables the tangle of wined breaths and grumbling gorges. His breath hangs over our saucestained plates, the green fairy's fang thrusting between his lips. Of Ireland, the Dalcassians, of hopes, conspiracies, of Arthur Griffith now, A E, pimander, good shepherd of men. To yoke me as his yokefellow, our crimes our common cause. You're your father's son. I know the voice. His fustian shirt, sanguineflowered, trembles its Spanish tassles at his secrets. M. Drumont, famous journalist, Drumont, know what he called queen Victoria? Old hag with the yellow teeth. *Vieille ogresse* with the *dents jaunes.* [...]

The blue fuse burns deadly between hands and burns clear. Loose tobaccoshreds catch fire: a flame and acrid smoke light our corner. Raw facebones under his peep of day boy's hat. How the head centre got away, authentic version. Got up as a young bride, man, veil, orangeblossoms, drove out the road to Malahide. Did, faith. Of lost leaders, the betrayed, wild escapes. Disguises, clutched at, gone, not here.

This gives a brilliantly sharp picture of Joyce sitting in a bar with the old Fenian in permanently nostalgic humour, reflecting on Stephens's escape, the explosion at Clerkenwell, his interest in the present state of the nationalist movement, but most of all his isolation in exile:

I was a strapping young gossoon at that time, I tell you. I'll show you my likeness one day. I was, faith. Lover, for her [Ireland's] love he prowled with colonel Richard Burke, tanist of his sept, under the walls of Clerkenwell and, crouching, saw a flame of vengeance hurl them upward in the fog. Shattered glass and toppling masonry. In gay Paree he hides, Egan of Paris, unsought by any save me. Making his day's stations, the dingy printingcase, his three taverns, the Montmartre lair he sleeps short night in [...]

Weak wasting hand on mine. They have forgotten Kevin Egan, not he them. Remembering thee, O Sion.

There is an apparent reference to his brother, John Stanislaus

Joyce's neighbour: 'Tell Pat you saw me, won't you? I wanted to get poor Pat a job one time.'[51]

This is Joyce's personal contact with the Fenian movement: some drinks in Paris with a sad old Fenian remembering past glories but capable of nothing else. Unforgetting, he is nonetheless forgotten. The Fenians who escaped to America rather than to France found a large coterie of like-minded Irish men and in many cases, like John Devoy or Jeremiah O'Donovan Rossa, played active roles in keeping the cause of revolution alive in Ireland. Stephens himself, however, fell out with the dominant American wing of the Irish revolutionary movement and spent years, apparently in poverty, in Paris until he was permitted to return to Ireland in 1891. He died ten years later.[52]

Stephens's escape after the abortive rebellion was much spoken of in Ireland because it was the only success of which the Fenian movement could boast. 'The man that got away James Stephens' was a catchphrase in Dublin, and it was reflected thus in *Ulysses*. In *Calypso* Bloom, thinking of going to Tara Street Public Baths for a wash, reflects that the 'Chap in the paybox there got away James Stephens, they say.'[53] A similar credit is given to others. In *Cyclops* the feat is attributed to the bombastic patriot of the Public House, the Citizen: 'There's the man, says Joe, that made the Gaelic sports revival. There he is sitting there. The man that got away James Stephens. The champion of all Ireland at putting the sixteen pound shot.'[54] Still later, the credit is given to Bloom himself at the height of his popularity in the hallucinatory *Circe* episode, after he has made a patriotic stump speech. John Wyse Nolan declares that Bloom is 'the man that got away James Stephens'.[55]

The Fenian movement never revived in its own right in Ireland, though its successor organization, the Irish Republican

Brotherhood, played a significant role in the Land League and in the 1916 rebellion. But the physical force tradition, which the Fenians epitomized, evolved and developed, was subsumed under the generic title 'Fenian'. During the Land War, from 1879, the term was generally applied to the perpetrators of agrarian murders.

On 6 May 1882, just after Parnell and other nationalist leaders had been released from a form of internment, leading to the resignation of the hardline Chief Secretary for Ireland, William Edward 'Buckshot' Forster, it was felt that a new era in Anglo-Irish relations had been inaugurated by the much admired British Prime Minister, W. E. Gladstone. That day, one of brilliant sunshine, saw the arrival of the new Chief Secretary, Lord Frederick Cavendish, a former Financial Secretary to the Treasury, a generous-minded Liberal and a nephew by marriage of Gladstone himself. Cavendish was not personally disliked, as Forster had been. His advent was seen as the beginning of a new and more friendly policy from which a lasting peace might have been expected. His murder was to seem to many a declaration of war to the death.

The new Chief Secretary, largely unrecognizable in Ireland, decided to travel alone from Dublin Castle where he had been officially welcomed, to the Viceregal Lodge in the Phoenix Park, a distance of about two miles. Near the entrance to the park he met Thomas Burke, the Under-Secretary and head of the Public Service, who was an Irish Catholic. They walked on together and were near the Viceregal Lodge when they were attacked by a group of seven men who stabbed them to death with surgical knives. The assassins were then picked up and driven away in hackney cabs, while other horse-drawn hackneys went in other directions to baffle pursuit.

The contemporary effect of this assassination can hardly be exaggerated and has been brilliantly chronicled in a number of works and is very palpable in *Ulysses*.[56] The initial reaction in Ireland was one of shock and shame. It was not simply shock at the extremely bloody nature of the crime itself. It was shock at the shattering, after only a few days, of the new departure which seemed to put an end to the atmosphere of armed and aggressive confrontation in Anglo-Irish politics. It was also alarm at the assassination of an amiable English nobleman, well connected with the liberal Prime Minister and his government who, unlike 'Buckshot' Forster, had earned no personal opprobrium in Ireland. There was also shock that a group capable of doing such a deed, soon identified as the 'Irish National Invincibles', had been able to organize quite unsuspectedly in Dublin. As the weeks and months after the assassinations went by, it became clear that the police, too, were at a loss. The government suspended habeas corpus, enacted repressive legislation and made belligerent statements; the police 'rounded up the usual suspects' and then released them again.

All this changed quite suddenly in January 1883. A long list of prominent, mostly impoverished nationalists were arrested or rearrested. Chief amongst them was James Carey, an apparently reputable builder and landlord, active in various Catholic pietistic societies and a married man with a numerous family. When, in February 1883, Carey was not produced amongst the defendants at the preliminary proceedings in the magistrates' court, but was brought in instead as a Crown witness, there was a sensation in Dublin the effects of which lasted for decades and are plainly

mirrored in *Ulysses*. The Lord Lieutenant, Lord Spenser, considered Carey's betrayal 'the greatest event since the landing of
[King] Henry II'.[57]

Carey 'swore up' in the magistrates' court and later at the trial
at the Dublin City Commission in Green Street. He withstood
cross-examination in a supercilious and sometimes jocose way.
Five men were hanged on the strength of his evidence and that of
other informers. The hanged men were regarded as simple-minded
and courageous, but utterly wrong-headed. Particular hatred was
directed at Carey because it was felt that he had induced these
much humbler men into the conspiracy and then ensured that they
were hanged for it while saving his own neck.

Later in 1883, after the executions, Carey and his family were
taken into a nineteenth-century equivalent of the witness protection
programme. He was given passage with his family to Cape Town
and then onwards to Durban on a ship called the *Melrose Castle*.
But while still on board he was recognized and shot dead by an
Irishman called Patrick O'Donnell.

It was this aspect of the case – the initiation of the conspiracy
by the upwardly mobile James Carey and his subsequent betrayal
of his underlings – that most impressed Joyce. When Bloom steps
into the Catholic Church in Westland Row to read his salacious
letter from Martha Clifford, his scheme for a meeting with Martha
leads to thoughts of Carey, whose Christian name, however, he
cannot remember:

Meet one Sunday after the rosary. Do not deny my request.
Turn up with a veil and black bag. Dusk and the light behind
her. She might be here with a ribbon around her neck and do

the other thing all the same on the sly. Their character. That fellow that turned queen's evidence on the invincibles used to receive the, Carey was his name, the communion every morning. This very church. Peter Carey, yes. No, Peter Claver I am thinking of. Denis Carey. And just imagine that. Wife and six children at home. And plotting that murder all the time. Those crawthumpers, now that's a good name for them, there's always something shiftylooking about them. They're not straight men of business either.[58]

This passage, and others on the same subject cited below, shows that the Invincible murders of twenty-two years before are not at the forefront of Bloom's mind, but lie close enough to it for him to think of them quite easily when something reminds him of them – the thought that Martha Clifford or Irish Catholics in general might be hypocritical in their lifestyle.

These references in Bloom's stream of consciousness to 'Their character [...] Those crawthumpers' in the context of moral hypocrisy and commercial dishonesty are significant. Bloom seems to regard the mass of the Catholic Irish as 'other' than himself, devious and shifty and well capable of producing the murderer and betrayer Carey. Carey's act in turning Queen's evidence is suggested by the thought of Martha Clifford betraying her religious principles. There is more than a hint of disapproval, but the murder does not seem more immoral than Carey's betrayal of his comrades, or Martha's putative betrayal of her religious principles, perhaps with Bloom himself.

The topic of the Invincibles murder comes up again, after Dignam's funeral, when the gentlemen are gathered in the office of the editor of the *Evening Telegraph*. The bombastic editor is telling a story of how details of the Invincibles affair were conveyed in a sort of code to the *New York World*, which had 'cabled for a special'. Getting the date wrong by a year, he says: 'That was in eightyone, sixth of May, time of the invincibles, murder in the Phoenix park, before you were born, I suppose.'[59] He recalls some of the participants a little uncertainly: 'Tim Kelly, or Kavanagh I mean. Joe Brady and the rest of them. Where Skin-the-Goat drove the car.'[60]

Skin-the-Goat was the nickname of the cab driver Fitzharris who drove the getaway cab. The editor's reference leads one of the men to remark: 'Skin-the-Goat, Mr O'Madden Burke said. Fitzharris. He has that cabman's shelter, they say, down there at Butt bridge.'[61]

Later in the same conversation a newspaper story brings to mind a more recent recollection of the Invincibles:

Professor MacHugh came from the inner office.
—Talking about the invincibles, he said, did you see that some hawkers were up before the recorder...
—O yes, J. J. O'Molloy said eagerly. Lady Dudley was walking home through the park to see all the trees that were blown down by that cyclone last year and thought she'd buy a view of Dublin. And it turned out to be a commemoration postcard of Joe Brady or Number One or Skin-the Goat. Right outside the viceregal lodge, imagine![62]

Number One was the assumed name of a man called Tynan, who claimed (unconvincingly) to have led the Invincible movement. It appears that in 1904 memorial cards for the executed men were still being sold in Dublin. To the drunken patriot, the Citizen, and those who think like him, the Invincibles are part of the litany of the patriot dead stretching back in an unbroken sequence to 1798 and beyond.

Much later in *Ulysses*, in the *Eumaeus* episode, Bloom rescues Stephen from drunken soldiers and other dangers of the night in the red-light district. Stephen is also by then quite drunk and is taken off by Bloom to the cabman's shelter near Butt Bridge. The keeper of this shelter, as we have previously heard, is said to be Skin-the-Goat Fitzharris. This leads to several reflections on Bloom's part about the Invincibles:

> Mr Bloom and Stephen enter the cabman's shelter, an unpretentious wooden structure, where, prior to then, he had rarely if ever been before, the former having previously whispered to the latter a few hints anent the keeper of it said to be the once famous Skin-the-Goat, Fitzharris, the invincible, though he could not vouch for the actual facts which quite possibly there was not one vestige of truth in.[63]

Having listened to some patriotic balderdash from the inhabitants of the shelter, he reflects:

> And as for the lessee or keeper, who probably wasn't the other person at all, he (B.) couldn't help feeling and most properly it was better to give people like that the goby unless you were a blithering idiot altogether and refuse to have anything to do with them as a golden rule in private life and their felonsetting, there always being the offchance of a Dannyman

coming forward and turning queen's evidence or king's now like Denis or Peter Carey, an idea he utterly repudiated.[64]

Bloom, while denouncing the crime ('personally, he would never be a party to any such thing'), also grudgingly admires it. He likens it to a *crime passionnel*, 'off the same bat as those love vendettas of the south, have her or swing for her', and feels some admiration for a man who had actually 'brandished a knife, cold steel, with the courage of his political convictions'. Then he qualifies this admiration when it occurs to him that Skin-the-Goat merely drove the car for the actual perpetrators of the outrage and so was not actually party to the ambush.

Bloom then becomes impatient of the aged figure, possibly the old Invincible. ('He ought to have either died naturally or on the scaffold high. Like actresses, always farewell positively last performance then come up smiling again.')[65] Here Bloom shows a certain resentment at the obscure survivors of long-past patriotic adventures such as Kevin Egan or Skin-the-Goat, if it is he. A long line of executed martyrs have raised the stakes, so to speak, for the proper behaviour of a martyred patriot: he owes his country a death, not a long and obscure retirement.

Bloom's recollection of how Skin-the-Goat avoided execution is historically accurate. He was charged with murder and was defended by Richard Adams. He was acquitted on the charge of murder but subsequently tried and found guilty of being an accessory after the fact and sentenced, in 1883, to penal servitude for life. He was released in 1899 and died in September 1910.[66]

Adams is recalled in the *Aeolus* episode as 'Dick Adams, the besthearted bloody Corkman the Lord ever put the breath of life in'.[67] Adams was appointed a county court judge by John Morley, Chief Secretary in Gladstone's last government, whose policy was to promote Irish Catholics and nationalists to positions of significance in the police, the army, the public administration and the judiciary. There had of course always been Catholics who rose to high rank in these areas, but they were generally drawn from the small group of Catholic Unionists. With Gladstone's new departure it became possible for a Catholic who was a Home Rule supporter to be so promoted. This caused immense resentment to the Unionist community. Adams himself had a brisk, not to say earthy, style on the bench and suffered the indignity of having the Catholic Bishop of Limerick advise against unnecessary attendance in his court due to the broad crudities to be heard there.[68]

In the end, as with Emmet, the Invincibles incident culminated on the scaffold, with five executions; but one especially, that of Joe Brady, represented the entire six weeks of hangings to most people. Brady was a strong, handsome young man who was widely admired and had an indomitable mother to speak of and for him. She pointedly said that, unlike the others, he took all that he knew to the grave with him and scorned to bargain for his life by offering Queen's evidence. In fact, however, a blood sacrifice was required by both sides. The English government needed to show that it had murder by the throat and that the terrible crime of 1882 had evoked a terrible vengeance by 1883.

But equally the Fenian tradition needed blood sacrifice as well and was nourished by it, as its balladry witnesses:

High upon the Gallows tree stood the noble hearted three
By the vengeful tyrant smitten in their bloom

But they met him face to face with the courage of their race
and they went with souls undaunted to their doom.

Never til the latest day shall the memory pass away
Of the gallant lives thus given for our land
But on the cause will go amidst joy and weal and woe
Til we make our isle a nation free and grand.[69]

This much-performed song was written in the aftermath of the
1867 execution of three Fenians, William Allen, Michael Larkin
and Michael O'Brien, for the murder of a Manchester policeman,
Sergeant Brett, during the rescue of other Fenian prisoners. No
doubt it nourished the patriotic sentiments of Joe Brady and the
others, all then children, just as the legend of their executions in
turn nourished the generation of 1916. But a hero figure, like Brady,
Allen, Larkin or O'Brien, must be dead.

Joyce was unimpressed by this patrimony of death, just as he was
undisturbed by the assassination of Lord Frederick Cavendish. As
in the case of Emmet, he portrays Brady's execution snidely, indeed
vulgarly, so as to puncture the solemnity of his death 'on the gallows
tree' and thus undermine his example.

In the *Cyclops* episode, the men in Kiernan's public house are
discussing capital punishment and the pros and cons of it:

—There's one thing it hasn't a deterrent effect on, says Alf.
—What's that? says Joe.
—The poor bugger's tool that's being hanged, says Alf.
—That so? says Joe.
—God's truth, says Alf. I heard that from the head warder

that was in Kilmainham when they hanged Joe Brady, the invincible. He told me when they cut him down after the drop it was standing up in their faces like a poker.

—Ruling passion strong in death, says Joe, as someone said.

—That can be explained by science, says Bloom.[70]

The fate of Joe Brady and the other Invincibles never inspired anything like the cult around the image of Robert Emmet. They were ill adapted to the role of romantic hero which Emmet filled to perfection. His attempt at rebellion, though it petered out in an hour, was a *pronunciamento* in the approved style – uniformed officers leading a charge in the streets near the seat of government. The Invincibles crime of 1882, by contrast, was a hole-in-the-corner knife attack on two unarmed men. Moreover, it occurred at a time when Anglo-Irish relations seemed about to take a dramatic turn for the better. Still more relevantly, events subsequent to the Invincibles murder of Cavendish and Burke were not such that an Irish nationalist could look on with any satisfaction. When the authorities, under the magistrate John Adye Curran and the famous policeman Superintendent Mallon, began to tighten the net around the members of the 'Irish National Invincibles', there was a scurry amongst the members of that group – including, as we have seen, their leader – to save their own necks by giving Queen's evidence. It was this aspect in particular that attracted Joyce's attention.

Ulysses, as we shall see in the following chapter, was banned for about a decade in the United Kingdom and the United States. It was never banned in Ireland, but for twenty years after its publication it was scarcely read and difficult to find. There was no lack of Catholic commentators ready to denounce the book as irreligious and obscene. As far I am aware, however, no published work condemned it for its mockery of Emmet, who was, in the early days of the Irish Free State and for a long time afterwards, a secular saint in Ireland. This is probably due to the fact that no one – absolutely no one – of an Irish nationalist persuasion read far enough into the book to see what Joyce had said about the 'felons of our land'.

Part III

7. Attempts to Suppress *Ulysses*

Even before its publication in book form in 1922, *Ulysses* provoked serious attempts to suppress it in America. Self-appointed censors, some describing themselves as 'Societies for the Suppression of Vice', took the lead. But the public authorities in Britain too – the Home Secretary, the Director of Public Prosecutions, Scotland Yard, the Civil Service – all showed themselves eager for the fight against 'this disgusting book'.

In America the public authorities were less eager, but felt they had no alternative but to assert a long-established legal view of 'obscenity'. They lacked enthusiasm, however: when the book was formally complained of to the Attorney General of New York, he sent a copy to the local Society for the Suppression of Vice, and that private body took it on from there. The litigation then set in train supplanted the traditional view of obscenity for ever. Ironically, the law that the US authorities sought to enforce was nineteenth-century English statute and case law.

Ulysses, the great modernist novel which described not merely the characters' hidden actions but even their innermost thoughts, was profoundly unacceptable to those whose thinking on 'obscenity' was rooted in the mid-Victorian age. But that was precisely the era when the law of obscenity had flourished. A decided case of that era, *R* v *Hicklin* (1868), was the legal standard for obscenity, both in England and America (see pp. 232–4). *Ulysses* could not possibly meet the Hicklin test, precisely because, as a 1922 reviewer said, 'All that is unmentionable, according to civilised standards has been brought to the light of day, without any veil of decency.'[1] But by 1936 *Ulysses* had beaten *Hicklin* and all it stood for.

The central moment in the process, the point of no return, was the decision of the US Court of Appeals for the Second Circuit (New York) in *US* v *One Book called Ulysses*, in late 1933. But the law of obscenity was based in the aggressive Evangelical Christian thought of the early nineteenth century. So it is to England that we turn first, England in the hour of its greatness, England at the high point of the long Victorian era.

The long Victorian era

When little Jix was born, or came alive,
The great Queen ruled and everyone was good,
And England stood, where Mr Gladstone stood,

Since then the times have changed, the clock has ticked;
Jix does not think so. Jix was brought up strict.

P. R. STEPHENSON, *Policeman of the Lord:
A Political Satire* (Sophistocles Press, 1929)

'Jix' was Sir William Joynson-Hicks (1865–1932), the most determined opponent of the publication of *Ulysses* in Britain. He was successively Paymaster General, Postmaster General, Financial Secretary to the Treasury and Minister for Health, after the fall of Lloyd George in 1922. When the Conservatives returned to power in 1924 Joynson-Hicks was appointed Home Secretary, one of the three great offices of state apart from that of Prime Minister.

Joynson-Hicks was a High Victorian somewhat out of his time. A man of strong religious views, he boasted as Home Secretary that he would shut down nightlife in London; led a vigorous campaign against immoral behaviour in public parks (which resulted, embarrassingly, in the arrest of the Clerk to the Privy Council), and campaigned ceaselessly against what he saw as immoral literature. Jix personified the strong but anachronistic forces of Victorian morality, which selected *Ulysses* as a particular target.

The Victorian era, during which Great Britain achieved an international political, economic, literary and linguistic hegemony unlikely ever to be rivalled, is epitomized for many in the image of the widowed old Queen who was an exemplar, or perhaps a prisoner, of a rigid Protestant morality. The Victorian age ended, chronologically, with the death of Queen Victoria in January 1901. She had reigned since 1837.

But the post-publication reception of *Ulysses*, to look no further, shows that the culture of the Victorian era, and the legal expressions of its morality, survived the old Queen by a good many years. The potency of this survival is perfectly epitomized in Joynson-Hicks. He was a religious enthusiast, to put it mildly. For his attempts to shut down nightlife in London he was thoroughly ridiculed, for example by Evelyn Waugh in *Vile Bodies*.

Joynson-Hicks's own statements show that there cannot have been a more enthusiastic book-burner since the High Victorian era. To judge from the official correspondence in the British archives, many senior civil servants and law officers of the time shared his views. They appear ridiculous figures by the standards of today, if undoubtedly sincere in their stern morality.

The law on obscenity, in the 1920s, was almost identical on each side of the Atlantic. But if the law was identical, the approaches taken in Great Britain and the United States respectively were very different. The English gentlemen, led by Joynson-Hicks as Home Secretary and Sir Archibald Bodkin as Director of Public Prosecutions, preferred to proceed on the basis of 'a word in the ear' of well-placed publishers, booksellers, academics and others, and to prevent the circulation of *Ulysses* by seizing copies entering the country rather than by public prosecution. The Americans did not shrink from the latter course.

It is worth looking first at the law of obscenity as it stood in Britain and in America in the early 1920s.

The rise of the Victorian law on obscenity

The first and second decades of the nineteenth century saw an evangelical revolution: a dramatic revival in the practice of the Anglican branch of the Christian religion by some of its members, more prone to God-bothering than the rest. They espoused a more self-critical, intense and sometimes fanatical form of religious practice. Under the influence of such revivalist ministers as John Wesley, founder of Methodism, many such individuals were 'born again' while remaining within the confines of the previously rather comfortable Anglican Church. Such people tended to be deeply critical of their own spiritual development and, more to our purpose, to be censorious of others, even to the point of the promotion of laws to regulate moral behaviour. William Wilberforce, the great opponent of slavery, was very admirable in that regard. But he also succeeded in having an Act passed to prevent swimming in the River Thames because of the risk to morality which he thought it represented. He and his like saw such risks everywhere.

As the century went on, this 'evangelical' tendency enlarged its sphere of activity. In 1857 the Lord Chief Justice of England was John Campbell, 1st Baron Campbell (1779–1861). In 1857 he was presiding over what he regarded as a particularly lurid pornography trial, which to his great frustration ended in an acquittal by the jury. As it happened, the trial was concluded at a time when Parliament was considering a bill to control the sale of poisons.

Campbell considered that the need to restrict what he saw as pornography was just as acute as the need to control dealings in prussic acid, strychnine and arsenic, because he regarded pornography as more deadly than the poisons mentioned. He accordingly drafted his own Obscene Publications Bill and saw it through Parliament (Campbell, as a member of the House of Lords, was a parliamentary as well as a judicial figure).

Up to that time, the battle against pornography had been in the amateur if enthusiastic hands of the Society for the Suppression of Vice, whose moving spirit and most active member was John Bowdler. Bowdler, who has given the English language the word 'bowdlerize', had achieved eminence of a sort by publishing sanitized versions of the works of Shakespeare and other classic writers. As Vice-President of the society he saw to the conduct of about forty prosecutions for selling obscene material at common law in the 1850s.

Lord Chief Justice Campbell's experience, however, led him to doubt whether juries would reliably convict people who simply published words in print, especially in view of the condign sentences that judges such as Campbell and his colleagues were capable of imposing on those who were convicted. Accordingly, in the bill which he drafted in 1857, he did not aim at jailing the author, publisher, or printer but he provided that the books themselves, if considered obscene, could be liable to an order for destruction by burning, made in a summary manner by the local magistrates. To facilitate this, the authorities, in various English port cities, maintained a 'King's Chimney' where books considered obscene by the local bench could be burned.

But Lord Campbell, for all that he was an active legislator in the House of Lords as well as the Lord Chief Justice, did not find it easy to pass his bill into law. There was opposition on the ground that, under its very general terms, works of genuine literary or scientific merit could be destroyed and that Britain might become an international laughing stock if works in general circulation in other countries were banned there. Liberal Members of Parliament, and Conservatives of a libertarian tinge, made their unhappiness with the bill quite clear. Accordingly, Campbell, addressing the House of Lords, gave a solemn assurance that the measure would apply: 'exclusively to works written for the *single purpose* of corrupting the morals of youth and of a nature calculated to shock the common feelings of decency in *any* well regulated mind' (emphasis added).[2] Campbell specifically assured the imperial legislature that literary works, even if they were of a 'polluting' nature, would be judged only by the force of public opinion and not by the law he was introducing. Their anxieties mollified by these assurances, the legislators passed the bill into law and it became known as Lord Campbell's Act.

Changes introduced by the Act

Before the Act of 1857 there was surprisingly little statute law on the question of obscenity. By the Vagrancy Act of 1824 it was illegal to 'expose for sale' any 'obscene books or prints', but this summary offence was judicially found to be a public order provision, to prevent obstruction of the roads or highways, rather than a criminalization of obscenity itself. The publication of obscene material was a common-law misdemeanour, but this required a full criminal trial on indictment, before a jury. Lord Campbell's own experience led him to think that a jury would not necessarily share his view of what was obscene, or find proof beyond any reasonable doubt.

Lord Campbell's novel insight, on which his bill was based, was that, rather than endure the uncertainties of a jury trial, it would be quicker, more certain and more economical to give magistrates a statutory power of destruction of such material. The Act accordingly provided for the seizure and summary disposition of any material deemed to be obscene, following information being laid 'before a Court of summary jurisdiction'. This latter phrase meant the magistrates' court, thus avoiding a jury trial.

The Act required that, following evidence of a common-law obscenity offence being given, usually by a policeman, the magistrates could issue a warrant to search the premises where the work was to be found and to seize any obscene material. The proprietor could then be called upon to attend court and give reasons why the material should not be destroyed. The ingenious aspect of the Act was that by concentrating on the destruction of obscene printed material, it avoided the standards, and in particular the burden of proof beyond reasonable doubt, required when it was intended to imprison an individual.

The Act offered no definition of obscenity. Therefore it was for the courts to devise such a test based on the common law. In practice, the magistrates' court, a largely lay tribunal of members of society regarded as particularly respectable, would decide what was obscene.

The Act of 1857 gave rise to a series of lower court decisions. Inevitably one of these cases came before the High Court, which gave a decision of general application and of an extremely restrictive nature. This case came to represent the law in England and America for many decades. The case is *R* v *Hicklin*.[3] The Hicklin in the title was a London magistrate. He had before him a case of one Henry Scott, who was said to have sold a copy of an anti-Catholic pamphlet entitled 'The Confessional unmasked: shewing the depravity of the Romish Priesthood, the iniquity of the confessional, and the questions put to females in confession'.

Magistrates ordered that 250 copies of the pamphlet, which had been seized under Lord Campbell's Act, should be burned. They did this over the protests of the owner of the pamphlet, who said that he was only concerned to expose the Church of Rome and not to harm or damage public morality. Hicklin accepted this and revoked the Order for Destruction on that basis. The authorities referred this decision to the High Court, which quashed it and reinstated the Order for Destruction.

The decision in this case was given by Lord Chief Justice Cockburn, a successor of Campbell's as Lord Chief Justice. He held: 'The test of obscenity is whether the tendency of the matter charged as obscenity is to deprave and corrupt those whose minds are open to such immoral influences and into whose hand a publication of this sort may fall.'4 These few lines encapsulate what was known for many decades in England and in America as the Hicklin test.

It has three important features. Firstly, the test is *objective*. If the tendency of the work *is in fact* to deprave and corrupt, then it does not matter that, as in the case of Henry Scott, it was written, published and sold without any *intention* of corrupting anyone. Secondly, the concept of depraving and corrupting can mean depraving or corrupting *any* person, and does not envisage a highly or even averagely educated adult readership or a professional readership but merely 'those whose minds are open to such immoral influences and into whose hand [the book] may fall'. Thirdly, the test does not require the work in question to be judged as a whole, or in context. If there is *any* obscenity with a tendency to deprave and corrupt, the case is made out, and the entire book condemned. In the case of a publisher or bookseller, the entire edition or stock of the book could be destroyed.

It is obvious that this test is a major deviation from the assurances given by Lord Campbell when he was introducing the Act. As we have seen, he considered that it would target only 'works written for the single purpose of corrupting the morals of youth and of a nature calculated to shock the common feelings of decency in any well regulated mind'.[5] But for Lord Cockburn, the purpose or intention of the publisher was irrelevant. Policemen, magistrates and Vigilance Committees throughout the English-speaking world had a power of enormous scope given to them by Lord Cockburn.

In 1857, and today, and apparently at all times in between, society in Britain and America (and Ireland) contained various groups of people determined to censor the works of others. By reason of the *Hicklin* decision a book could be banned if it had a tendency to corrupt *any* class of readers likely to get hold of it. Accordingly, Dr Havelock Ellis's *Studies in the Psychology of Sex*,[6] a work of impeccable medical content, was ordered to be destroyed in 1898. It was unlikely to corrupt the medical readership at whom it was aimed, but, under *Hicklin*, that did not matter. The censors, or would-be censors, were prone to emphasize that a book which could shock or corrupt any person – even a child in the nursery – was a work which it was illegal to sell in England.

This aspect of the law was particularly dear to Sir William Joynson-Hicks. Speaking to a Church body in 1928 he said: 'There must be some limit to the freedom on what a man may speak or write in this great country of ours. That freedom, in my view, must be determined by the question as to whether what is written or spoken *makes one of the least of these little ones offended.*' (Emphasis added.)[7] It cannot be too strongly emphasized that the effect of the Hicklin test was to render unpublishable anything which could not be given to the tiniest child of reading age. 'The least of these little ones' is of course a biblical reference, but the effect of adopting it as a legal standard was to restrict what could be written for an adult audience to what would be given to an innocent child.

The result of the battle to publish *Ulysses*, both in America and in Britain (about two years later), was to lead to the abandonment of the Hicklin test in both jurisdictions.

8. The American Trials of *Ulysses*, 1919–1933

O f the various legal controversies to which *Ulysses* has given rise, none was more significant in the long term, or decided at a higher judicial level, than the 1933 case entitled *US* v *One Book called Ulysses*.

My account of this case is very largely based on the papers of the law firm Greenbaum, Wolff & Ernst of New York, who acted for Random House, the publishers of the first American edition of *Ulysses*. These papers, which contain internal memoranda as well as correspondence with the other side and legal pleadings, including the 'briefs' or written submissions of the parties, were bound by the law firm itself. In red leather on the spine is written '*United States* v *Ulysses*' and the name of the firm is in black leather on the lower spine. I was fortunate to be loaned these documents by the present owner.

The fact that the law firm bound their file of papers in this way, so as to resemble a law report, is evidence of their (in my view entirely justified) pride in their work and their consciousness of the significance of the case. The documents allow us to trace the lawyers' tactics with considerable clarity. This appears to have been the first time that Joyce and *Ulysses* were represented on the obscenity issue by serious lawyers who knew precisely what they were doing and who were ahead of the other side at every stage of the case. But they were not the first lawyers called to defend Joyce's book.

In 1921, the United States became the first country formally to find *Ulysses* obscene. This occurred as a result of a prosecution in a New York City police court, on the complaint of John S. Sumner, secretary of the New York Society for the Suppression of Vice, leading to a judgment against the book in February 1921. The defendants were Margaret Anderson and Jane Heap, proprietors of the *Little Review* (see pp. 238–9).

Twelve years later, in 1933, the United States Federal District Court in New York City not only held that the book was not obscene but, in the person of Judge John Woolsey, endorsed it as great literature. The prosecutor, the United States Treasury Department, which had intercepted the book in transit, appealed to the United States Court of Appeals for the Second Circuit. There, the verdict of acquittal in the district court was upheld by a majority of two to one.

In part, these conflicting decisions reflect changing public opinion: the first case coincided with the institution of Prohibition in the US and the second with its repeal. There are other, most unusual aspects to the two cases. In each, the prosecution seems to have been set up and in part orchestrated by the defendants themselves. Secondly, the defence was badly conducted in the first trial (see p. 240); on the second occasion it was conducted with ingenuity and remarkable professionalism by the very expert obscenity lawyer Morris Ernst. Moreover, the reputation of Joyce and of *Ulysses* itself had been transformed in the interval: on the second occasion the defence was able to quote enthusiastic endorsements of the book by leading American and English writers, some of whom compared Joyce to Shakespeare and Homer. Moreover, the United States Secretary of the Treasury had already deemed *Ulysses* to be a 'classic', thereby permitting its import for private perusal. At the first New York trial the book was proclaimed as mere filth, but in the second trial, and particularly on the appeal, the prosecutor Sam Coleman said only: 'No-one would dare attack the literary value of this book... but there is obscenity in it.'[1] This, it will be recalled, represents the Hicklin test: if there was any obscenity in the book its overall literary value did not matter.

Anybody who has read Richard Ellmann's biography of the writer, or indeed John McCourt's account of Joyce's years in Trieste,[2] will recall just how irritated and frustrated he was at the constant difficulties placed in the way of publication of his short story collection *Dubliners* by the British law of obscenity and the law and conventions about respect for the monarch. The United Kingdom (which of course then included Ireland) did not operate a system of prior restraint: instead, a publisher was liable to be criminally tried after the event for publishing obscenity, as Penguin Books were in relation to *Lady Chatterley's Lover* in the 1960s. This system had what the American courts would call a 'chilling effect' on printers and publishers, each of whom (together with booksellers) was liable for an obscene publication. This in turn explains some of the apparently very petty anxieties of English printers. Their concerns in relation to *Dubliners* seemed to have centred on the use of mild vernacular epithets such as 'bloody', the whole of the story 'An Encounter', in which two boys 'miching' from school meet a rather strange man near the Dublin docks, references to King Edward VII in 'Ivy Day in the Committee Room' and to certain businesses which were going concerns at the time, notably a railway company and four public houses. It is very difficult to see, as Joyce himself pointed out, how any of this last category of references could have been construed as libellous.

His attention shifted seven years later to the United States, when attempts were made to have *Ulysses* published there by way of serial publication or in book form.

The statute and common law of the United States in 1920 prohibited the publication of obscene materials. Over and above that general prohibition, the United States Post Office, a federal entity headed by a Cabinet member, the Postmaster General, was mandated not to distribute obscene publication in the mails: in practice, the Post Office maintained a list of dubious or prohibited materials which were, as the *Little Review* discovered, found to be 'non-mailable'.

Between March 1918 and December 1920, Joyce had sent successive episodes of *Ulysses* to the *Little Review*. This was a small, avant-garde review run by two American women, Margaret Anderson and Jane Heap. They had been introduced to Joyce by Ezra Pound. The two women were most anxious that *Ulysses* should be serially published in their magazine, and it was. The devoted but somewhat unrealistic attitude of the joint directors of the magazine is summarized in the comment Richard Ellmann attributes to

Margaret Anderson on reading the opening of the *Proteus* episode ('Ineluctable modality of the visible').[3] She said: 'This is the most beautiful thing we'll ever have. We'll print it if it's the last effort of our lives.'[4] To borrow another of Ellmann's observations, 'They did in fact start the book in the March 1918 issue of the *Little Review*, and nobly piloted the magazine towards the reef of censorship on which it temporarily foundered.'[5]

In view of subsequent events relating to attempts to censor *Ulysses* in the United States, the details of this foundering may be of some interest. The edition of the *Little Review* for January 1919, containing the *Lestrygonians* episode, was confiscated. So too was the May edition containing *Scylla and Charybdis*.

But the first trial of *Ulysses* was provoked by the July–August 1920 edition, containing an instalment of the *Cyclops* episode. Both sides, however, acted with coolness and premeditation. Although the Post Office confiscated all the relevant editions of the *Little Review*, they subsequently permitted 500 copies to continue their journey to the magazine's subscribers. This, a step no doubt taken on legal advice, was so that it could be shown that Anderson and Heap had actually distributed the magazine containing the episode objected to, to specific individuals. This would be a necessary proof if it were later decided to prosecute them for obscenity, and not merely to confiscate copies of the magazine.

In fact, however, Margaret Anderson herself did everything that her opponents could wish in this regard. She provoked the first prosecution by sending a copy of the edition containing the *Nausicaa* episode to a young lady whom she knew, the daughter of a well-known New York lawyer of conservative views. She calculated, rightly, that the girl would show the magazine to her father and, again rightly, that the latter would notify the authorities. He contacted the Attorney General for the State of New York. As a result of the lawyer's complaint the material was drawn to the attention of John S. Sumner of the New York Society for the Prevention of Vice, who made an official complaint in September 1920. It was this that led eventually to a trial, commencing on St Valentine's Day 1921, in the New York City police court which led to the conviction of Margaret Anderson and Jane Heap on obscenity charges.

Both the authorities and the publishers wished to keep the prospect of prosecution alive. From the point of view of the publishers, it would seem that the notoriety of a prosecution was thought to confer commercial and reputational advantage. The case for the defence at the trial was conducted by the Irish-American lawyer and well-known dealer in paintings and manuscripts, John Quinn. He seems to have operated in a somewhat 'seat-of-the-pants' way and lacked the profound knowledge of the contemporary law of obscenity that was so marked a feature of the defence case in the 1933 trial. Worse still, in the opinion of his clients, he appeared eventually to put forward the mitigation, to which the magistrates had shown themselves prone, that the two lady publishers could not really have understood what exactly was being described in the *Nausicaa* episode. In the upshot, the publishers were convicted and fined $50 each. They appear to have regretted not being sent to jail. Quinn undertook on their behalf that they would publish no more 'filth' and assured the magistrates that *Nausicaa* was as bad as it got: the book contained nothing worse. In fairness to Quinn, he may have thought it important to avoid a formal finding of obscenity until *Ulysses* could be published in book form in the US. As it was, the book had only a clandestine existence for more than a decade.

The Customs Court case

While the *Little Review* case is well known to literary scholarship and is mentioned in all of the standard works, very little attention has focused on a judgment of the United States Customs Court dated 1 August 1928 in the case of *Heymoolen* v *United States*. I am aware of it because the brief judgment of a Judge Tilson is the first document in the file of papers of the law firm of Greenbaum, Wolff & Ernst. From the Customs Court decision it is clear that the legal form of the 1928 case was a 'protest' against the decision of the Collector of Customs at the port of Minneapolis, who decided to exclude from the United States a cargo of forty-three books, including copies of eleven separate titles. One of these, of which there were seven copies, was *Ulysses*. Some of the titles of the other works involved would suggest that they were works of frank pornography. They had been excluded under section 305(a) of the Tariff Act 1922. Copies of the books were introduced in evidence by counsel for the government; there was no appearance by the importer. From the location of the hearing in Minneapolis it is possible that the importation was from Canada. The judge held:

> Only a casual glance through the books in evidence is sufficient to satisfy us that they are filled with obscenity of the rottenest and vilest character. If merchandise of this character is admitted to the United States then s.305 of the Tariff Act of 1922 should be erased from the Statute Books. The plaintiff states in his brief that these books are 'of undoubted merit and literary value'. If it could be argued that books abounding in obscenity, filth and rottenest are books of undoubted

merit and literary value then all these are masterpieces [...] as to all the books which were introduced in evidence, we unhesitatingly affirm the actions of the collector in excluding and refusing to permit entrance of the same, and as to those books which were not introduced in evidence, there was no evidence introduced to overcome the presumption of correctness attaching to the actions of the collector, and as to those books also the action of the collector is affirmed.

This is a significant judgment because it is the recorded judgment of a judge specifically holding that *Ulysses* was obscene and it was a major item in the government's arsenal in the later litigation. It is not, however, as can be seen from its terms, a reasoned or erudite judgment. It refers to no authority and is unimpressive as a piece of legal exposition.

By the early 1930s Morris Ernst, a partner in Greenbaum, Wolff & Ernst, was incontestably the leading legal expert on obscenity in the United States. He was an archetypal New York liberal Jew and subsequently became President of the American Civil Liberties Union (ACLU). In 1928 he had written a book on censorship, *To the Pure*, and shortly afterwards he represented the *The Well of Loneliness* by Radclyffe Hall when it was accused of being obscene. Later again, but before the *Ulysses* case, he represented the publishers of Dr Marie Stopes's book, attacked because of its advocacy of artificial contraception. In the course of the *Ulysses* litigation, his pre-eminence in the field was openly acknowledged by his opponents. The lawyers for the United States Attorney for New

York actually held a conference with him and asked him to direct them to the leading judicial authorities on obscenity. This suggests a high level of respect both for his learning and for his integrity.

Ernst had an assistant in his firm, a young lawyer called Alexander Lindey. His name is written on the inside cover of the book of papers on which I have drawn for this chapter. Lindey was then an idealistic young liberal lawyer who, in August 1931, wrote to Ernst: 'I still feel very keenly that this [the legal defence of *Ulysses*] would be the grandest obscenity case in the history of law and literature and I am willing to do anything in the world to get it started.'

Random House founder Bennett Cerf's memoir *At Random* (1935) tells the story of how he got in touch with Ernst:

> I heard the great lawyer say one night that the banning of *Ulysses* was a disgrace and that he'd like to wage a fight to legalise it. So in March 1932 I had lunch with Ernst and I said 'If I can get Joyce to do an edition of *Ulysses* for America, would you fight the case for us in court?' I added 'We haven't got the money to pay your fancy prices' – he was a very high powered lawyer – 'but if you win the case you will get a royalty on *Ulysses* for the rest of your life.'[6]

This is precisely what occurred.

Lindey acted throughout the litigation as what the Americans call 'second chair', i.e. like a junior counsel in Ireland or England or a partner's assistant in a large firm of solicitors. As is often the case in such arrangements, a great deal of the actual work was done by him, though according to Ernst's direction, and Lindey was the signatory on much of the firm's correspondence to do with *Ulysses*.

Some legal background

In view of the present controversy in the United States judicial and legislative circles as to whether it is proper to cite a foreign judicial authority in the US Supreme Court, it is interesting to note that, according to the United States government, the American law of obscenity in 1933 was precisely that laid down in the mid-Victorian English case, *R* v *Hicklin*. It commended itself to the government because it laid down three propositions. Firstly, that the obscenity of a book could be established by proving that an isolated passage was obscene, without regard to the tenor of the work as a whole. If more than one such passage could be identified, then of course the case was strengthened. Secondly, a book's obscenity was to be judged by the susceptibility of its *most vulnerable audience* to be corrupted or led into 'lewd and lascivious' thoughts and not by its effect on the hypothetical reasonable man, or any more sophisticated reader. Thirdly, obscenity was a question of fact – the motive or intention of the writer or publisher was irrelevant.

The *Ulysses* litigation took place in New York City, probably the most liberal part of the United States. The appeal from the trial court was therefore to the United States Circuit Court of Appeals for the Second Circuit. The Second Circuit was, at the time, dominated by the personality and legal genius of Judge Learned Hand, widely regarded as the most distinguished American judge never to have been appointed to the Supreme Court. The other members of the court that dealt with the *Ulysses* case were Judge Augustus Hand, a cousin of Learned's, and Judge Martin Manton, a Catholic who was later imprisoned for accepting bribes, the first federal judge so convicted. He dissented from the judgment of Augustus Hand in the *Ulysses* case.

Every lawyer involved in litigation makes it his or her business to learn the proclivities and the previous decisions of the members of the appellate tribunal for the courts before which he or she practises. Ernst and Lindey, therefore, would have been aware that Judge Learned Hand had given a widely known judgment on obscenity in a case called *The United States* v *Kennerley*, as a judge of the United States Federal District Court, in 1913. This judgment was given on a motion by the defendant, a publisher, to dismiss an indictment in an obscenity case. On such a preliminary motion, a judge is obliged to take the most favourable view possible of the other side's case: to incline against dismissal of the action without trial. Hand voted to reject the motion, and followed *Hicklin*, though only on the ground that that case had been 'accepted by lower federal courts until it would no longer be proper for me to disregard it'. But he continued:

> I hope it is not improper for me to say that the rule as laid down, however consonant it may be with mid-Victorian morals, does not seem to me to answer to the understanding and morality of the present time. I question whether in the end men will regard that as obscene which is honestly relevant to the adequate expression of innocent ideas, and whether they will not believe that truth and beauty are too precious to society at large to be mutilated in the interest of those most likely to pervert them to base uses. Indeed, it seems hardly likely that we are even today so lukewarm in our interest in letters or serious discussion to be content to reduce our treatment of sex to the standard of a child's library

in the supposed interest of a salacious view, or that shame will for long prevent us from adequate portrayal of some of the most serious and beautiful sides of human nature.

Judge Learned Hand also said, in *Kennerley*: 'I scarcely think that society would forbid all which might corrupt the most corruptible, or that society is prepared to accept for its own limitations those which may perhaps be necessary to the weakest of its members.' And: 'To put thought in leash to the average conscience of the time is perhaps tolerable, but to fetter it by the necessities of the lowest and least capable seems a fatal policy, because it would drastically reduce the scope of literary expression in an open society.'

Setting up the prosecution – by the defence

The significance of this 1913 case to the lawyers for *Ulysses* cannot be overstated. It showed that the most eminent and influential member of the Second Circuit's Appellate Bench was more than open to a departure from the authority of *Hicklin*. This was a strong reason for seeking to ensure that any litigation about *Ulysses* took place in the state of New York. This, in turn, led the lawyers to take a very bold step to ensure that that was what happened: they effectively invited prosecution. If they had not taken these proactive steps, it would have been open to the authorities of any part in the United States where the book was published or sold to launch a prosecution there. As we shall see, a notably liberal-minded judge in New York City was somewhat taken aback by the contents of Molly Bloom's soliloquy; no great imaginative effort is needed to guess at the reaction of a jury in the Bible Belt to that same text.

How the lawyers got involved

The law firm's papers contain a letter to Morris Ernst of 23 March 1932 from Mr Bennett A. Cerf of Random House. This letter enclosed a copy of the publishing contract that the firm of Random House were offering Joyce for *Ulysses*. The rest of the letter consists of Cerf's understanding of the basis on which the lawyers were acting and is very interesting. There is provision for:

(1) A payment of $500 by way of retainer immediately.
(2) A 'straight royalty' of 5 per cent 'on our trade edition of the book, in the event that the book is legalised'.
(3) A 2 per cent royalty on all copies of the book sold in a reprint edition.
(4) 5 per cent of any net sum realized by Random House from the sale of *Ulysses* to a book club or similar organization at a special figure.
(5) Extra compensation in the event of jury trial based on the number of days 'that you are tied up in court'.

The bulk of the lawyers' remuneration, in other words, was a cut of the publisher's profits. This probably made sense in view of the fact that both Random House and its proprietor were very much in a start-up situation (Cerf was still under thirty years of age).

On the following day, the lawyers replied through Alexander

Lindey pointing out that, by their oral agreement, the publishers were to bear any out-of-pocket costs – those of printing briefs, court fees, cables, photostats and the like. He also pointed out that their fee for attending the jury trial would not be less than $50 a day. But he presciently advised: 'In my opinion a [jury] trial does not loom as a serious practical possibility. The United States Attorney would relish spending three weeks in court reading *Ulysses no more than ourselves.*' (Emphasis added.) As will be seen, the lawyers took important steps to ensure that there would not be a jury trial.

Lindey pointed out that the lawyers were also to have 5 per cent of any limited edition of the book, as well as the same percentage on the trade edition. He then advised Cerf that it was time to arrange to send 'the proper edition' through the Customs. He also advised:

In any test case involving the legality of the book, statistics as to its use by educational institutions will have considerable effect. We suggest that you prepare and send out a circular letter to one hundred or more colleges and universities requesting information as to whether (a) Joyce is considered in any course given by the institution on contemporary literature and (b) whether *Ulysses* is used as collateral or prescribed reading.

The lawyers' plan is made still more clear in a letter they wrote Cerf on 25 April of the same year, 1932:

No doubt you have already arranged for the sending of a copy into the United States, and for cable advices indicating the date of shipment and the book and the boat. As soon as you receive such advices we suggest that you communicate with us so that we in turn may inform the customs authorities of the impending arrival of the book. *You will realise, of course, that it is an essential part of our plan that the book be stopped by customs: and we do not wish it to slip through either by inadvertence or because of lack of advance information.* [Emphasis added.]

In a letter of 2 May 1932, the law firm wrote to the Collector of Customs for New York telling him that:

a copy of James Joyce's novel *Ulysses* has been dispatched into this country addressed to our client. We are informed that the volume left on the 'Bremen' on April 28th and is due at the port of New York on Tuesday, May 3rd, 1932.

We are transmitting this information to you because we do not wish the book to slip through Customs without official scrutiny. As you may know, *Ulysses* during the past two decades has been praised by critics as probably the most important contribution to the world literature of the twentieth century. Entirely apart from its profound literary significance, we are convinced that *Ulysses* is not violative of the Tariff Act. In saying this we are not unmindful of the adverse attitude of your department with regard to the book in the past. We feel, however, that in view of such recent decisions as [the lawyers cite five contemporary cases] there is no longer any legal sanction for such attitude.

It is clear from that letter that the lawyers were ostentatiously 'putting it up to' the Customs authorities, who were of course part of the Treasury Department. The latter took the bait and by letter of 13 May, the Assistant Collector advised the lawyers that:

> The book in question is detained as in violation of s.305 of the Tariff Act as obscene. For your further information you are advised that the book *Ulysses* was the subject of a customs court decision contained in Treasury decision 42907 in which the Court affirmed the action of the Collector in excluding and refusing to permit entry of the book.

In other words, the Customs authorities, like good bureaucrats, considered themselves bound by and reliant upon the decision of the court in Minneapolis in 1928.

The Customs authorities could not possibly miss the book on its way in. Accordingly, the *defence* lawyers set up the ensuing prosecution. But they took other steps as well. On 19 April 1932, Lindey wrote to Joyce's friend Paul Léon in Paris asking him 'to purchase the latest edition of *Ulysses* and to paste critiques of the book into the front of it, because thereby they become, for legal purposes, a part of the book and can be introduced in evidence'.

This was undoubtedly an important tactical step. As the lawyers had guessed, the authorities were not at all anxious to read large chunks of *Ulysses* aloud to a jury nor to give the whole book to each member of a twelve-person jury and invite them to read it. The state lawyers wanted, on the contrary, simply to emphasize the passages they believed to be obscene and then, on the authority of the Hicklin decision, to claim that if the jury agreed with them about those passages, the whole book should be found obscene, confiscated and burned.

This letter to Léon was written because, on that very day, 19 December 1932, the prosecution and the defence entered into a 'stipulation' or formal agreement:

> That the book *Ulysses* be annexed to and become part of the libel [indictment] filed herein and by this reference herein is the said libel incorporated as if entirely restated and recapitulated. It is further stipulated that the claimant [Random House] waives its right to trial by jury and further that both parties hereto will move for judgment herein and that upon such motion the Court may consider, pass upon, and decide all questions of law and fact herein involved and the Court may after such consideration, render general findings of fact and conclusions of law.

In other words, the parties agreed to a 'bench trial' without a jury but with binding effect. The prosecutors also agreed that the very copy of *Ulysses* seized would become part of the indictment, with all the additional material Paul Léon had pasted into it. All this would be available for the court's consideration.

It is important to note that it was the particular copy of *Ulysses* actually imported which was the subject of this stipulation. Furthermore, the reviews posted into it could not be amended in any way because they were part of the indictment. This included immensely laudatory critiques of the book by authoritative literary figures. Equally, the prosecuting lawyer, Sam Coleman, underlined in the book the passages he considered to be obscene, which is very useful for scholars. As might be expected, the last episode, *Penelope*, dominates these citations.

Another document casts an interesting light on the case as it developed. This is a letter of 7 August 1933, showing the degree of co-operation between prosecution and defence. This letter is from the law firm to Mr Nicholas Atlas of the United States Attorney Office and refers to 'our conference of this morning'. Enclosed are a number of books, notably the defence law firm's brief, or written argument, in an important obscenity case called *US* v *Dennett*, the brief in another case, *US* v *Berg* and other material. Furthermore it transpires that Mr Coleman had asked the defence lawyers for 'a list of recent obscenity cases, so as to enable him to ascertain the present trend of judicial attitudes'. The lawyers sent him an itemized list of cases heard between 1930 and 1933 with additional comments. They also referred to a number of cases which had been thrown out in the magistrates' court and still others in which the grand jury had declined to indict. He referred to the firm's brief in *People* v *Wendling*,[7] decided only a few months previously. This is the case about the stage production of *Frankie and Johnny*.

This is a very significant letter, going into great detail and sharing with the prosecution the obviously very considerable research the firm had done. From the number of the cases cited in which the firm was engaged for the defence, it is clear that they were the leading obscenity lawyers in New York, and probably in the United States, at that time. The fact that the prosecution requested the defence lawyers to direct them to the relevant case law would be recognized by lawyers then and now as an enormous compliment, an acknowledgement of their pre-eminence in that field of law and an act of faith that they would not mislead their opponents.

Morris Ernst wrote a memoir of the case for its twenty-fifth anniversary, from which it can be seen that Sam Coleman's high opinion of him was fully reciprocated. Ernst commented: 'Sam Coleman (now an esteemed judge) carried [out] with vigour his duty of seeking the truth by adversary relationships and unlike most prosecutors was not [merely] interested in producing convictions.'[8]

In view of the lawyers' great care to introduce opinion evidence in the form of the opinion of reviewers, it is significant to note the case of *Halsey* v *New York Society*.[9] This was a case about Théophile Gautier's novel of 1835, *Mademoiselle de Maupin*. There the Court of Appeal had emphasized the importance of a bibliography of scholarly writing about the book in question showing the trend of critical opinion. Accordingly, the lawyers sent the prosecution an essay listing eighteen books and sixty-two articles dealing with *Ulysses* or Joyce's work more generally. They refer to articles by foreign writers such as André Maurois and to the French, German, Spanish and Japanese translations of *Ulysses*, as well as to a number of books, previously banned, which were now openly available in the United States. They also enclosed a map of the United States showing the location of the libraries directed by the librarians whose opinion they proposed to rely on.

The 'classic' ploy

One reason the lawyers had readily to hand the material just summarized was that, prior to the letter in question, they had used some of it in having *Ulysses* recognized as a 'classic' by no less a person than the Secretary of the Treasury himself, a member of President Harding's Cabinet. This arose in the following way.

Like many revenue statutes, the Tariff Act was revised almost annually. In the debate on the 1926 Tariff Act, Senator Bronson Cutting ventilated a complaint by a constituent, a doctor of mature years and undoubted respectability, that he could not import *Lady Chatterley's Lover* by D. H. Lawrence. Cutting wanted to permit by statutory amendment the importation of classics. This was opposed tooth and nail by the Senator for Utah, who said that Lawrence's book would be imported into America only 'over my dead body'. However, Cutting settled, presumably on Ernst's advice, for a discretionary provision allowing the Secretary of the Treasury to admit the so-called classics or books of recognized and established literary or scientific merit into the United States, when imported for 'non-commercial purposes'.[10]

Relying on this provision, Lindey on behalf of the law firm had on 1 June 1933 asked that *Ulysses* be admitted into the United States under the provisions of the Act of 1930 on a similar basis.

The lawyer, in making this request, was careful to 'state specific-ally that I do not consider that *Ulysses* is not admissible under the general provisions of section 305'.[11] This very necessary disclaimer was put in to prevent his request to import the book as a classic from being construed as an admission that it *was* indeed obscene and therefore could *only* be imported under the discretionary provision, as a classic which happened also to be obscene.

The second section of the law firm's papers consists of the petition for admission of the book to the US as a classic. It is a magnificent document and anticipates the firm's tactics in the sub-sequent trial. In his covering letter, Lindey relied on the undisputed reputation of James Joyce as a writer of first-rate importance, generally on the worldwide acclaim which had been accorded to *Ulysses* as the foremost prose masterpiece of the twentieth century, and specifically on the evidence contained in the exhibits annexed to this petition.

The petition goes on to claim that Joyce 'is the only man in English literature worthy of a place beside Shakespeare'. Lindey justified this admittedly extravagant statement on the basis of a large number of testimonials from such persons as Edmund Wilson, H. L. Mencken, Malcolm Cowley, Theodore Dreiser, John Cowper Powys, Louis Untermeyer, F. Scott Fitzgerald and John Dos Passos. He went on to say:

> One persuasive proof of the significance of *Ulysses* may be found in the fact that important men have written important books and articles about it and its author.
>
> *Ulysses* has been translated into French and German: stupendous tasks, when one realises the length of the book and especially its linguistic idiosyncrasies. To say that only a work of exceptional merit would have prompted such Herculean enterprises in translation is to state a truism which will bear no denial.
>
> In introducing the stream of consciousness method and developing it to a high degree of perfection Joyce has, in *Ulysses*, made an epochal contribution to letters. There can be no doubt that his book is a modern classic in every sense of the word.

As a result of this petition the United States Treasury Department, in a letter serendipitously dated 16 June 1933 and addressed to the Acting Collector of Customs for New York, permitted its import as a classic. The 16th of June was, of course, the anniversary of the day in which *Ulysses* is set, Bloomsday. The significance of this decision for the subsequent litigation cannot be overstated. A book whose condemnation and destruction was sought by the authorities had been acknowledged to be a classic by the Secretary of the Treasury.

As a matter of logic, there is no reason why a classic should not equally be obscene. But the book's officially recognized standing as a classic obviously made it easier to argue that it was not obscene, or that any obscenity it did contain was subordinate to a high literary purpose. As to why the Secretary of the Treasury declared the book (which he almost certainly did not bother to read) to be a classic, one can only speculate that the very strong opinions of eminent American writers must have had a huge impact on his decision. Classic status, however, only permitted the importation of a single copy for personal, non-commercial, use. The authorities were entitled to proceed with their claim in the Federal Court for the confiscation and destruction of the book based on the proposition that it was obscene, whether or not it was a classic. That is precisely what they did. Defence lawyers, who would have been very familiar with every judge on the United States District Court for New York, were determined that, if at all possible, the case would come for trial before Judge John M. Woolsey. They managed to arrange this by a policy of artful adjournment in which they appear to have had a large measure of co-operation from the prosecutors. Richard Ellmann incorrectly attributes to Woolsey the title *Justice*: in the United States, that title is reserved for a member of a Supreme Court, whether state or federal (all other holders of judicial office are designated *Judge*).

Woolsey was at the time a plump, dapper, sharply dressed man aged fifty-six. His record in censorship cases had been uniformly liberal; he had authorized the importation into the United States of Dr Marie Stopes's book. He had a reputation as a *littérateur*, and particularly as an expert on eighteenth-century literature, specifically the works of Samuel Johnson. He was also known as a connoisseur of colonial-era American furniture. During the course of the argument before him, Ernst, in attempting to illustrate the 'stream-of-consciousness' technique, emphasized that even when one is trying hard to concentrate the mind will wander into unpredictable byways. Woolsey acknowledged this and said that though he was concentrating as hard as he could on Ernst's argument, his mind had several times uncontrollably wandered to a contemplation of Ernst's fine Hepplewhite chair standing empty in the courtroom behind him. In Ernst's memoirs he paid the following tribute to Judge Woolsey: 'John S. Woolsey was one of those rare jurists who was a rounded, physically as well spiritually, human being who, unlike many members of the Bench and Bar, read widely in fields remote from his professional interests.'[12]

Over the decades since the case was heard, Woolsey's judgment has achieved far more fame than that of the appellate court, the United States Federal Court of Appeals for the Second Circuit. In the first American edition of *Ulysses*, and in very many subsequent editions up to the 1960s, including all those published by Random House, Woolsey's judgment was printed in full, thereby arguably making it the most publicized judicial pronouncement of the twentieth century. As we shall see, Woolsey's judgment went very far indeed towards an absolutely permissive attitude to publication. It had four main points.

Firstly, Woolsey held that a judge should consider not only the work impugned but the criticism written about the book. He said:

I have read *Ulysses* once in its entirety and those passages of which the government particularly complains several times. In fact for many weeks my spare time has been devoted to the decision my duty requires me to make in this matter.

Ulysses is not an easy book to read or to understand. But there has been much written about it and in order properly to appraise it it is advisable to read a number of other books which have become its satellites.

Woolsey listed eleven books on *Ulysses* he had read, nearly all of which were readily available in New York. As can easily be illustrated, they were all highly favourable to Joyce. Valéry Larbaud was amongst the authors read. He compared Joyce to Swift, Stern, Fielding and Homer. T. S. Eliot likened *Ulysses* to the *Odyssey*. Stewart Gilbert made comparisons between Joyce and Ovid, Shakespeare, Ibsen and Proust.

These reviews must be considered against the background that the United States Secretary for the Treasury had already certified the book to be a classic.

Secondly, in a finding which considerably extended the boundaries of the law but was not endorsed by the appellate court, Woolsey held that 'literature' and 'obscenity' are mutually exclusive. Woolsey, in other words, regarded obscenity as the *deliberate* excitation of lustful thoughts for their own sake and without any redeeming or countervailing context or purpose. In relation to *Ulysses*, however, he held that: '*Ulysses* is a sincere and honest book and I think the criticisms of it are entirely disposed of by its rationale.' And: 'in spite of its unusual frankness I do not detect anywhere the leer of the sensualist'.

This observation can only be relevant to the legal approach taken by Judge Woolsey on the basis that the intent of the author is central to the question of obscenity. So far from being a mere pornographer, in Woolsey's view 'Joyce sought to make a serious experiment in a new literary genre'. This is, clearly, a major departure from the law as laid down in *Hicklin*.

This second point is central to Woolsey's approach to the case and its exposition occupies rather more than two-fifths of the entire judgment.

Thirdly, and very favourably from Joyce's point of view, Woolsey again declined to follow *Hicklin* and held that the effect on the averagely robust reader, and not on the most vulnerable imaginable reader, was the standard for the assessment of obscenity. He likened this averagely robust person to the 'reasonable man' so beloved of lawyers in stating duties in other areas of the law and also to the person described in the French phrase *l'homme moyen sensuel*.

Finally, Judge Woolsey held that the book should be considered *as a whole*. This is a central finding because, as Joyce and the publishers privately conceded, parts of the book are obscene. Woolsey certainly thought so. He said: 'I'm worried about the last part of the book [...] there is that soliloquy in the last chapter. I don't know about that.' This, however, was said in the course of argument, and not in the judgment. Woolsey had obviously overcome his reservations.

Woolsey attempted to sum up the stream-of-consciousness technique as follows:

Joyce has attempted – it seems to me an astonishing success – to show how the screen of consciousness with its ever-changing kaleidoscopic impression carries, as it were, on a plastic palimpsest, not only what is there focused of each new observation of the actual things around him, but also in a penumbral zone, residua of past impressions, some recent and some drawn up by association from the domain of the subconscious.

The appeal

An appeal from Woolsey's decision was taken by the state to the Court of Appeals for the Second Circuit. Learned Hand and his cousin Augustus Hand constituted the eventual majority and Martin Manton dissented.

The prosecution did not ask the court to read the entire book, the prosecutor saying: 'I'll give you a generous sampling.' In fact he asked the court to read twenty-five passages which he underlined in their copy of the book and stated that he was relying on them 'with particular reference to the stream of thought soliloquy of Mrs Molly Bloom'.

It appears to have been decided at an early stage, at least by the Hands, that the judgment would be written by Augustus Hand. Learned Hand was a brilliant judge, a fine stylist and a notable legal innovator. By 1933, however, this had gained him something of the reputation enjoyed by Lord Denning in England in the late twentieth century: admittedly brilliant, but not necessarily sound or predictable. According to his biographer, Professor Gerard Gunther, young appellate lawyers in the 1930s were taught to 'cite Learned but follow Gus'. Judge Augustus Hand was thought to be more respectful of precedent and of established positions of law while Learned was seen sometimes as simply enthusiastic.

The Second Circuit was unique in an important respect amongst United States appellate courts then or (as far as I know) now. All other courts, including the US Supreme Court, held a conference shortly after each hearing at which the members of the court expressed their views verbally. These were tentative initial views, not binding. In the Second Circuit, however, there was no meeting for this purpose; instead each judge provided a very brief written note of his thinking. From these it can be seen that Learned Hand and his cousin were profoundly impressed by *Ulysses*. They did not particularly admire the judgment of Judge Woolsey, thinking it over-enthusiastic and insufficiently legal. Learned Hand's biographer refers contemptuously to literary critics of the time who thought they were praising Judge Woolsey's judgment by comparing it to a particularly intelligent book review. Nevertheless, Learned Hand, while believing that there were passages in the book which were undoubtedly obscene, opined that: 'the offending passages are clearly necessary to the epic of the soul as Joyce conceived it'. Turning specifically to Molly Bloom's soliloquy, on which the prosecution relied so heavily, he said: 'Perhaps the monologue of Mrs Bloom in its immediate effect *is* erotic but on the whole it is pitiful and tragic, and much of the book is so.'

As was noted at the beginning of this book, Judge Augustus Hand said that Joyce, like Milton, was concerned with 'Things unattempted yet in prose or rhyme'. It is difficult to imagine a more serious compliment from a traditionally educated upstate New York Yankee.

The United States Court of Appeals for the Second Circuit therefore upheld the decision of Judge Woolsey in the Federal District Court for New York: *Ulysses* was not obscene. The reputation of the Court of Appeals, and of Judge Learned Hand in particular, meant that it was a practical impossibility after that to ban the book in any common-law jurisdiction, effectively the whole English-speaking world. The American decision took the heart out of the English campaign to suppress the book, which collapsed in 1936.

In 1926, Ireland had introduced its own statutory censorship scheme. It relied heavily on the reference of books entering the country to a Censorship Board. If *Ulysses* had reached that body, there is no doubt it would have been banned. But the book was never referred to the board because few if any Irish people attempted to import it. Apart from a small number of individuals, Ireland and Joyce ignored one another from the birth of the Irish Free State in 1922 to Joyce's death in 1941. Joyce never sought an Irish passport. His funeral in Zurich was attended by the British Minister in Berne, Lord Derwent. Derwent's Irish diplomatic equivalent was told to 'explain inability to attend funeral' and to 'find out if Joyce had died a Catholic'.

In retrospect, it is perhaps difficult to imagine a sophisticated New York court of the 1930s condemning *Ulysses* as obscene. Its literary value was uncontroverted, even by the prosecution. Nevertheless, Greenbaum, Wollf & Ernst could not have advised Bennett Cerf and his company simply to import the book and distribute it in the US. It would have been liable to seizure under the two previous decisions and he might have lost the whole of his investment. The fact is that the authorities were constrained by their own court victories in the early and mid-1920s, in New York and Minneapolis respectively. When the lawyers wrote and asked them, in effect, if they had changed their mind about *Ulysses*, a bureaucrat could not have replied other than the Customs' lawyer did: no, they had not changed their mind. The book, after all, had not changed and the authorities were still contending for the validity of the view of the law under which the book had been condemned. But there is no sign of enthusiasm on the part of the state, and their lawyers did nothing to stop the defence manoeuvring to draw the highly favourable Judge Woolsey. The brief in favour of *Ulysses* is a mighty document which inspires the admiration of a lawyer after more than eighty years. But one has a feeling reading it that the arguments being advanced by Ernst are ones whose time has come: public opinion was ready for those arguments. It is very instructive that the state does not appear to have filed *any* written argument. Moreover, the Solicitor General of the United States, who was in charge of the federal government's litigation, refused the state of New York permission to appeal to the Supreme Court; this is probably just as well, as the United States Supreme Court at that time was in an extraordinarily conservative phase. As it is, *Ulysses* was liberated, the very restrictive Hicklin test abandoned for ever and a strong defence based on literary considerations was made available to publishers by this litigation. The prestige of the courts by which this was done and the plangent language in which it was expressed made it very unlikely that any respected and self-respecting common-law court would thereafter declare the book obscene. But Joyce and his publishers were extremely lucky to find judges of striking cultural sophistication, as well as high legal attainments, in the federal courts in New York. Their decision opened the American market to *Ulysses* and, as Joyce understood very well, the market of the rest of the English-speaking world.

9. 'This Disgusting Book': *Ulysses* in England

Sylvia Beach's Shakespeare and Company published the first edition of *Ulysses* in Paris in February 1922 in a print run limited to 1,000 numbered copies. In October 1922, Harriet Shaw Weaver's the Egoist Press issued a second printing of 2,000 copies of which five were seized and destroyed by the New York Post Office Authority as a result of the New York magistrates' decision that the book was obscene. The American suppression started earlier than its British equivalent because, as I have described, John S. Sumner of the New York Society for the Suppression of Vice had not waited for *Ulysses* to appear in book form. He moved on the serial publication of the *Nausicaa* episode of *Ulysses* in the *Little Review*, published by Margaret Anderson and Jane Heap. The episode was condemned as obscene in February 1921 by a magistrates' court in Manhattan, leaving little doubt that the book as a whole would meet the same fate if published in America.

There is no evidence that the American case had any impact on British official opinion, though it may have inflamed certain individuals against the book. British officialdom became involved in the campaign on 12 December 1922. On that day a copy of *Ulysses* was confiscated by the Customs at Croydon Airport, near London. The Customs acted according to their powers under the Customs Consolidation Act (1876). It appears that the importer 'protested the seizure' on the grounds of the work's literary merit. In those circumstances, the Customs authorities asked the Home Office whether the book should be detained as being indecent or returned to the owner. They told the Home Office: 'The importer describes it as a noteworthy work of art by an author of considerable repute which is being seriously discussed in the highest literary circles.'[1]

The difficult question raised by the Customs arrived on the desk of Mr Sidney Harris, a senior Home Office official. He despatched the book to Sir Archibald Bodkin, Director of Public Prosecutions, with the observation that: 'There is no doubt as to the obscenity of the passage referred to on pages 704 and 705.'[2] These references are to Molly Bloom's soliloquy, and specifically to the passages now found at pages 620–21 in the Bodley Head edition. The soliloquy constitutes the whole content of the eighteenth and last episode of the book *Penelope*.

It is very striking that Bodkin's eye fell immediately upon Molly Bloom's long and almost unpunctuated soliloquy. This was, as we have seen, the episode that most troubled the notably liberal Judge John Woolsey in New York, and the episode on which the prosecutor, Sam Coleman, focused in providing extracts for the Federal Court of Appeal in 1934. It appears that, certainly in the case of Bodkin and his peers, their reaction to the themes of the episode was heightened by a sense of oddity or, worse, the fact that the speaker is a woman, and one who appeared to them to be an uneducated Irish charwoman. Certainly, *Penelope* was unique in terms of anything published up to 1922 in putting highly erotic, even lustful, sentiments in the mouth of a woman.

Bodkin's response to the Home Office is extremely instructive, both in manner and matter. He said:

> As might be supposed I have not had the time, nor may I add the inclination to read through this book. I have however read pages 690 to 732. I am entirely unable to appreciate how those pages are relevant to the rest of the book or indeed what the book itself is about. I can discover no story. There is no introduction which gives a key to its purpose and the pages above mentioned, written as they are as if composed by a more or less illiterate vulgar woman, form an entirely detached part of the production. In my opinion there is more, and a great deal more than mere vulgarity or coarseness, there is a great deal of unmitigated filth and obscenity.
>
> The book appears to have been printed as a limited edition in Paris where I notice the author, perhaps prudently, resides. Its price no doubt ensures a limited distribution. It is not only deplorable but at the same time astonishing that publications such as *The Quarterly Review*, *The Observer*, and *The Nation*, should have devoted any space to a critique upon *Ulysses*. It is in the pages mentioned above that the glaring obscenity and filth appears. *In my opinion the book is obscene and indecent*

and on that ground the Customs authorities would be justified in refusing to part with it.

It is conceivable that there will be criticism of this attitude towards this publication of a well-known writer; the answer will be *that it is filthy and filthy books are not allowed to be imported into this country.* Let those who desire to possess or champion a book of this description do so. [Emphasis added.]³

Bodkin is, of course, quite wrong in thinking that *Penelope* is 'an entirely detached part of the production'. As we shall see, Molly Bloom comments on various themes featured in other parts of the book, such as notorious trials; she reflects specifically on the case of Mrs Maybrick; Freemasonry and specifically whether Bloom is a Freemason; her own affair with Boylan and Bloom's reaction to it; life insurance and whether Paddy Dignam made any provision for his wife and children; drinking and its effect on Bloom and his circle; Bloom's superiority to his drinking companions as a husband and father and, it seems, his superiority as a lover to the flamboyant Boylan. It can also be seen that Bodkin blames the respectable periodicals mentioned for having noticed *Ulysses* at all. His overall reaction is that the extract he specifically mentions is sufficient in itself to establish *Ulysses* as 'a filthy book' and that 'filthy books are not allowed to be imported into this country'. The last sentence of his comment is not without irony, since Bodkin was to take every step within his power to ensure that absolutely no one could possess or champion *Ulysses*.

Bodkin's note to the Home Office, and other references in the official correspondence, make it clear that reviews of the book had come to the attention of the authorities. It was specifically noted, by Bodkin and, later, by the Home Office civil servant Sydney Harris in his reply to the Customs authorities, that there was a review by Shane Leslie (later Sir Shane Leslie) in *The Quarterly Review* (1922). Leslie, who was an Irish landowner, said that he found the book 'unreadable, unquotable and unreviewable'. He also wrote, in a passage that was to become celebrated, that the book was: 'an attempted Clerkenwell explosion in the well-guarded, well-built, classical prison of English literature. The bomb has exploded [...]. All that is unmentionable, according to civilised standards has been brought to the light of day without any veil of decency.'[4]

'Clerkenwell explosion' refers to the famous Irish Fenian bombing of the London prison of that name in 1867 in an attempt to free prisoners, a bombing that killed twelve bystanders (see pp. 267–8). Here, and elsewhere in the reviews and official correspondence, is a sly hint that the objectionable features of the book are rather 'Oirish'.

Bodkin, Harris and other Home Office officials all referred to the price of the volume. It was on sale in Paris for 136 francs (about £2), but the reviews mentioned by Bodkin had generated such interest that there was a black market in London at around £40.

Having been thus advised by Bodkin, Sydney Harris made a note for his political master, the Home Secretary, Sir William Joynson-Hicks, whom we encountered on pp. 243ff. He said, in part:

I have discussed this with the DPP and agree entirely with his opinion. The passages, which he has marked, are foul in their obscenity and cannot be justified by any literary motive

[…] [he condemned the papers that had reviewed the book and continued] but for these notices few people would have heard of the book which is being talked about and obtained no doubt by private purchase in Paris. Fortunately the book is too expensive to command a wide circle of readers. The fear is that other writers with the love of notoriety will attempt to write in the same vein. *I think we may safely advise the Customs that the book is obscene and should be forfeited.*

Harris then made practical suggestions:

The question arises whether we ought not to make discreet enquiries amongst the booksellers in London as to whether the book is being obtained; but on the whole I think it best to take no further action at present. *A prosecution might only give the book further publicity.* The Customs should also be asked to seize any further copies that may be forfeited and the Post Office and the Police informed.[5] [Emphasis added.]

He went on to suggest that interception warrants should be signed by the Home Secretary to allow postal packets to be searched for copies of the book. He drafted a suitable note to convey this decision to the Customs.

The extracts from the official correspondence quoted above perfectly express the attitude of British officialdom and, it must be noted, of not a few in literary circles as well.

It is impossible, at this distance in time, to know what particularly moved Mr Harris to outrage. It seems not unduly speculative to suggest that Molly Bloom's appreciative recollection of her sexual encounter with Boylan[6] and her preceding account of Leopold Bloom's sexual preferences may have stiffened Mr Harris's already jaundiced attitude to the book.

The effect of Bodkin's decision

The effect of Sir Archibald Bodkin's decision, and of the occasional reminders of it whispered in suitable ears in the succeeding years, was to prevent any large-scale commercial importation of *Ulysses* into Britain until the year 1936. It also, naturally, prevented publication or printing of the book in Britain itself, since any publishing company able to undertake that venture would risk the loss of its entire investment by the confiscation of the book. Bodkin was very happy with these results.

That is not to say that there were no copies of *Ulysses* at all available in England. Especially in 'advanced' circles, copies were indeed to be had, sometimes at very inflated prices indeed, as the reference to copies changing hands at £40 each illustrates. There was also a widespread and less commercially motivated passing of copies from hand to hand. These copies were sometimes purchased by individuals on trips to Paris and simply smuggled through Customs; others came in the post from Paris or elsewhere. The control of incoming postal packets was not, of course, quite watertight. Thus in 1932 George Orwell speaks of 'the friend who was going to lend me *Ulysses* has at last got his copy back and I shall go up to town one day to collect it'. Two years later he remarked to another friend, Arnold Bennett, 'I managed to get my copy of *Ulysses* through safely this time.'[7]

Two incidents

It is worth chronicling two specific incidents, one already well known, to illustrate the diligence and focus of the Home Office and the Director of Public Prosecutions in suppressing any importation of *Ulysses* and use of it in the case of successful importation.

Dr F. R. Leavis (1895–1978) was one of the towering figures in the academic study of English literature of the twentieth century, an austerely serious moralist critic. In 1926, however, he had yet to be appointed to any academic position and was giving an external course on English prose in Cambridge University. He asked the Cambridge bookseller Charles Porter, of the firm of Galloway and Porter, to request permission for him to import a copy of *Ulysses* for the purpose of his lectures, and a further copy to be placed in a university library. What followed appears clearly from the British Official Archives, and from the account which Leavis gave of the affair in a letter to *The Times Literary Supplement* in May 1963. As with the records relating to the original banning of *Ulysses*, one cannot do better than let the official mind speak for itself.

Porter's application crossed the desk of Sydney Harris, whom we have met in his previous role in the reception of *Ulysses* in England. He minuted:

> This is an amazing proposition. A lecturer at Cambridge, who proposes to make this book a text book for a mixed class of undergraduates must be a dangerous crank. Permission must of course be refused but I agree that it would be very useful to have the advice of the DPP [Sir Archibald Bodkin].

The suggestion of the involvement of Bodkin had been made by a more junior civil servant, Mr H. Heuston, who minuted his superior, Harris:

> From my knowledge of the book I am inclined to doubt its suitability for the education of the boy and girl undergraduates who may attend lectures and I am inclined to say that so far from removing the ban we should take steps to prevent the lectures taking place. The introduction of obscene literature into Oxford and Cambridge is a matter that for some time past has been handled – and admirably handled – by the Director and if we might trespass on his time in this case I have no doubt but that this somewhat alarming proposal could be suitably and speedily dealt with. Send to Director of Public Prosecutions.

The response from Bodkin makes it perfectly clear that, on the topic of the suppression of *Ulysses* in Great Britain, he was a crusading figure. He wrote to the Chief Constable of Cambridge, noting that: 'You have already been informed from the Home Office that *Ulysses* is an obscene work by one James Joyce.' He contemplated the possibility that the booksellers were the victim of a student prank or hoax, and therefore asked him to report immediately as to who Dr F. R. Leavis was and whether, indeed, he was seriously intending to lecture on *Ulysses*. He reminded Chief Constable Pearson: 'You will, I am sure appreciate that the enquiries as to Dr Leavis must be made discreetly.'

He then noted that:

> having discussed this matter with the Home Office *it is quite*

clear that the ban on this disgusting book will certainly not be removed; that no facilities whatsoever shall be given for lecturing upon its subject; and that if it be discovered that any other bookseller in Cambridge or elsewhere have in some way procured copies and sell them, I shall have to consider very carefully the advisability of instituting proceedings. [Emphasis added.]

But the institution of public criminal proceedings, with the publicity that that would give the book, and the risk of failing to get a conviction, was not Bodkin's preferred course of action. Very significantly, he added: 'I am further desirous of taking some steps with the University Authorities *to prevent such lectures from being delivered* whether to a mixed University Class or otherwise'. (Emphasis added.)[8]

The Chief Constable replied that the book was not on sale in any other booksellers, 'they all having been previously warned with respect to the sale of this book'.

Sir Archibald Bodkin's next step was to write to the Vice-Chancellor of Cambridge University, the academic head of the university. This was a Professor Albert Seward, who was an academic botanist by background. Bodkin said he was writing to him 'upon a delicate and important matter which has been reported to me by the Secretary of State, Home Office [i.e. Joynson-Hicks]'. Speaking of *Ulysses*, he wrote:

There is a notorious book called *Ulysses* by one James Joyce which for some reasons, the chief of which is probably owing to its disgusting character, was published in Paris in 1922.

Attention was drawn to it as an indecent publication and, not by H.M. Customs but by myself acting under the directions of the Home Secretary, *every effort has been made to secure and destroy any copies found coming into or circulating within this country*. [Emphasis added.]

These two last quoted letters show exactly the strategy of the British authorities in suppressing *Ulysses*. Booksellers were warned about selling it, apparently by the local constabulary, and were hardly likely to take the risk of doing so. Bodkin's letter to the Vice-Chancellor makes it quite clear that active efforts were made to prevent any importation of the book. Turning to the bookseller's application to import a copy for Dr Leavis's lectures, Bodkin said: 'It was hardly credited that this book shall be proposed as the subject of lectures in any circumstances but above all that it should be the subject of discussion and be available for the use of a mixed body of students.'

Repeating the estimate of *Ulysses* which he had formed in 1922, he said:

I do not pretend to be a critic of what is, as I suppose, literature, but the book *Ulysses* which contains seven hundred and thirty-two pages is an extraordinary production of which, to use a colloquialism, I am unable to make head or tail, but there are many passages in it which are indecent and entirely unsuitable to bring to the specific attention of any person of either sex.

The book concludes with reminiscences, as I suppose they may be called, of an Irish chamber-maid, in various parts of which grossness and indecency appear. I should be quite prepared, if you desire it, to lend you a copy of *Ulysses* for the purpose of satisfying yourself that my observations are justified, as also is the prohibition which attaches to it. I am confident that no English publisher would take the risk of publishing such a book.

Dr Leavis's attempt to import the book for academic purposes led to a new departure, an intrusion by the arms of state in the form of the Home Office and the Director of Public Prosecutions into the syllabus of one of the ancient universities.

We know from Dr Leavis's 1963 letter what happened as a result of Bodkin's letter to the Vice-Chancellor. The latter sent for Leavis (and told the DPP that he would be seeing him in the next day or two). When Leavis presented himself, the Vice-Chancellor simply handed him Bodkin's letter without comment. Leavis said that he did not see why anyone who wanted to read the book should not do so, and pointed out that the book already had a distinguished reputation in literary circles. But he also said that he had never entertained what he called 'the absurd idea' of prescribing the book for study for the English Tripos. He continued his report of the conversation:

I could have easily got a copy by letting myself be put in touch with one of the disreputable agents every bookseller knows of. 'I am glad you didn't do that', the Vice-Chancellor replied, '*letters get intercepted.*' And he touched with an admonitory finger one of the pigeon holes of the desk at which he was sitting. He didn't seem at all disturbed and I think he replied to the public prosecutor in terms of my explanation. [Emphasis added.]

From this it appears, firstly, that Leavis could have got his hands on a copy of *Ulysses* without undue difficulty and, secondly, that he felt it necessary to assure Seward that he was not in fact teaching the book. Thirdly, it is significant to note that the Vice-Chancellor of Cambridge University felt it necessary to warn the junior lecturer that 'letters get intercepted'. This simple action gives an excellent sense of the atmosphere in Britain at the time, even amongst highly intelligent, self-confident figures in elite institutions.

Bodkin replied to the Vice-Chancellor, obviously unhappy with the bland tones of the latter's letter:

This is not the first occasion in which I have known a book containing disgusting passages being favourably reviewed by the literary critics. What I am concerned in *is to prevent any knowledge of this book, Ulysses, spreading amongst university students of either sex*. [Emphasis added.]

Bodkin then set out very clearly the motivation of the censors:

Knowledge of it may awake curiosity, and curiosity may lead to possibly successful attempts to obtain it. If I learn that any copy has come into the hands of any university student, I shall take every step which the law permits to deal with the matter, and I can hardly avoid remarking that if I have to take any such steps, inevitably the source from which knowledge of the book arose will be known, and the publicity will hardly tend to increase the reputation of the university, or the subject matter of the lectures.

I trust you will think right to bring every influence to bear on Dr. Leavis to impose upon this book as complete a ban as the authorities impose upon booksellers and others who might be likely to deal with it.

In writing to the Chief Constable, Bodkin suggested that he might find a way to monitor Leavis's lectures and see if he referred to *Ulysses*. If that occurred, 'I should then probably consider it right to address a communication to Dr. Leavis personally.'

Commenting on this correspondence, Sir Ernley Blackwell, the Assistant Secretary (Legal) in the Home Office, said:

The Vice-Chancellor's letter is evasive. Can he have read the book? He said that he would not trouble the Director to send him a copy. It is hoped that the Director's last letter will have the desired effect. If not, a publication of any bookseller found dealing with the publication would bring the Vice-Chancellor and Mr Leavis to their senses.

Commenting on the book itself, Blackwell remarked: 'If the last forty pages of this book [that is, Molly's soliloquy] can be called literature there is a whole lot of it running to waste every day in the airing courts at Broadmoor.' The long-serving Sydney Harris told his superior that Bodkin's letter was 'a model of the way to address Vice-Chancellors'.

From these notes it can be seen that British officialdom was deeply and actively committed to the suppression of *Ulysses*. It had a marked preference for doing so by more or less oblique warnings, coupled however with threats of prosecutions. The civil servants were, in general, satisfied with the efficacy of such tactics.

Commenting on the matter almost forty years later, in his letter to *The Times Literary Supplement*, Leavis referred to 'the potency of convention' and the subtle sort of damage that that had inflicted upon him personally. He said that:

> It was very natural at the time of Lawrence's death, and later, for ordinary conventional academics to say, with an untroubled conscience, when asked how Leavis had earned so marked a disfavour: 'We don't like the books he lends undergraduates'. After the notorious scandal, to have gone on like D. H. Lawrence and T. F. Powys was, in those days, asking for it.[9]

The Home Office papers disclose several exploits in the suppression of *Ulysses* along the same general lines. They also reveal that individuals quite well known in the literary world of the day were not above making complaints to the Home Office or the police with a view to suppressing the book. For example, in 1930 Arthur Mee, the editor of the *Childrens' Newspaper*, told the police that he had noticed that a bookseller in Museum Street, London was advertising a mint-condition 1922 first edition of *Ulysses* at a price of twelve guineas. A police inspector was sent round to the shop and discovered that the book was included 'accidentally, in their stock'.

Lord Birkenhead's copy of *Ulysses*

Frederick Edwin Smith, 1st Earl of Birkenhead (1872–1930) was a brilliant and flamboyant Tory lawyer and politician of the day. He dominated the English Bar in the period prior to the First World War and earned a truly enormous income. A Tory MP since 1906, he strongly supported the Ulster Unionist cause, coming close to treason in doing so. He famously acted as Sir Edward Carson's 'galloper' during the militarized rallies of the Unionists, thereby earning the nickname 'Galloper Smith', which stuck to him for life. He was Attorney General (in which capacity he prosecuted Sir Roger Casement) and under the Liberal–Tory coalition headed by Lloyd George he rose to be Lord Chancellor. In that capacity he was one of the delegation that signed the Anglo-Irish Treaty in 1921. He was later Secretary of State for India (1924–8). He died in September 1930. In December of that year the poet and writer Alfred Noyes telephoned Scotland Yard and spoke to a Constable Grub. Noyes told Grub that a copy of the suppressed book, *Ulysses*, was in the catalogue of sale of books belonging to the late Lord Birkenhead which was shortly to take place at Birkenhead's residence, 32 Grosvenor Square, by Messrs Hampton, auctioneer. No steps were taken immediately and Noyes then returned to the attack, saying that at the suggestion of Lord Darling, a distinguished former judge, he intended to contact the DPP. The police then sent an inspector to deal with the matter, who reported:

I saw the Director of Public Prosecutions and the Home Office. Last evening I saw Lady Birkenhead's Private Secretary and told her that a complaint was made about the sale of this book, and there was a possibility of some adverse comment being made in the press or elsewhere, with the result that she will make arrangements to have the lot withdrawn. If Mr Noyes rings again, we can say that the matter has been 'dealt with' – that is quite enough.

Alfred Noyes (1880–1958) was an English poet, short-story writer and playwright. He is best known today for his ballads 'The Highwayman' and 'The Barrel-Organ'. Noyes was quite a considerable literary figure at that time. In 1928, after the death of his first wife, he converted to Catholicism. Later in life he was a strong advocate of the view that Roger Casement's 'Black Diaries' were forged and just before his death wrote a book, *The Accusing Ghost*, defending that position. I am not aware of any specific reason why he took such great exception to Joyce's novel. He had seen the Casement diaries during the First World War, when he worked for the Foreign Office. It is possible that his *animus* may have been against Birkenhead, rather than Joyce, on the basis of the lawyer's rather unscrupulous use of them to deny Casement a reprieve.

Birkenhead was a brilliant but extremely cynical man who had been classically educated and whose occasional poems (in Latin as well as English) show a considerable literary gift. It is interesting that he had acquired a copy of *Ulyssses*. But the principal interest of the Noyes complaint and the police reaction to it is to show that the banning of *Ulysses* remained very actively on the official agenda as late as 1930.

From 1930 onwards, however, the resolution of officialdom to keep the book banned was beginning to weaken. In 1930 a Dr S. Herbert, who was a medical practitioner, a Justice of the Peace and an established medical author, applied to be permitted to import the book. He was granted permission to do so for private use. At much the same time, however, Harold Nicolson, the aristocratic ex-diplomat, author and future MP, who was giving some literary talks on the BBC, was forbidden by no less a person than Lord Reith, the formidable Director General of the BBC, to mention *Ulysses*.

In January 1934 the literary critic Desmond MacCarthy applied for permission to import a copy of *Ulysses*. He was delivering a series of lectures at the Royal Institution in London and wanted to consult the book. At the same time the Bodley Head made it clear that they were going to attempt a British publication of *Ulysses*. This fact led the Home Office to think that it would be 'impolitic' to refuse Desmond MacCarthy's request. A new civil servant, a Mr Henderson, wrote a memo to his superior speaking of MacCarthy's application:

> This is an awkward enquiry at this moment when there has been paragraphs in the Press about John Lane's (Managing Director of the Bodley Press) having posted a copy of the book to himself from Paris (he says it got through) and about his intention to publish *Ulysses* here.

The Home Office consulted the (new) DPP, who advised:

> The problem is not easy. The authorities regard a book for the purpose of action as obscene or not according to the use to which it may be put (not perhaps according to its recipient). In practice it is suppression of the trade and publicity in obscenities that is aimed at.

If the initial American decision to ban *Ulysses* in 1921 had no obvious effect in Britain, the same cannot be said for the decision of the Federal District Court, and subsequently the Federal Circuit Court of Appeals for the Second Circuit in 1933 to hold that the book was not obscene. This was noted by the Foreign Office. Joyce himself summed up the position after the United States Court of Appeal decision in that case in a letter to T. S. Eliot:[10] '*En Somme*, one half of the English-speaking world has given in. The other half, after a few terrifying bleats from *Leo Britannicus*, will follow – as it always does.'[11] That is more or less exactly what happened.

Mr Henderson, now a very senior official, drily noted of the American Court of Appeal decision that 'this doesn't help us very much'. Nothing definite happened, however, for a further two years. In September 1936 Mr Henderson informed the (new) Home Secretary that 'an extremely awkward situation has now arisen'. This was because Foyles, the booksellers, had indicated that a limited edition of *Ulysses* was to be published very soon. He reported:

I have had preliminary word with the DPP along the lines that a book costing £6.6.0 or £3.3.0 was not likely to get into the hands of anyone likely to be corrupted by it *and that probably the prudent course would be to do nothing.*

It now appears that the book was published last Saturday by John Lane of the Bodley Head. *The Morning Post* says that John Lane consulted the Home Office but there is no record of such consultation on the file [...]

The last time it was discussed in the Home Office was when Mr T. S. Eliot and Mr Mosley of Faber and Faber came to see me in January 1934, being introduced by the present Attorney

General. It was then decided to await developments and see if the book was published here and if there were any protests. It was agreed in 1922 that the customs and post office should seize copies. No doubt many copies got through. [Emphasis added.]

The upshot of this was that a conference between the Home Office, the Attorney General and the DPP was convened.

On 8 October 1936 *The Morning Post* reported that 1,000 copies of *Ulysses* were on sale in London. The paper said there was 'brisk demand' for copies of the work that was advertised by Bodley Head as the banned book read by Lord Chancellors (presumably a reference to Birkenhead) and the subject of Cambridge University lectures. Against that background, the bureaucratic conference finally took place on 6 November 1936. It was noted:

Sir David Somervell, the Attorney General, said that the definition of obscenity in *R* v *Hicklin* was inadequate. In his view the question of intention of the writer has to be taken into account, as in the criminal law generally. The context or general setting also has to be considered. No-one today would hold that books such as [those] by Havelock Ellis on sexual matters or medical books on sexual aberrations were obscene.

Standards in these matters are constantly changing. Having applied these tests to *Ulysses* he was of the opinion that the book was *not obscene* and having regard in addition to its established position in literature he has decided to take no action. [Emphasis added.]

That was the end of the official commitment to suppress *Ulysses*. A week later a confidential note cancelled the interception warrants granted in 1923. The first unlimited edition of *Ulysses* appeared in Britain in 1937. There was no cheap edition until the Penguin version of 1968, by which time the novel had become a classic.

Joyce, perhaps typically, greeted the news that his book could now be published in English and in England with the observation: 'Now the war between England and me is over, and I am the conqueror.'[12] It does not seem likely that England, outside a very small official and literary elite, was aware that it was at war with Joyce. But the England of Sir William Joynson-Hicks was yielding to a new world, a world safer for literary innovators like James Joyce.

To a reader in the early twenty-first century, what is very striking about the English official correspondence concerning *Ulysses* is the total self-confidence of politicians and bureaucrats who were still expounding and enforcing High Victorian values in the 1920s and 1930s. Equally striking is the elitism they manifest: what possible value could be the 'memoirs' of 'an Irish chamber-maid' have? Why should such things be published? This, of course, would have particularly outraged Mrs Molly Bloom, a major part of whose persona was that she was the daughter of an officer and a gentleman, Major Tweedy. This self-confident elitism is reminiscent of the demeanour of Joyce's one-time mentors, the Irish Jesuit Fathers, who flourished in Ireland as late as the 1960s. Another parallel was the paternalism, not to say patriarchalism, of Joynson-Hicks, Bodkin, Henderson and the rest. It was for them to decide, they confidently believed, what was and was not suitable for 'boy and girl undergraduates' to read and to control the excesses of uppity young dons like Leavis. They took no pleasure, they loudly assured each other, in having to read filth like *Ulysses*, but since it was their regrettable duty to peruse it, their superior intellects, high education and wide experience enabled them instantly to discern the central piece of filth that the book contains, and to identify it very precisely.

The group of London mandarins, political and bureaucratic, who took the decisions about *Ulysses* in the 1920s and 1930s was also a mutual admiration society. Henderson was loud and repetitious in his admiration for Bodkin; Sir Ernley Blackwell, an enthusiastic circulator of Casement's 'Black Diaries' a decade or so before, could hardly contain his admiration for Bodkin's draft reply to the Vice-Chancellor of Cambridge University.

This was a group of exceptionally clever men. They *were* all men, though their views were shared by some very clever women such as Virginia Woolf. Their actions and correspondence show no sign that they knew they were fighting a losing battle, or that High Victorian *mores* were being progressively undermined. They were probably right, from their own point of view, to display no cracks in their self-confidence, no doubt that the morality they espoused was shared by every decent person. But they were in fact like a herd of dinosaurs about to face extinction. The difference in establishment opinion as manifested by Sir Donald Somerville, QC, Attorney General in the mid-1930s, in comparison with that of Bodkin shows precisely how one age was yielding to another.

It is irresistible for an Irish man writing about these events a whole long lifetime after they took place to remark that it would be difficult to think of an Irish politician or opinion-former of the time who would express views quite as rigid as those of Bodkin or Joynson-Hicks. The question of whether to ban *Ulysses* in Ireland never arose because interest in the work was so slight that it was never submitted to the Censorship Board. If it had been, I am quite sure that it would have been banned but I do not think that any Irish minister or high civil servant of the 1920s or 1930s would have left on record views quite as peculiar as those quoted in this chapter.

Appendix: The Trial
of Robert Emmet

Robert Emmet's trial was, of course, the occasion for his famous speech. The speech in turn, and in particular its final paragraph, was throughout the nineteenth century, in 1916 and for decades afterwards, *the* sacred text of Irish nationalism.

The actual trial of Emmet, in the received nationalist version of history, is seen almost exclusively as the context in which the great speech was delivered.

Even at the time it took place, in September 1803, the trial was regarded as very dubious. It had none of the forensic integrity that had seen the acquittal of Hardy and the other radicals of the London Corresponding Society less than a decade before. The legal points which had ensured their acquittal, on the same charge of treason, were never raised at Emmet's trial in Dublin and his original defence counsel, the eminent Irish nationalist lawyer and politician John

Philpot Curran, father of Emmet's beloved Sarah, withdrew from the case just before the trial opened and his successor, Leonard McNally, made no attempt to counter the case for the prosecution by cross-examining their witnesses or otherwise mounting an effective defence.

In the decades after the trial the reasons for this began to leak out. In the early 1820s the British government in Ireland under the Lord Lieutenancy of the Marquess of Wellesley, brother of the Duke of Wellington, discovered, apparently to their great surprise, that Leonard McNally had been for almost thirty years a spy in the pay of Dublin Castle. McNally had been a leading radical lawyer of the day in Dublin and held a brief in most of the state trials. It transpired that throughout that period he had been reporting secretly to the Castle on his clients' plans and dispositions. This was discovered, almost incredibly, when his widow and family sought the continuation after his death of the secret 'pension' or bribe which he had been paid annually.

News as dramatic as this could not be kept secret. By the late 1820s McNally's treachery was widely spoken of and by the early 1840s it was written of, without contradiction, in Dr Madden's very influential *The Life and Times of Robert Emmet*.

The authorities' attitude to these revelations was to state that it was all a long time ago and things were done differently then, and to insinuate that McNally's treachery, though unfortunate and dishonourable, had had no practical effect because the case against Emmet was so strong. Even in recent times (2003) a reputable historian, Dr Marianne Elliott, has endorsed this point of view.

But nationalist and mainstream opinion was extremely sceptical of the trial and felt there was something wrong with it while not being able to say exactly what had corrupted the proceedings. The street ballad from 1900 quoted on p. 195 contains the strongly felt but very general assertion that 'he was betrayed, and shamefully treated'.

In 1904 Michael MacDonagh published a book, *The Viceroy's Post-bag*,[1] which was the fruit of serious research in the English archives. It revealed a great deal of general historical interest: for example, the full details of the payment of lavish bribes to secure the passage of the Act of Union in 1800. In relation to Emmet's trial, it published the actual correspondence between Leonard McNally and his masters in Dublin Castle. It also revealed the Irish government's own view that it had only a very dubious case against Robert Emmet and the extraordinary steps which it took to cut Emmet off from any effective defence by threatening his inamorata, Sarah Curran.

The first fruit of these threats was that John Philpot was forced to withdraw as Emmet's counsel because of his daughter's compromised position. This left the case for the defence in the hands of the Castle's creature, Leonard McNally. His betrayal of his own client's interest was manifestly disgraceful. From a professional point of view he simply failed to argue points that must have been obvious to him and which had saved the lives of other defendants in treason trials.

Thus the passage of time, the discovery of documents and the fact that Balfour's and Asquith's governments of the early twentieth century cared much less than their predecessors had done about the events of 1803 led to the revelation that Emmet's trial had been indeed a show trial and that the famous speech which echoes so plangently in *Ulysses*, an 'allocution' in terms of the law of the time, was the only significant part of the trial not to have been contrived by the Castle.

The trial, as we have seen, took place in Dublin's Green Street Court House, which was also the setting of the Childs murder case. This building housed the principal criminal court of the day, the Dublin City Commission. It had previously been the location of a great number of the trials which followed the Rebellion of 1798. As the century wore on it was the venue for many more political trials, usually followed by executions, such as those of the five Invincibles hanged in May and June 1883.

In those days, and particularly in the early nineteenth century, it was customary for the trial to be followed almost immediately by the execution: Emmet was hanged the day after his conviction. The high point of his trial, from a nationalist point of view, was the very striking speech which he made from the dock. But from a lawyer's point of view the interest of the trial is quite different. For despite the forced withdrawal of the great anti-Union barrister John Philpot Curran and his replacement by the government placeman Leonard McNally, Emmet also had other, uncorrupted lawyers. Moreover, there is dramatic evidence from the government side that, three weeks before the trial, the government still considered the case against Emmet dangerously weak and expressly contemplated, in correspondence with the imperial government in London, the possibility that Emmet might be acquitted.

McNally's correspondence with the Lord Lieutenant of Ireland, the Earl of Hardwicke, was published in MacDonagh's ground-breaking book of 1904. This reveals amongst other things the steps the government took to secure Emmet's conviction. They ensured that Emmet made no attempt to defend himself, and that inadmissible evidence was produced against him without objection, all made possible by threatening to implicate Sarah Curran in Emmet's treason if he mounted any defence.

The trial and the events immediately surrounding it also have a broader interest. The trial transcript, the official and the private correspondence about it, the love letters to and from Sarah Curran and the well-recorded interrogation of Emmet before the Irish Privy Council are a virtual time capsule of early-nineteenth-century Ireland. Various notables of the day – Curran, Lord Norbury, McNally himself, William Wickham and Lord Lieutenant Hardwicke – are shown in oblique and fascinating lights. Other than Curran, their very names would now scarcely be known but for their connection with Emmet. Light is also thrown on such ephemera of cultural history as the notion of 'honour' shared by political opponents and the attitude that this led them to adopt to women – at once patronizing and highly favourable.

Emmet's was a show trial in three different senses. Firstly and most obviously, the result was rigged. Secondly, the trial and execution were a badly needed demonstration that the Irish administration had indeed cracked the conspiracy that had produced the alarming events of 23 July 1803. Thirdly, the trial provided an opportunity for various ambitious men who had opposed the Union only three years before ostentatiously to change their stance and for others to affirm their loyalty. All these things are salutary to reflect upon even today.

Their result was to turn the trial into a foregone conclusion. The effect of doing so was to ensure that, in Emmet's own words, 'the sentence was already pronounced at the Castle before your jury was empanelled'.[2] This enabled the government to turn the prosecution of Emmet into a show trial in two other and quite separate ways. It may help an understanding of the trial to discuss them briefly. The Irish government, under Philip Yorke, Earl of Hardwicke as Lord Lieutenant and William Wickham as Chief Secretary, had been grossly embarrassed by the rebellion and the weakness and confusion of the government's response to it. Hardwicke's brother, who was a British minister, wrote privately to him telling him that letters from Ireland were feeding hysterical newspaper and parliamentary outbursts which Hardwicke had to answer immediately if his government in Ireland was to continue. The government remained under severe parliamentary attack and Hardwicke and his associates continued to construct long, self-justifying accounts of their failure to predict and suppress the rebellion.

In the immediate aftermath of 23 July, the government decreed the suspension of habeas corpus and caused the passage, or rather revival, of the Insurrection Act, conducting mass arrests and searches. All this gave the impression of activity, but the principal strategy was a policy of state trials followed by almost immediate executions in Dublin from 31 August on. This, they felt, was the best answer to their critics. Hardwicke's wife wrote to a friend at that time:

> The ignorant or angry letters from Dublin were believed in England [...] They loudly declared their belief that no jury would dare to find the rebels guilty, or that, if they did, would Government dare to punish them. In spite of all their violence, they have seen that the slow but steady march of justice can overtake the offender, even in this lawless country [...] The sentence being put in force the following day has struck much

awe on the minds of those who talked so loud of the fear or weakness of their rulers.[3]

The principal difficulty in this strategy was that most of the prisoners tried and executed were, as Wickham himself admitted, 'miserably poor', and plainly not leader figures. When Emmet was captured the Lord Lieutenant said only, 'There is every reason to believe that he was deeply implicated in the affair of 23 July, but I confess that I had imagined that he had escaped.'[4] Almost immediately, however, it became possible to portray Emmet as the sole leader of the rebellion, now brought to justice. This accounts for much of the hyperbole in the prosecution speeches at the trial. The government desperately needed a prominent, and Protestant, victim on whom the whole rebellion could be blamed. It was not, they thought, credible that a group of impoverished Catholics could have organized it.

The trial also allowed for a conspicuous display of loyalty and attachment to the government by some of those who had previously been bitter opponents. Most obvious amongst this group was William Conyngham Plunket. He had been a patriotic parliamentarian who in 1800 had promised to oppose the Union settlement with his blood. It is thus certainly true that, in the understated phrase of the Chief Secretary, 'He had not previously been associated with the government.' But he was instructed as the third of the seven counsel who prosecuted Emmet and he controversially exercised the Crown's right of reply, although the defence neither called evidence nor addressed the jury. His speech was in effect a declaration of his conversion to the government side, where it caused absolute glee. Speaking of the speech Wickham wrote to his predecessor:

It was delivered on purpose to show his entire and unqualified renunciation of his former principles, his determination on long and mature reflection to support the Union after having been its inveterate opposer, and to stand or fall with the present Administration. You may naturally suppose that this is the prelude to closer connection, and that it will be the death-blow to the anti-Union party at the Bar.[5]

Before the year ended Plunket was appointed Solicitor General and he went on to enjoy a remarkable political career both in Ireland and in England.

A similar though more private act of conversion occurred with John Philpot Curran, whose daughter's involvement with Emmet was a cause of gross embarrassment. This, paradoxically, forced him into closer contact with the administration.

These men represented new supporters of the Union settlement and of the government. Their older and more reactionary predecessors were typified by Lord Norbury, Chief Justice of the Common Pleas, who presided at the trial. He was the practitioner *par excellence* of the extraordinary system of jobbery that characterized the government of Ireland in the late eighteenth and early nineteenth centuries. He had held every lucrative legal office under the pre-Union parliament and his price for his services had been his own ennoblement and appointment to judicial office. Since it did not suit him to accept these rewards until after the Union was passed in 1800, he had extracted a down payment in the form of the elevation of his wife to the peerage in 1795. He was aptly labelled by Daniel O'Connell a 'judicial bully, butcher and buffoon'.[6] A more sympathetic commentator, the former Irish Chief Secretary Charles

Abbot, described him in September 1802 as 'scarcely fit for the situation to which he has been raised'.[7]

The case against Emmet

It is often thought that the case against Emmet was one of irresistible strength so that, for example, the corruption of his defence counsel, though deplorable, made no difference. For instance, the participants in an RTÉ programme broadcast on Monday, 8 September 2003 mistakenly though that Emmet had pleaded guilty so that there was 'very little role' for McNally. Contemporary records disprove this proposition, both in terms of the evidence that was available and of the applicable law.

On 26 August 1803, the day after his arrest, Emmet was committed to Kilmainham Jail. The register of the prison shows that this was on the authority of Chief Secretary William Wickham, for the offence of high treason. But Wickham was not then confident that he could convict Emmet of this offence. On 28 August Wickham wrote to the Home Office, explaining his fear that if Emmet denied having involvement in the conspiracy he might go free. He listed the evidence then available to the Crown under seven headings. Five of these were documentary, including the original draft of the proclamation of the provisional government. The other two were circumstantial – his attempted escape when arrested and his request to the owner of the house where he was staying not to put his alias on the list of persons resident there, which, under martial law regulations, was required to be displayed on the door. Wickham's difficulty was that Emmet's handwriting could not be proved.

He recorded: 'Those who know his handwriting in better days cannot say that they believe the papers of which we are in possession to be written by him.'[8] Because, in Wickham's words, 'He was very much beloved in private life', he was pessimistic about getting other witnesses to say they recognized Emmet's handwriting. Worse than that, the documents did not appear to have been written by the same person, so that 'on account of the dissimilarity of the handwriting it would probably be thought more prudent not to produce them'.[9] Wickham concluded:

> If the prosecution against him should fail, it will probably be on account of his changing frequently his manner of writing. We cannot, I fear, convict him without producing as his handwriting different papers written apparently by different persons.[10]

Furthermore, although the authorities had available to them a man who had been captured by the rebels and saved from summary execution by their leader, this person, Patrick Farrell, would not identify the leader as Emmet. In those circumstances the persons present at the prosecutor's meeting described by Wickham gave serious consideration to bringing forward what he called 'secret information'. In the context, this can only be the evidence of Leonard McNally, the ostensibly radical nationalist lawyer who was supposed to be acting for Emmet. The group discussed this possibility, but Wickham recorded: 'There is but one opinion on the subject [...] [I]t were a thousand times better that Emmet should escape than that we should close forever a most accurate source of information.'[11] Leonard McNally appears to be the only source available to the government in August 1803 who fits that description.

It thus appears that, as of the date of Wickham's letter, there was no direct evidence available to implicate Emmet in the offence of high treason. There were documents which were highly incriminating but could not be proved. This situation did not change: after the trial Wickham wrote to Hardwicke's brother, Charles Yorke, who was then the British Home Secretary:

> Though he was educated at the College and had resided so much in Dublin there was no person to be found who could prove his handwriting in a legal manner [...] Singular as it may appear, though we were in possession of several letters and papers that were written by him, it was impossible to obtain proof of his handwriting.[12]

The other evidence available at the end of August 1803 was not believed even by Wickham himself to amount to a sufficient case of high treason.

Notwithstanding, on the day after the trial Lord Lieutenant Hardwicke was able to report to the Home Secretary that it was 'universally admitted that a more complete case of treason was never stated in a court of justice'.[13] Accordingly, the principal legal mystery of the case against Emmet is to explain how a prosecution weak almost to the point of non-existence – so weak that those in charge of it seriously considered exposing their most effective and most secret agent to shore it up – became one of irresistible strength in a period of less than three weeks.

It is striking that Emmet was charged only with treason and

not with the murder of Lord Kilwarden, who had been killed on Thomas Street after Emmet had withdrawn. This is particularly strange because, to the outraged loyalist community, the murder of a distinguished judge and notable moderate had caused more fear and distress than any other aspect of the rebellion. But to have charged Emmet with murder would have required explicit evidence of his participation in the crime or his ordering of it, or of the murder of government officials generally. Since the government had no evidence whatsoever along these lines it adopted the much easier expedient of charging him with treason, which could be inferred, so the judge directed, from very oblique proofs.

Interrogation and muzzling of the defence

On 30 August Emmet was taken from Kilmainham Jail to Dublin Castle for interrogation before the Irish Privy Council. The members present were Lord Redesdale, the Lord Chancellor, Standish O'Grady, the Attorney General, Wickham and the Under-Secretary, Alexander Marsden. At this session the Crown were presented with a solution to their dilemma, though they did not at first recognize it. Emmet confirmed his identity and stated: 'Having now answered my name I must decline answering any further questions.'[14] He declined to say whether he had been in France; when he had first heard of the insurrection; whether he had had any previous knowledge of it; whether he had been in Dublin during it; or whether he had corresponded with persons in France. He refused to say whether he was acquainted with a number of persons whose names were put to him; whether he would identify his handwriting; whether he had seen the proclamation of the provisional government in various forms.

He was then asked: 'By whom are the letters written that were found on your person?' He replied, 'As to the letters taken out of my possession by Major Sirr, how can I avoid this being brought forward?'[15]

This was the turning point of the interrogation and, indeed, of the whole case against Emmet. At the time of his arrest he had been in possession of unsigned letters from Sarah Curran. They appeared to be love letters, though the Crown did not accept them at face value. She had particularly asked him to destroy them but he had not done so. Emmet was also in possession of some locks of her hair which he, in his distracted state, thought might also lead to her identification. When Sarah's letters were referred before the Privy Council Emmet immediately began speaking volubly. He asked whether 'anything has been done in consequence of those letters being taken? May I learn what means, or what has been done to them?' On being told that this was not possible he said:

> You must, gentlemen, be sensible as to how disagreeable it would be to one of yourselves to have a delicate and virtuous female brought into notice. What means would be necessary to bring the evidence in those letters forward without bringing the name forward? Might the passages in those letters be read to me?

He eventually said, 'I would rather give up my own life than injure another person.'[16]

In this and later stages of the examination before the Privy

Council Emmet sought to appeal to conventional contemporary notions of honour. The Attorney General rather graciously said, 'We knew before you came into the room that this would be the line you would take.'[17] Emmet then effectively prefigured the arrangement subsequently come to, saying:

> I am glad you have had that opinion of me. Have any proceedings been taken on those letters? I will mention as near as I can the line I mean to adopt. I will go so far as this: if I have assurances that nothing has been done, and nothing will be done, upon those letters I will do everything consistent with honour to prevent their production [...] I would do anything to prevent the production of those letters [... W]ith notions of honour in common persons may have different principles but all might be agreed as to what a person might owe to a female. Personal safety would weigh nothing if the production of those letters could be prevented.[18]

Although this seems very plain in hindsight, the extraordinary fact is that the prosecutors and Emmet were at cross purposes. The government men were firmly of the opinion that 'The language of a love intrigue had been assumed as a means of misleading the government.'[19] They thought the letters were military communications in a cipher that had not been cracked and which had actually been penned by Emmet's sister on the instructions of some other conspirator. This appears from a note later added by the Under-Secretary to the record of the interrogation, in order to explain the apparent obtuseness of the interrogators to the British Home Office.

The interrogators then used two techniques to increase the pressure on Emmet. First, the Attorney General said that the letters 'formed evidence against the person who wrote them'. Emmet, in what was very definitely a pre-feminist attempt to exculpate Sarah Curran, replied:

> I can only say that a woman's sentiments are only opinions and they are not reality. When a man gives opinions it is supposed that he has actions accordingly; but with a woman the utmost limit is only opinion. I declare on my honour as a man that the person had only opinions.[20]

Emmet, however, refused to make any specific disclosures about the insurrection, but said that he would consider what he might do if he could have an interview with a named lawyer. This was refused. He was reminded of the disclosure made by his brother Thomas Addis Emmet and William McNevin in 1798, but said the two cases were different. At the end of the interrogation he was asked whether he would like the author of the letters to be produced before him. He took this as an indication that Sarah Curran was already in custody and the interview ended with the Lord Chancellor observing that 'Mr Emmet's feelings are a good deal affected.'[21]

On 7 September Emmet was arraigned and pleaded not guilty. He nominated John Philpot Curran as his counsel and Leonard McNally, a son of the barrister of the same name who was secretly informing on his clients, as his solicitor. The next day, in an extraordinarily ill-advised move, he was sufficiently distracted to write a letter to Sarah Curran under her own name and at her father's address. This he entrusted to a prison warder whom he thought was trustworthy; it was immediately placed in the hands of the authorities. The result was a raid led by Major Sirr on the Curran household, the Priory, Rathfarnham, in the course of which Sarah seems to have suffered a sudden nervous collapse. Ironically, the principal subject of the letter was his guilt at implicating her by non-destruction of the letters. Upon the belated realization of the identity of his correspondent, the Castle's anxieties about the trial were at an end. The letters were regarded as remarkable, both in themselves and in the identity of their writer. They were passed for private perusal to the Home Secretary and to the King himself. The former observed that 'Mademoiselle seems to be a true disciple of Mary Wollstonecraft.'[22]

An immediate consequence of the raid was that John Philpot Curran, in a terse and frigid letter, withdrew as Emmet's counsel. He did not refer in detail to the reasons for this but suggested 'That if those circumstances be not brought forward by the Crown, which from their humanity I hope will be suppressed, it cannot be of any advantage to you to disclose them to your agent or counsel.' This, undoubtedly, was Curran attempting to protect his own and his daughter's position, and perhaps not unreasonably so. It is clear from McNally's secret dispatches that the government had made him fully aware of Sarah Curran's compromised position. Curran had in fact been ordered by the Lord Lieutenant to withdraw as Emmet's counsel, but it must be said that he could scarcely have continued to act with propriety, since vigorous defence, such as he had often provided for other prisoners, might have led to his daughter's public exposure. Emmet wrote him a long letter in reply. Most of it is devoted to an attempt to exonerate Sarah in her father's eyes. He also, very generously, stated that he had not expected

Curran to be his counsel, and 'I nominated you because not to have done so might have appeared remarkable.'[23] Responding to the tone rather than the content of Curran's note, he memorably said: 'A man with the coldness of death on him need not be made to feel any other coldness.'[24] Leonard McNally and Peter Burrowes were nominated as alternative counsel. Given what we know about other state prisoners' choice of counsel in September 1803 and for many years before that, it was entirely predictable that if Curran dropped out, McNally would replace him, especially as McNally's son was Emmet's solicitor.

It unfortunately appears that Curran was severely compromised, politically and professionally, by the revelation of his daughter's romance. One of McNally's secret dispatches records that Curran was very unpopular in radical circles because he returned Emmet's brief. He also returned his other rebellion briefs. The reason for this is more than hinted at in a Dublin Castle memorandum of 2 October 1803. Speaking of a pending case which raised a point embarrassing to the government, it said: 'I am very sorry to think we are likely to have this question brought forward, but there is no avoiding it in the circumstances. It is fortunate that Mr Curran is completely in our power.'[25]

When Curran's political allies unexpectedly came into power at Westminster in 1806, the Whig grandees felt that 'the transaction between Mr Curran's daughter and Robert Emmet' made his appointment to political office impossible.[26] So untouchable was he that Henry Grattan, with grim humour, suggested that he be made an Irish bishop. He was eventually made Master of the Rolls in Ireland, an office which was then only quasi-judicial and had recently been held by a layman. He did not shine in it and resigned, miserably, in 1814.

Once the interception of the letter to Sarah Curran became known to him, Emmet apparently thought of nothing but how to protect her. Leonard McNally in one of his reports to the Castle said:

On this subject his mind seems wholly bent, and cruelly afflicted. For his own personal safety he appears not to entertain an idea. He does not intend to call a single witness, nor to trouble any witness for the Crown with a cross-examination, unless they misrepresent facts. [He will not] controvert the charge by calling a single witness.[27]

This, of course, is an extraordinary letter for a defending counsel to write to the prosecution before the trial. It is confirmed by what the other counsel involved, Peter Burrowes, told Thomas Moore thirty years later: that Emmet had 'made the most earnest entreaties to the government that if they suppressed the letters in the trial he would not say a word in his defence but go to his death in silence'.[28]

Effect of the Crown's blackmail

Two moments in particular during the trial show that an agreement was made along the lines suggested by the government. The Attorney General, in opening the case, actually quoted from one of Sarah Curran's letters a passage in which she raised the question of whether French assistance was or was not desirable. This, however, he ascribed to 'a *brother* contributor acquainted with his schemes and participating in his crimes'.[29] He also quoted a passage suggesting the view that the Irish people were 'incapable of redress and unworthy of it', and that this accounted for the rebellion's failure.

The other revealing event occurred during the evidence of Major Sirr, the 'Town Major' or police chief of Dublin. He said that he had found certain letters on Emmet at the time of his arrest. The letters were produced and laid on the table of the court. Lord Norbury said: 'If the prisoner wishes to have any other part of these papers read [other, that is, than the part already read by the Attorney General] he may.' This appears to be a judicial intervention of the utmost fairness, but its true significance is apparent from the response of Peter Burrowes, Emmet's uncompromised defence counsel, who said: 'My Lord, the prisoner is aware of that, and throughout the trial will act under that knowledge.' Emmet was being reminded of what precisely his position was and that any attempt at defence would lead to Sarah Curran's exposure. Immediately afterwards, Burrowes attempted to address the jury but, according to what he later told Thomas Moore, Emmet stopped him from doing so, saying: 'Pray do not attempt to defend me – it is all in vain.'[30]

Just before that intervention the Attorney General had attempted to get Sirr to read from a very incriminating letter to the government allegedly found in the room where Emmet had been arrested. No objection was taken, but the court itself intervened, saying that 'nothing can be read but what is legally proved', an attitude which of course was embarrassing to the prosecution since they had no proof of handwriting. Extraordinarily, McNally declared that no objection was being taken to the admissibility of the letter. Norbury said that the court had wanted to protect Emmet from the admission of any evidence 'which is not strictly legal', but having consulted with his colleagues after McNally's intervention, he still admitted it.[31]

Any possibility that the Attorney General's misrepresentation of the sex of Emmet's correspondent might have been accidental is removed by a letter from the Chief Secretary to the British Home Office on the day of the trial, where he said:

Mister Yorke [the Home Secretary] will have observed that the attorney general when he gave in evidence such parts of the young lady's letter found upon Emmet as it was found necessary to produce, stated boldly that the letter from which the extract was made had been written by a brother conspirator.[32]

The word 'brother' was underlined in the original. He went on to say that information about the true identity of the correspondent might leak out, but that it was important that it should not be seen to do so from the government in either country.

It is accordingly clear that, before the trial, the government had ensured that Emmet would make no attempt to defend himself. The seeds of this arrangement, which was quite improper but which Emmet was very willing to come to, were to be found in the recorded notes of the interrogation before the Privy Council; its fruits are clear from the trial itself. It is probable, though the details are at this stage irrecoverable, that the arrangement was finalized by and through McNally.

As a result of this arrangement the government were able to introduce in evidence without objection highly incriminating though legally unprovable documents. If this had not occurred, even on the government's own view, they were liable to lose the case.

They were also able to supplement this evidence with that of three witnesses, Fleming, Colgan and Farrell, who had been in the depot on Thomas Street, which had been Emmet's headquarters immediately before the insurrection, to identify him as having been there in a position of authority. The first of these, Fleming, had been by his own admission thoroughly involved in the rebellion. He said of Emmet: 'He was the headman of it. He gave directions to Quigley, and he to the others.' Fleming was a painfully weak witness who claimed that he had 'given himself up to the government to become a good subject'.[33] He said he had come to no arrangement with them and could not say whether or not he expected to be prosecuted. He was precisely the sort of witness who, in other trials arising from the insurrection, had been devastatingly cross-examined by advocates such as John Philpot Curran, but no serious attempt was made to contradict his account.

The next witness, Colgan, was a tailor who claimed that he had been drinking in a neighbouring public house and fallen asleep. He then woke up in a dark outhouse where he was forced to work for the rebels making uniforms. He also put Emmet in the Thomas Street depot. He admitted that he would not have given evidence or information if he had not been arrested. At the end of his brief evidence he contradicted himself by saying to a juror who enquired, presumably struck by the incredibility of his story of having been shanghaied while in a drunken slumber, that he had actually fallen asleep not in the public house, but in the depot.

The last witness of this sort was Patrick Farrell, who genuinely had stumbled on the depot a day or two before the insurrection and had been held there against his will. It will be remembered that this was the man who, according to Chief Secretary Wickham's letter, had been unable to identify Emmet when given the opportunity to do so between 25 and 28 August. He now identified him clearly and without doubt. It seems manifest that the process of identification could have been explored and challenged, but no attempt was made to do so. Instead – incredibly – McNally cross-examined him only to establish that he had been well treated while he was held, and that he had heard no discussion of French aid amongst the rebels. He actually apologized for doing so much: 'At the express wish of my client, I shall be excused in putting such questions as he suggests to me, and which will be considered as coming directly from him.'[34]

Two prisoners were acquitted in the 1803 Commission because identifying witnesses had collapsed on cross-examination. Not to cross-examine here was virtual acquiescence in a conviction.

Emmet had been known to the government since his brother's participation in the United Irishmen in 1798, and his own expulsion from Trinity College following the celebrated visitation to the college by the hardline anti-Catholic Lord Chancellor, John FitzGibbon, in that year. But he was not a major, publicly known agitator in the intervening period and there had been no great hue and cry for him after the insurrection. He had not been identified, for example, as the gorgeously uniformed figure leading the rebels along Thomas Street. The direct evidence of his involvement was remarkably weak and came from very questionable sources. Both the opening and closing prosecution speeches heavily relied on the documents which could be attributed to him because his counsel failed to object to them. McNally's annual pension from the government in respect of his work as an informer amounted to

£300 a year. For his actions and failures to act in the Emmet case he was paid a special bonus of £200. He died in 1820 with his activities still unrevealed: as has been noted it was the extraordinary act of his family in seeking to have his pension continued after his death which alerted a later historian, W. J. Fitzpatrick, to his double life. £100 of his bonus was paid on 14 September 1803, five days before the trial: it is tempting to link this with his conveying an absolute assurance that the trial would be a walkover.

Treason

One of the most obvious defects in the defence of Robert Emmet was the omission to take any issue at all as to whether the activities of Emmet actually constituted treason, as alleged in the first count of the indictment. Treason had always been a controversial charge because of its peculiar place in English law. It was the first common-law offence to obtain statutory definition, in 1351 under a statute of King Edward III. This, ironically, was introduced because the vagueness of the offence at common law made it a valuable and flexible weapon. Accordingly, count 1 of the indictment against Emmet charged treason in the classic form, that of 'compassing or imagining the death of the King'. This mental act was the offence: specific overt acts were merely the evidence of it. Over the centuries, there had been a tension between a narrow interpretation requiring an actual intention physically to kill the king, and a broader approach, whether statutory or otherwise, which validated an offence of constructive treason whereby an intention to imprison, depose or restrain the king was regarded as including an intent to kill him.

The 1790s were a time of considerable radical activity in England as well as in Ireland. In 1794 there was a great state trial of persons concerned with the London Corresponding Society, a group favouring universal suffrage, annual parliaments and, it was alleged, the overthrow of the King. In the trial for high treason of its leader, Thomas Hardy, the prosecution and defence were conducted by two luminaries of the English Bar, Lord Eldon and Thomas Erskine respectively. Eldon contended that it was sufficient if the persons performing the overt acts intended 'to put the King in circumstances in which, according to the ordinary experiences of mankind, his life would be in danger'. Erskine contended for a literal construction of the Act, as requiring an intention physically to kill the King. He admitted that an intention to depose was something which entitled the jury to draw an inference that the prisoner intended to kill the King, but said that this was a matter for the jury, and that unless they did draw that inference, Hardy could not be convicted of treason even though he had, by an overt act, manifested an intention to depose the King. Chief Justice Eyre then left the issue of intention to the jury. This was not done in Emmet's case, where the jury were simply told that if they accepted the evidence of the witnesses the offence of treason was complete. His counsel took no objection, and ignored the point on which Thomas Erskine had saved the lives of Hardy and many others only nine years earlier.

Immediately following Hardy's acquittal, Pitt's government introduced an Act[35] that extended the definition of treason from compassing the death of the King to compassing, imagining or intending his death, destruction, or any bodily harm tending to death or destruction, maiming, wounding, imprisonment or restraining the person of the King, or levying war with him in order to change his policy, or in order to overawe either or both of the Houses of Parliament. It also criminalized as treason conspiring with any foreigner to invade any part of the King's dominions. This would certainly have snared Emmet's acts as we know them. But this Act did not apply in Ireland.

In the Irish state trials between 1798 and 1803 a much broader definition of treason than that available at English common law was used. Specifically, the question of intent to kill the King was regarded by the judges as conclusively proven by proof of an act of rebellion, or an intention to depose, and never left to the jury. In his *A History of the Criminal Law of England*, Sir James Fitzjames Stephens wrote:

> The doctrine against which Erskine is supposed to have prevailed in the trials of 1794 was applied to many later cases without hesitation. This occurred in the trials for the Irish Rebellion in 1798 and in particular of two brothers, Henry and John Sheares.[36]

That is the very point: the cases in which the English decision of 1794 was ignored were all Irish cases.

It should also be noted that, in relation to Irish cases, there was an additional difficulty in maintaining a constructive intention to kill the King from an act of rebellion in Ireland. King George III had never resided in or even visited Ireland. In the English state trials Lord Eldon had contended that deposing the King endangered his life 'according to the ordinary experiences of mankind'. This, of course, is much harder to maintain if the overt acts of rebellion take place on a different island. But that point, too, was ignored by McNally.

The speech from the dock

Emmet's speech from the dock is by far the best-known aspect of the trial. It is much more than that: it is a defining statement of Irish nationalist aspirations – 'Our object was to affect a separation from England' – made very shortly after the Act of Union which was intended to put an end, once and for all, to the historic dissentions of the Irish people. It was eloquent in an extraordinary degree, as was recognized in the Chief Secretary's dispatch to London on the following day. It was addressed, explicitly, over the heads of the judges and persons present in court to a wider public, but more particularly to posterity. It became one of the most famous speeches of any sort in the nineteenth century and beyond, familiar to Abraham Lincoln and part of the general information of the American political class at the time.[37]

By contrast, others have always been uneasy about the speech and sought to belittle it. Roy Foster, in his justly celebrated *Modern Ireland 1600–1972*, described it as 'Emmet's attitudinizing in the dock', a dismissal which shows an extraordinary blind spot in a great historian.[38] Kevin Myers, in a 2003 *Irish Times* article, cast doubt on whether the speech was made at all, describing it as one of the 'facts' of Irish historiography. Norbury, he said, would not have let Emmet speak for so long, nor would he have permitted a shorthand writer to be present, and in any event the trial took place, in Myers's view, 'long before anyone else in the world knew [...] all the arts of shorthand'.[39]

Alas for Kevin Myers, two shorthand versions of the speech were taken, one by a *prosecuting* counsel, William Ridgeway, who published it immediately afterwards, as he had published accounts of most of the Irish state trials in 1798. His account was widely used in the contemporary newspapers. The other version was by John Angell, and was the basis for the account of the nationalist historian Dr Madden. So far from the arts of shorthand being unknown in Ireland at the time, Angell's father had published a textbook on the subject. The first English text on shorthand appeared in 1588. Samuel Pepys wrote part of his celebrated diary in shorthand in the mid-seventeenth century. Verbatim or purportedly verbatim accounts exist for all the major trials of the era in both Ireland and England. Myers's bland assertion to the contrary is rather puzzling.

An understanding of Emmet's speech is greatly enhanced by being seen in the context of the trial. For reasons already discussed, at the end of the prosecution case Emmet's counsel did not address the jury or call evidence. In the ordinary way, the judge would in those circumstances have proceeded to deliver his charge to the jury. The prosecution had a right of reply but normally did not exercise it in circumstances where, because of the defendant's silence, there was nothing to which to reply.

On this occasion, however, William Plunket delivered a lengthy and obviously prepared address to the jury on behalf of the prosecution. McNally did protest about this. Plunket's speech was in itself and in its content a totally political act. As has been noted, he had been a stern and – verbally – sanguinary opponent of the Act of Union. He had been an intimate of Emmet's brother, Thomas Addis Emmet, after the latter had left the medical profession for the Bar. However, like many of his class, he was beginning to come to terms with the Union now that it was an established fact.

Plunket's acceptance of the brief for the prosecution, and still more his speech, as we have seen, caused glee in government circles.

The Lord Lieutenant wrote that it would completely destroy the spirit of opposition at the Bar, which he regarded as a matter of political significance. The Chief Secretary described Plunket's speech as masterly, though surprisingly disjointed in delivery.

Contemporary accounts of the trial show that Emmet, who had been impassive during most of the evidence, appeared deeply angered by Plunket's speech. It set out to do a number of things wholly unacceptable to Emmet. Firstly, it sought to associate him with the excesses of the French revolutionaries, and to suggest that he would have introduced their bloody practices to Ireland if his rebellion had succeeded. Secondly, it sought to portray Emmet as the entire reason for the rebellion – 'the man in whose veins the very life's blood of the conspiracy ran' – and to discount the role of the United Ireland movement more generally. And thirdly, he praised the loyalty, contentment and dutiful subservience of the Irish population as a whole.

After the speech Norbury briefly charged the jury, telling them, as noted above, that if they believed the evidence, the offence was made out. The jury then consulted for only a minute or two before returning a verdict of guilty (only one verdict is recorded, though there were three counts) without leaving the box.

The immediate lead-in to the speech was the court clerk's routine question to Emmet as to whether he had anything to say as to why sentence of death should not be passed upon him in accordance with law.

Emmet started his speech by declaring quite frankly that he had nothing to say as to whether sentence of death should not be passed upon him, and making it clear that he wished to address a wider audience than he saw before him. If a strict view of the purpose of the allocution – the court clerk's question to the prisoner as to whether he had anything to say – were being taken, that was the time to take it. But it was not taken, then or much later, until Emmet began to attack the government and the judges. This omission suggests to me that the contemporary Irish courts routinely tolerated, on the allocution, speeches in vindication of the prisoner – and even speeches which, unlike Emmet's, challenged the verdict. Almost a third of Emmet's lengthy speech was devoted to an attack on the French revolutionary governments; a statement of his view that they had no intrinsically benevolent attitude to Ireland; a statement that he would only have co-operated with them under a treaty similar to that which Benjamin Franklin had secured before French intervention in the American revolutionary war; and a denunciation of the despotism which the French revolution had ushered in, in France and many other European countries. This was all very acceptable to the judges and to the government. Indeed, the latter took pains to make sure that this part of the speech was transmitted to France, to the confusion of the United Irishmen's agents there, led by Thomas Addis Emmet.

Being portrayed as a French agent in the Ireland of 1803 had much the same effect as being portrayed as a Communist agent in the United States of the 1950s. Emmet was certainly not a revolutionary in the French sense: his proclamation asserted the protection of property, other than that of the established Church, and a strong commitment to freedom. He said: 'We must fight so that all may have a country after which each shall have his religion.'[40] Emmet was more than conscious that the thrust of the government's attempt at his vilification was to portray him as a French stooge. This must account for the enormous emphasis on his critique of the French revolutionaries.

Emmet's speech was, in its later stages, interrupted seven times – six times by Lord Norbury and once by the clerk of the court. We have Emmet's word for it, in his very last letter to William Wickham, that these frequent interruptions, mounting in hostility of tone, caused him to end his speech without saying all that he had planned. Ironically, of course, the realization that he was being silenced led to the extempore conclusion which is by far the most impressive part of a truly powerful speech, and which has echoed down the years ever since.

The trouble began when Emmet ceased dissociating himself from the French and began to say what his positive purposes had been. Once he announced that his object had been to effect a separation from England, Norbury pointed out that he was making an avowal of treason, saying that though the court would give Emmet 'the utmost latitude of indulgence', it would not allow him to justify the crime of treason as 'the dangerous medium of eloquent but perverted talents'.[41] Emmet continued to attempt to explain his objective and was persistently harried by Norbury, on whom he launched an extraordinary attack:

> By a revolution of power we might change places though we could never change characters. If I stand at the Bar of your Court and dare not vindicate my character, what a farce is your justice.

This eventually led Norbury to take a view of the right on allocution much narrower than the one he had articulated perhaps ten minutes earlier: 'If you have anything to urge *in point of law* you will be heard.' Emmet replied:

The form prescribes that you should put this question; the form also confers a right of answering. This no doubt may be dispensed with, and so might the whole ceremony of the trial, since sentence was already pronounced at the castle before your jury was empanelled. Your lordships are but the priests of the oracle, and I submit, but I insist on the whole of the forms.[42]

It is clear that Emmet particularly resented suggestions that he was responsible for the bloodshed – notably the murder of Lord Kilwarden and his nephew, which had taken place after he had withdrawn from the Thomas Street area – and similarly that he was in league with a foreign oppressor. He said:

The proclamation of the provisional government speaks my views: no inference can be tortured from it to countenance barbarity or debasement. I would not have submitted to a foreign oppression for the same reason that I would have resisted tyranny at home.[43]

Norbury then made his final and longest interruption. In effect, he accused Emmet of being a traitor to his family, upbringing and class. He pointed out that Emmet was a gentleman by birth, whose father filled 'a respectable station under the government'. He referred to his eldest brother Christopher Temple Emmet, who had died young after a short but brilliant career at the Bar. He accused him of ignoring his heritage when he conspired 'with the most profligate and abandoned and associated [himself] with hostlers, bakers, butchers and such persons'. '[Y]our heart', Norbury told Emmet, 'must have lost all recollection of what you were.'[44]

The tone of this long intervention on the printed page indicates what must have been the angry and outraged manner of its delivery. It was clear that Emmet would be allowed to proceed little further and, with the exception of a few lines about the character of his father (whose views appear to have been a great deal more radical than Norbury knew), he went directly into his famous peroration. This cannot possibly have been scripted in advance because its whole theme, apart from an oblique reference to Sarah Curran, is that the state through Norbury has not allowed him to complete his vindication. These lines are the essence of Emmet's legacy: a contemptuous silence in the face of a government which will not allow him to vindicate himself, the epitaph unwritten and the tomb uninscribed 'until other times and other men can do justice to my character'.[45] It is mainly as a result of this exalted passage that Emmet, to use the Yeatsian description, 'died, and immediately became an image'.[46]

Execution and the last letter

Emmet was sentenced to be hanged, drawn and quartered by an overwrought Norbury, who was now weeping. Though the sentence was pronounced in the ancient form, the practice for many years had been simply to hang a prisoner convicted of treason and then decapitate him. Prisoners sentenced for other offences were merely hanged. The method of hanging had been by strangulation caused by pushing a noosed prisoner off a low plank.

In 1793, however, the new Kilmainham Jail and the new Newgate Prison at Green Street had been equipped with hanging platforms at the front. The hangings were still carried out publicly, but by the drop method which usually, though not invariably, caused a more merciful death by breaking the neck.

For the executions of 1803, however, there was a reversion to an older practice. All the prisoners hanged in September 1803 were taken to a place near the scene of their participation in the rebellion or alternatively to the vicinity of their own houses, which were sometimes burned down in front of them. There they were hanged on makeshift scaffolds and by the strangulation method, since there were no facilities for a drop. Moreover, the 'hanging processions' which had been a feature of the former practice were revived in 1803: Emmet was taken to the adjacent Newgate Prison immediately after his sentence, but then transported to Kilmainham, from where the procession began the next day shortly after one o'clock. He was actually being led out of jail when he requested to be allowed to write a final letter. It was to William Wickham, Chief Secretary for Ireland, and extraordinarily it was a letter of thanks, exoneration and profound respect. It was written, Wickham noted, 'in a strong, firm hand without blot, correction or erasure'.[47] It thanked Wickham for 'The delicacy with which I feel with gratitude I have personally been treated'.[48] Emmet wrote that, had he been permitted to do so at the trial, he had intended to exonerate the government 'of any charge of remissness in not having previously detected a conspiracy which from its closeness I know was impossible to have done'. He acknowledged the mildness of Wickham's administration, but said that this circumstance 'under the peculiar situation of this country, perhaps rather accelerated my determination to make an effort for the overthrow of a government of which I do not think equally highly'.[49]

Less than two hours later, Emmet was hanged, his head hacked off with a butcher's knife and shown to the people as the 'head of a traitor'.

Wickham received the letter shortly after three o'clock, by which time the execution had taken place. It had an extraordinary effect on him. In a letter he wrote in 1835, enclosing a copy of Emmet's letter to a friend, he said that 'For the long space of 32 years it has been my constant companion.'[50] In fact, it changed his life dramatically. He resigned his office in December 1803, pleading ill health – but the real cause of his resignation was, as he said, 'more than suspected in higher quarters and amounted in its very nature to absolute exclusion'.[51] He had lost confidence in his government's policy in Ireland, and had come to believe that there was much justice in Emmet's cause. He knew that his resignation would 'place an almost insuperable barrier to my further advancement and condemn myself to a life of retirement, without a chance of any provision for my family, probably for the remainder of my days'. Indeed, apart from a brief spell in the Treasury during the short-lived pro-Emancipation government of Lord Grenville in 1806-7, he never held office again.

Despite this, he considered that Emmet had done him 'a direct and important service' by writing to him as he did. Wickham knew that he had made himself an outsider; that, in his own words, 'The manner in which I have suffered myself to be afflicted by this letter would be attributed to a sort of morbid sensibility rather than to its real cause.'[52] Emmet was famously fastidious about his epitaph, but even he might have accepted the words of Wickham, into whose character he seems to have had an insight. Wickham spoke of the 'almost intolerable' burden he felt from being 'compelled by the duty of my office to pursue to the death such men as Emmet and Russell', and of his depression at his status as an outsider after his resignation. Yet, he wrote in his 1835 letter, 'How light the strongest of such feelings must appear when compared to those which Emmet so nobly overcame even at his last hour, on his very march to the scaffold.'[53]

And, Wickham famously declared, 'Had I been an Irishman, I should most unquestionably have joined him.'[54]

Wickham was not merely a patriotic Englishman and politician. He had been engaged for fifteen years in the most secret aspect of English government: the maintenance of a vast intelligence network on the Continent, and a system of what he called 'preventative police' in England.[55] He was a spymaster par excellence. Though a loyal supporter of William Pitt who had wanted to resign when Pitt left office in 1801, he had been prevailed upon to go to Ireland by the new government simply because he was too important to lose. His attitude, and indeed his whole life, were radically changed by his brief encounter with Robert Emmet. The words that provoked this response from such a man were something more than mere 'attitudinizing'.

Notes

1. Contexts: Joyce, History, Law and England

1. Arthur Power, *Conversations with James Joyce*, ed. Clive Hart (Lilliput Press, 1999), p. 98.
2. T. S. Eliot, '*Ulysses*, Order and Myth', *The Dial*, November 1923, reprinted in *The Complete Prose of T. S. Eliot: The Critical Edition*, vol. 2, ed. Anthony Cuda and Ronald Schuchard (Johns Hopkins University Press and Faber & Faber, 2014).
3. Quoted in Michael Schmidt, *The Novel: A Biography* (Harvard University Press, 2014), p. 606.
4. *U* 18:1007–8.
5. *U* 7:1–2.
6. Joyce to Grant Richards, 5 May 1906. See James Joyce, *Letters*, vol. 2, ed. Richard Ellmann (Viking, 1966), p. 134.
7. Quoted in George D. Painter, *Marcel Proust: A Biography* (Chatto & Windus, 1959–65).
8. Declan Kiberd, *Ulysses and Us* (Faber & Faber, 2009), pp. 6, 7, 8.

9. *U* 1:638–49.

10. *U* 16:1148.

11. *U* 16:1160–65.

12. *U* 16:1169–71.

13. *U* 2:264.

14. Richard Ellmann, *James Joyce* (OUP, 1982), pp. 91–2.

15. There are, by my count, thirty-two separate law cases in *Ulysses*, eighteen of which are criminal trials. These vary from gruesome murders to police court cases, allegations of breaches of water regulations, etc. All the serious cases, and all but a handful of the others, are real-life ones. In *Finnegans Wake* the trial and 'Starchamber Quiry' into HCE's possible crime are major themes, and the Maamtrasna case, the Invincible Murders of 1882, the Parnell Commission and the Dreyfus case also feature.

16. Census of Ireland, 1901.

17. James Joyce, 'The Dead', in *Dubliners*, ed. Jeri Johnson (OUP, 2000), pp. 147ff.

18. *U* 16:74–5.

19. *U* 17:178.

20. James Joyce, 'A Peep into History', in *James Joyce: Occasional, Critical, and Political Writings*, ed. Kevin Barry (Oxford World Classics, 2000) (henceforth *OCPW*), p. 84.

21. Ibid., n. 7/ p. 307.

22. *U* 12:33–51.

23. James Joyce, *A Portrait of the Artist as a Young Man*, ed. Jeri Johnson (OUP, 2000), p. 12.

24. Power, *Conversations with James Joyce*, p. 65.

25. *U* 14:1459–60.

26. James Joyce, *Finnegans Wake*, ed. Seamus Deane (Penguin Classics, 2000), p. xiii.

27. Patrick Geoghegan, *King Dan* (Gill & Macmillan, 2008) and *The Liberator* (Gill & Macmillan, 2010). Also David George Boyce, *Nineteenth-Century Ireland* (Gill & Macmillan, 2005).

28. James Joyce, 'The Shade of Parnell', *Il Piccolo della Sera*,

16 May 1912. See Barry (ed.), *OCPW*, p. 196.

29. Joyce, *A Portrait of the Artist as a Young Man*, p. 25.

30. Ibid., p. 28.

31. Ibid., pp. 32–3.

32. *FW* 73:19.

33. On Healy, see Frank Callanan, *T. M. Healy* (Cork University Press, 1996).

34. *U* 16:77.

35. Power, *Conversations with James Joyce*, p. 99.

36. Seamus Heaney, 'Gravities', *Death of a Naturalist* (Faber & Faber, 2009).

37. Ellmann, *James Joyce*, p. 645. For the life of Joyce's father, see Peter Costello and John Wyse-Jackson, *John Stanislaus Joyce* (Fourth Estate, 1997).

38. *FW* 85:23–4.

39. *FW* 85:27.

40. *FW* 78:21.

41. 'Honorbright Merreytrickx' (*FW* 211:33).

42. See Vincent Deane, 'Bywaters and the Original Crime', in *Finnegans Wake: 'Teems of Times'*, ed. Andrew Treip, *European Joyce Studies* 4 (Rodopi, 1994), pp. 165–204.

43. By the Criminal Appeal Act 1907, 7 Edw. 7c 23.

44. For an account of these events see Ellmann, *James Joyce*, pp. 184–5.

45. *Dictionary of Irish Biography*, ed. James McGuire and James Quinn (Cambridge University Press/Royal Irish Academy, 2009), Gerald Fitzgibbon.

46. See Callanan, *T. M. Healy*.

47. Maurice Healy, *The Old Munster Circuit* (Michael Joseph, 1939).

48. *U* 9:624–5.

49. *U* 8:881–4 and 1151–5.

50. See the Appendix in Richard Ellmann, *Ulysses on the Liffey* (OUP, 1972), pp. 186 ff.

51. *U* 7:776; 836–7.

52. *U* 10:1176–282.

53. *U* 12:1621–34.

54. *U* 16:224–6.

55. *U* 18:996–9.

56. *U* 11:502–15.

57. *U* 18:374–9.

58. *U* 18:878–87.

59. *U* 18:769.

60. *U* 18:397.

61. *U* 18:397–405.

62. *U* 18:606–11.

63. *U* 2:268–72.

64. *U* 2:278–80.

65. *U* 2:242–54.

66. *U* 2:346–51.

67. *U* 1:666–8.

68. *U* 1:431–2.

69. *U* 1:480.

70. *U* 1:648–9.

71. *U* 1:434.

72. *U* 1.62–3.

73. *U* 1:51–3.

74. *U* 1:506.

75. *U* 12:1364–75.

76. *U* 15:4434–7.

77. *U* 15:4497.

78. *U* 15:4525–30.

79. *U* 15:4611–16.

80. *U* 15:4618–19.

81. *U* 15:4621–4.

82. *U* 15:4597–8.

83. *U* 15:4628–9.

84. *U* 15:4630.

2. Outrages in Ireland and England: Maamtrasna, Great Wyrley and Judicious Doubt

1. James Joyce, 'Ireland at the Bar' ('L'Irlanda alla Sbarra'), in Barry (ed.), *OCPW*, p. 147.

2. *FW* 57:16–61:35.

3. Barry (ed.), *OCPW*, pp. 145–7.

4. Ellmann, *James Joyce*, p. 197.

5. Ibid., p. 255.

6. Barry (ed.), *OCPW*, p. 145.

7. Ibid., p. 146.

8. Lord Spencer to Lord Granville, 17 September 1882, quoted in Myles Dungan, *Conspiracy: Irish Political Trials* (Royal Irish Academy, 2009), p. 139.

9. See Dungan, *Conspiracy*, and Jarlath Waldron, *Maamtrasna: The Murders and the Mystery* (Edmund Bourke Publishers, 1992). Much of the detailed account that follows is taken from these sources.

10. Joyce, 'Ireland at the Bar'.

11. Timothy Harrington, *The Maamtrasna Massacre: Impeachment of the Trials* (Dublin, 1884), p. 35.

12. Spencer to Harcourt, 23 November 1882 in Waldron, *Maamtrasna*, pp. 135–136.

13. Spencer to Queen Victoria, 11 December 1882, cited in Dungan, *Conspiracy*, p 156.

14. See Waldron, *Maamtrasna*, pp. 142–3.

15. Lord Spencer to Mr Justice Barry cited in Dungan, *Conspiracy*, p 156.

16. Harrington, *The Maamtrasna Massacre*.

17. T. M. Healy, *Letters and Leaders of My Day Vol. 1* (Thornton Butterworth, 1928), p 187.

18. Waldron, *Maamtrasna*, pp. 150–51.

19. *The Times*, November 1835.

20. Ronan Fanning, *Fatal Path: British Government and Irish Revolution 1910–1922* (Faber & Faber, 2013), p. 11.

21. Ibid.

22. Ibid., p. 28.

23. *U* 6:473–5.

24. *U* 8:419.

25. *U* 16:77.

26. For the Edalji background generally see Russell Miller, *The Adventures of Arthur Conan Doyle* (Harvill Secker, 2008), Chapter 15. For the trial and subsequent campaign see Gordan Weaver, *Conan Doyle and the Parson's Son* (Vanguard Press, 2006).

27. Letter from the Rev. Edalji, *The Times*, 16 August 1895.

28. The Crown told the jury that 'possibly the most important issue is – who wrote the anonymous letters?' *The Times*, 24 October 1903.

29. See, generally, *The Times*, 13 October 1905.

30. See *The Times*, 4 November 1903; 28 August 1907.

31. *The Times*, 29 January 1907: 'The matter merits further

public enquiry without delay.'

32. *The Times*, 11 February 1907. The Committee was 'to enquire into circumstances of the conviction of George Edalji for the Great Wyrley outrages'. There were three members, one of whom turned out to be a cousin of the Staffordshire Chief Constable.

33. *The Times*, 7 November 1934.

34. *FW* 85:22.

35. *U* 6:469ff. and *passim*.

36. *U* 5:62.

37. *U* 10:630.

38. See Miller, *The Adventures of Arthur Conan Doyle*, Chapter 15.

39. *FW* 57:16–17.

40. E.g. *FW* 361:20–21 and 86:32ff.

41. *FW* 104–25.

42. *FW* 104–7.

43. *FW* 107:23–32.

44. *FW* 107:36–108:1.

45. George Orwell, 'The Decline of the English Murder', *Tribune*, 15 February 1946.

46. Ken Whiteway, 'The Origins of the English Court of Criminal Appeal', *Canadian Law Library Review*, vol. 33 (2008), pp. 309–12.

47. *U* 2:7–8.

48. *U* 2:48–53.

49. *U* 2:54–5.

50. See *U* 16:1297–8.

51. (Palgrave Macmillan, 2011), p. 6.

52. Margot Norris, *James Joyce Quarterly*, vol. 44, no. 3 (Spring 2007), pp. 455–74.

53. Courts of Justice Act 1924, s. 8; Criminal Appeal (Northern Ireland) Act 1930, s. 1.

54. See, generally, Rosemary Pattenden, *English Criminal Appeals 1844–1944: Appeals Against Conviction and Sentence in England and Wales* (Clarendon Press, 1996).

55. See Whiteway, 'The Origins of the English Court of Criminal Appeal'.

3. Law, Crime and Punishment in Bloomsday Dublin

1. See, for example, *U* 16:1297–1306.
2. *U* 5:434–41.
3. See, for example, *U* 12:33–51.
4. *U* 12:1025.
5. *U* 6:997–8.
6. *U* 12:760–64.
7. *U* 8:406–13; 16:75–82 and *passim.*
8. *U* 6:470–71; 7:741–9; 17:792 and *passim.*
9. *U* 6:690ff.
10. J. J. Molloy features as a character in the *Aeolus* and *Cyclops* episodes.
11. *U* 6:231–6.
12. See, for example, *U* 8:1151ff.
13. *U* 15:4541–2.
14. *U* 18:234–45.
15. Ibid.
16. See R. Barry O'Brien, *Russell of Killowen* (Smith, Elder & Co., 1901) for an admiring life of Russell with details of his involvement with Mrs Maybrick's case.
17. See my 'A Gruesome Case: James Joyce's Dublin Murder', in *Librarians, Poets and Scholars: A Festschrift for Donall Ó Luanaigh*, ed. F. M. Larkin (Dublin, Four Courts Press, 2007).
18. See my article 'Murder Most Joyce' in *The Dubliner* (June 2006), p. 79.
19. Based on contemporary newspaper accounts and see my article cited above.
20. See *DIB* entry by Patrick Maume.
21. *U* 7:752.
22. Don Gifford with Robert J. Seidman, *Ulysses Annotated* (University of California Press, 2008), p. 145.
23. See the recitals in the bill which set out the history leading to the divorce.
24. See A. M. Sullivan, *Old Ireland* (Thornton Butterworth, 1927) and Healy, *The Old Munster Circuit.*

25. R. B. McDowell, *Land and Learning: Two Irish Clubs* (Lilliput Press, 1993).

26. Ellmann, *James Joyce*, pp. 108, 222, 225.

27. Hansard, vol. 56, cols 1018–24 (25 April 1898).

28. John Garvin, *James Joyce's Disunited Kingdom and the Irish Dimension* (Barnes & Noble, 1977).

29. *U* 12:1330–50 and *passim*.

30. *U* 16:79.

31. *U* 8:445–6.

32. *U* 8:449.

33. *U* 8:407–3 and 419–22.

34. Frederick Moir Bussy, *Irish Conspiracies: Recollections of John Mallon (the Great Irish Detective) and other Reminsences* (Everett, 1910).

35. *U* 16:1191–2.

36. *U* 16:1192–4.

37. *U* 16:1052–4.

38. *U* 16:1054–5.

39. *U* 5:546–7.

40. *U* 16:205–10.

41. *U* 12:33–51.

42. *U* 7:383; 12:1086–91.

43. *U* 7:698–704.

44. *U* 10:470–75.

45. C. P. Curran, 'Figures in the Hall', in C. Costello (ed.), *The Four Courts: 200 Years* (Dublin Incorporated Council for Law Reporting, 1996).

46. *U* 10:625–31.

47. *U* 16:964–8.

48. Rhadamantus, *Our Judges* (Dublin, 1890).

49. *U* 16:915–17.

50. *U* 12:762–4.

51. And 32 Vict. c. 144.

52. [1890] 25 LRIR 372.

53. [1905] 2 IR 1.

54. *U* 15:1640.

55. [1901] 2 KB 1.

56. *U* 12:1048–9.

57. *U* 16:1240–41.

58. *U* 11:901–2; 1078–80.

59. Joyce called this the 'Messianic Scene': *U* 15:859–954.

60. Joyce, *A Portrait of the Artist as a Young Man*, pp. 29ff.

61. Ellmann, *James Joyce*, p. 33.

62. *U* 16:1364–82.

63. *U* 16:1352–3.

64. *U* 16:1370–79.

65. *U* 16:1366–8.

66. *U* 16:1330–31.

67. *U* 16:1395–1400.

68. For an illuminating account of this subject see Frank Callanan, *The Parnell Crisis* (Cork University Press, 1992).

69. June Jordan, *Kitty O'Shea: An Irish Affair* (Sutton, 2005), p. 189.

70. Ibid.

71. *U* 15:945–6.

72. *U* 5:318ff.

73. *U* 5:434– 41.

74. [1875] 1R 10 CL104.

75. [1897] 2 IR 426.

76. [1906] 1 IR 247.

77. *U* 8:396; 16:74.

78. *U* 9:625.

79. *U* 8:1151–61.

80. *U* 12:1094–110.

81. Sir Frederick R. Falkiner, *Literary Miscellanies, collected with notes biographical and otherwise by his daughter May* (Hodges Figgis, 1909).

82. McDowell, *Land and Learning*, p. 77.

83. *U* 7:502–3.

84. *U* 7:794–808.

85. See Sullivan, *Old Ireland*, pp. 62, 63, 71.

86. [1938] IR 526.

87. McDowell, *Land and Learning*, p. 138.

88. *U* 8:881–4.

89. See his obituary in *Irish Law Times and Solicitors Journal*, 25 September 1937.

90. See his obituary in ibid., 10 March 1928.

91. Dodgson Hamilton Madden, *The Diary of Master William Silence: A Study of Shakespeare & of Elizabethan Sport* (Longmans, Green, 1897).

92. Sir Dunbar Plunket Barton, *Links between Ireland and Shakespeare* (Maunsel and Company, Ltd, 1919) and *Links between Shakespeare and the Law* (Faber & Gwyer Ltd, 1929).

93. Sir Dunbar Plunket Barton, *Timothy Healy: Memories and Anecdotes* (Faber & Faber, 1933).

94. Healy, *The Old Munster Circuit*, pp. 43–4.

95. Ibid., p. 36.

96. *U* 16:1069.

97. For Adams generally see Sullivan, *Old Ireland*, pp. 75ff., 93, 119ff.; Sullivan, *The Last Serjeant* (McDonald and Co., 1952), pp. 50–54; Healy, *The Old Munster Circuit*, pp. 260–61.

98. J. B. Lyons, *James Joyce and Medicine* (Dolmen Press, 1973); see also J. B. Lyons, *Thrust Syphilis Down to Hell and Other Rejoyceana* (Glendale Press, 1988).

99. Ellmann, *James Joyce*, p. 140 (law), pp. 97, 111, 113ff. (medicine).

100. Not in *Ulysses*.

101. *U* 7:836–7.

102. *U* 17 :787–94.

103. See Costello and Wyse-Jackson, *John Stanislaus Joyce*.

104. *U* 3:105–6.

105. Healy, *The Old Munster Circuit*, p. 279.

106. *U* 7:262–7.

107. See his obituary in *Irish Law Times*, 10 September 1910.

108. See A. Farmar, *Ordinary Lives* (A. and A. Farmar, 1991, 1995), pp. 22ff.

109. *U* 6:229–36.

110. *U* 7:292–305.

111. *U* 12:1022–30.

112. *U* 10:764–6.

113. *U* 12:455–64.

114. *U* 12:415–31.

115. *U* 12:525ff.

116. Ed. by James J. O'Neill (Martin Lester, n.d.).

117. *U* 12:500.

118. See, for example, scenes in Joyce, *A Portrait of the Artist as a Young Man*, pp. 50–58; and 'An Encounter' in *Dubliners*; *U* 12:1330–59; *U* 15:1013–21.

119. See *The Times*, letter from *In Partibus Maris*, 13 June 1904; response from George Bernard Shaw, 14 June 1904.

120. *U* 12:1354–9.

121. See, for example, s. 37 of the Larceny Act 1916, and s. 5(4)

of the (Irish) Public Safety (Emergency Powers) (No. 2) Act 1923, which authorized the whipping with a birch rod of anyone convicted of armed robbery.

4. 'A Gruesome Case'

1. *U* 14:960.
2. *U* 6:470.
3. *U* 7:744–5.
4. *U* 14:1010–37.
5. *U* 6:469–75.
6. *U* 6:476–82.
7. Joyce, *Dubliners*, 'Grace', p. 122.
8. Ibid., p. 124.
9. *Irish Times*, 23 October 1899.
10. Freeman's Journal, 23 October 1899.
11. Ellmann, *James Joyce*, p. 92.
12. *U* 15:760–63.
13. *U* 3:174–83.
14. *Daily Express*, 20 October 1899.
15. Ibid.
16. Ibid.
17. Ibid.
18. Ibid.
19. Ibid.
20. *U* 7:737–40.
21. *U* 7:750–80.
22. *U* 14:955–60.
23. *U* 7:800–01.
24. Michael J. F. McCarthy, *Five Years in Ireland, 1895–1900* (Hodges, 1901).
25. *U* 15:999–1001.
26. *U* 15:1009–10.
27. *U* 16:75–82.
28. T. M. Healy, *Letters and Leaders of My Day* (T. Butterworth, 1928).
29. *Irish Times*, 23 October 1899.
30. Ibid.
31. Constantine Curran, *Under the Receding Wave* (Gill & Macmillan, 1970).

5. The Mortgaged Life

1. *U* 18:45–6.
2. *U* 6:1–30.
3. *U* 17:1841–2.
4. *U* 5:468–9.

5. *U* 16:1250–53.

6. *U* 15:1210.

7. *U* 15:1232.

8. *U* 6:1–542.

9. *U* 6:564–6.

10. *U* 6:570–73.

11. *U* 6:535–6.

12. *U* 17:1855–67.

13. *U* 15:3837–43.

14. *U* 18:1279–83.

15. Joyce, *Dubliners*, 'Grace', p. 122.

16. *U* 12:760–75.

17. *U* 13:1225–31.

18. *Thom's Official Directory of the United Kingdom of Great Britain and Ireland* (Dublin: Thom's, 1904).

19. (1890) XXV LR IR 372.

20. *U* 5:127–37.

21. *Thom's Directory*, p. 1517.

22. *U* 6:311–12.

23. *U* 12:331–6.

24. *U* 7:601–2.

25. *U* 15:199–201.

26. For more on this, also see Jaya Savige, 'Underwriting *Ulysses*: Bloom, Risk, and Life Insurance in the Nineteenth Century', in John Nash (ed.), *Joyce in the Nineteenth Century* (Cambridge, 2013), pp. 77–94.

27. *Tit-Bits*, 11 June 1904, cover.

28. *Tit-Bits*, 4 June 1904. See Savige, 'Underwriting *Ulysses*', p. 77.

29. Daniel Defoe, *An Essay on Projects*, ed. Joyce D. Kennedy, Michael Seidel and Maximillian E. Novak (AMS Press, 1999), cited in Savidge, 'Underwriting *Ulysses*', p. 83.

30. Ibid., p. 84.

31. Barry Supple, *The Royal Exchange Assurance, 1720–1970* (Cambridge University Press, 1970), quoted in ibid., p. 86.

32. Clive Trebilcock, *Phoenix Assurance and the Development of British Insurance* (Cambridge University Press, 1985), vol. 1, quoted in ibid.

33. Quoted in ibid., p. 87.

34. Trebilcock, quoted in ibid., p. 87.

35. *U* 6:307.

36. *U* 6:564.

37. *U* 6:537–9.

38. *U* 10:955–65.

39. *U* 10:1–6.

40. *U* 7:262–7.

41. *U* 8:939–41.

42. *U* 8:960–68.

43. *U* 12:775–9.

44. *U* 18:1222–7.

45. *U* 8:184–6.

46. *U* 15:758–60.

47. *U* 18:381–2.

48. *U* 18:1271–9.

49. *U* 10:625.

50. *U* 9:671.

51. *Thom's Directory*, 1900.

52. at p. 711 *Washington et al* v *Glackskey Ltd* (1927) 521 US 711.

53. (2nd edn, 1979), p. 711fn.

54. *Harvey* v *The Ocean Accident*, p. 37.

55. *U* 17:1881.

56. *U* 6:335–42.

57. *U* 6:343–9.

58. *U* 6:359–64.

59. *U* 6:527–32.

60. *U* 17:1903–4.

61. *U* 17:1930–32.

6. Political Violence: Emmet and the Invincibles

1. Geoghegan, *Robert Emmet: A Life* (Gill & Macmillan, 2002), pp. 253–4.

2. *U* 16:1055–72.

3. William John Fitz-Patrick, *The Sham Squire; and The Informers of 1798* (W. B. Kelly, 1872), p. 208.

4. Treason Act 1351.

5. Ian J. Gentles, *Oxford Dictionary of National Biography sub tit.* Harrison, Thom's.

6. Forfeiture Act 1870, s. 31.

7. Thomas Moore (1779–1852), Irish poet, singer, songwriter and entertainer, wrote *Irish Melodies*, 'The Minstrel Boy', 'The Last Rose of Summer' and many other songs and poems, and edited Byron's letters.

8. *U* 10:718ff.

9. *U* 10:761–3.

10. *U* 10:764–6.

11. Marianne Elliott, *Robert Emmet: The Making of a Legend* (Profile Books, 2003).

12. *U* 12:479–83.

13. 'Written Immediately after Reading the Speech of Robert Emmet', *Poetical Works*, vol. 1 (Longman, Green & Co., 1871).

14. 'On Robert Emmet's Grave', Edward Dowden, *The Life of Percy Bysshe Shelley* (Kegan Paul, Trench, 1887).

15. See Dr R. R. Madden, *The Life and Times of Robert Emmet* (1847) and *The United Irishmen* (2nd edn, 1860); Lord John Russell, *Memoirs Journals and Correspondence of Thomas Moore* (8 vols, 1853–6); Elliott, *Robert Emmet* and, especially, Geoghegan, *Robert Emmet*.

16. *Dictionary of Irish Biography* *sub.tit.* Emmet, Robert.

17. Saulsbury to Lincoln, 7 February 1865, *Lincoln Papers at the Library of Congress, series one.* This is quoted in Geoghegan's *Robert Emmet*.

18. *Uncollected Prose of W. B. Yeats*, ed. John P. Frayne and Colton Johnson (Macmillan, 1975).

19. P. H. Pearse, *How Does She Stand? Three Addresses* (Maunsel, 1915).

20. R. F. Foster, *The Irish Story* (Allen Lane, 2001), *Irish Times*, 21 September, 2003.

21. *DIB* entry, *supra*.

22. Ibid.

23. Ibid.

24. See Joseph Denieffe, *A Personal Narrative of the Irish Revolutionary Brotherhood* (The Gael Publishing Company, 1906), pp. vii–x.

25. V. A. C. Gatrell, *The Hanging Tree: Execution and the English People* (OUP, 1994), p. 87.

26. *U* 6:973–8.

27. *U* 10:769–71.

28. *U* 11 *passim*, esp. 569–1082.

29. *U* 11:1274–5.

30. *U* 11:1276–80.

31. *U* 11:1284–94.

32. See *U* 11:1131–41.

33. *U* 12:523–4.

34. *U* 12:525–678.

35. *U* 12:525–31.

36. *U* 12:533–4.

37. *U* 12:542–3.

38. *U* 12:551–2.

39. *U* 12:554.

40. *U* 12:562.

41. *U* 12:614–24.

42. *U* 12:624–6.

43. *U* 12:626–35.

44. *U* 12:547–51.

45. *U* 12:635–9.

46. *U* 12:658–69.

47. Joyce, 'Fenianism: The Last Fenian' (originally published in Italian, 1907), in Barry (ed.), *OCPW*, pp. 138–9.

48. Ibid., p. 139.

49. Ellmann, *James Joyce*, p. 107.

50. *U* 8:457–61.

51. *U* 3:216–64.

52. *DIB sub tit.* Stephens, James.

53. *U* 4:490–91.

54. *U* 12:880–82.

55. *U* 15:1533.

56. Senan Molony, *The Phoenix Park Murders* (Mercier, 2006); James Fairhall, *James Joyce and the Question of History* (CUP, 1993); Tom Corfe, *The Phoenix Park Murders* (Hodder & Stoughton, 1968).

57. Molony, *The Phoenix Park Murders*, p. 174.

58. *U* 5.375–84.

59. *U* 7:632–3.

60. *U* 7:639–40.

61. *U* 7:641–2.

62. *U* 7:697–704.

63. *U* 16:320–25.

64. *U* 16:1048–54.

65. *U* 16:1071–3.

66. Molony, *The Phoenix Park Murders*, p. 279.

67. *U* 7:679–80.

68. See Sullivan, *Old Ireland*, pp. 75ff., 93, 119ff.; Sullivan, *The Last Serjeant* (McDonald and Co., 1952), pp. 50–54; Healy, *The Old Munster Circuit*, pp. 260–61.

69. A. M. and D. B. Sullivan, 'God Save Ireland'.

70. *U* 12:455–64.

7. Attempts to Suppress *Ulysses*

1. Shane Leslie, review of *Ulysses*, *Quarterly Review* (October 1922), pp. 219–34. Reprinted in Robert Deming, *James Joyce: The Critical Heritage*, vol. 1: *1907–1927* (Routledge & Kegan Paul, 1970), pp. 206–11, 211.
2. Hansard 1803–2005, Fifth Series (Lords), vol. 146, House of Lords Debates, 25 June 1857, p. 329.
3. [1867–68] LR 2QB 360.
4. Ibid., p. 370.
5. Hansard 1803–2005, Fifth Series (Lords), vol. 146, House of Lords Debates, 25 June 1857, p. 329.
6. Vol. 1, 1897.
7. *The Spectator*, 20 October 1928.

8. The American Trials of *Ulysses*, 1919–1933

1. Paul Vanderham, *James Joyce and Censorship* (Macmillan, 1998), p. 111.
2. John McCourt, *The Years of Bloom: James Joyce in Trieste, 1904–1920* (Lilliput Press, 2000).
3. *U* 3:1.
4. Ellmann, *James Joyce*, p. 421.
5. Ibid., p. 421.
6. (Random House, 1977), p. 90.
7. 258 NY 451.
8. Michael Moscato and Leslie LeBlanc (eds), 'The United States of America v. One Book Entitled Ulysses by James Joyce: Documents and Commentary: a 50-year Retrospective' (Maryland, 1984), p. 45; Morris Ernst, 'Reflections on the *Ulysses* Trial and Censorship', in *James Joyce Quarterly*, vols 3–4 (1965), p. 3.
9. 231 NY 1.
10. Paul Vanderham, *James Joyce*

and Censorship: the trials of
Ulysses (New York, 1977, 2016
edition), p. 223.

11. Moscato and LeBlanc, p. 185.

12. Ernst, 'Reflections', p. 3.

9. 'This Disgusting Book': Ulysses in England

1. British National Archives, Home Office papers (HO) 144/20071; Ian Pinder, *Joyce* (London, 2004), p. 101.

2. BNA HO 144/20071; Celia Marshik, *British Modernism and Censorship* (Cambridge, 2006), p. 160.

3. BNA HO 144/20071.

4. Shane Leslie, review of *Ulysses*, pp. 219–34.

5. BNA HO 144/20071.

6. U 18:584–95.

7. George Orwell, *An Age Like This* (Secker & Warburg, 1968).

8. BNA HO 144/20071.

9. FR Leavis, *Letters in Criticism* (London, 1974), p. 98.

10. Of 18 September 1933.

11. Joyce, *Letters*, vol. 3, p. 295.

12. Ellmann, *James Joyce*, p. 693.

Appendix: The Trial of Robert Emmet

1. Published by John Murray.

2. Geoghegan, *Robert Emmet*, p. 252.

3. Elliott, *Robert Emmet*, p. 69.

4. MacDonagh, *The Viceroy's Post-Bag* (London, 1904), p. 335.

5. Elliott, *Robert Emmet*, p. 79.

6. M. R. O'Connell (ed.), *The Correspondence of Daniel O'Connell* (8 vols, IMC, 1972–80), vol. 3, p. 323.

7. MacDonagh, *The Viceroy's Post-Bag*, p. 156.

8. William Wickham to Pole Carew, 28 August 1803 (MacDonagh, *The Viceroy's Post-Bag*, p. 339).

9. Ibid., pp. 339–40.

10. Ibid., p. 339.

11. Ibid., p. 340.

12. Ibid., p. 397.

13. Ibid.

14. Ibid., p. 347.

15. Ibid., pp. 348–9.

16. Ibid., p. 349.

17. Ibid.

18. Ibid.

19. Ibid., p. 351.

20. Ibid., p. 350.

21. Ibid., p. 352.

22. Ibid., p. 361.

23. Ibid., p. 391.

24. Ibid., p. 393.

25. Elliott, *Robert Emmet*, p. 92.

26. PM Geoghegan, *Robert Emmet: a Life* (Dublin, 2002), p. 239.

27. Report of Leonard McNally, 12 September 1803 (MacDonagh, *The Viceroy's Post-Bag*, p. 390).

28. Geoghegan, *Robert Emmet*, p. 221.

29. Ibid., p. 230.

30. Elliott, *Robert Emmet*, p. 79.

31. Geoghegan, *Robert Emmet*, p. 239.

32. MacDonagh, *The Viceroy's Post-Bag*, p. 398.

33. *Trial of Robert Emmet upon an indictment for high treason* (London, 1803), p. 103.

34. Geoghegan, *Robert Emmet*, p. 235.

35. Geo. 3 c. 7.

36. (CUP, 2014), p. 278.

37. Geoghegan, *Robert Emmet*, Introduction.

38. R. F. Foster, *Modern Ireland 1600–1972* (Penguin, 1989), p. 286.

39. *The Irish Times*, 24 July 2003.

40. Geoghegan, *Robert Emmet*, Appendix C.

41. Ibid., p. 250.

42. Ibid., p. 252.

43. Ibid.

44. Ibid., p. 253.

45. Ibid., p. 254.

46. Ibid., p. 266.

47. Public Record Office of Northern Ireland (PRONI), T/2627/5/Z/13.

48. Robert Emmet to William Wickham, 20 September 1803 (BL Add. MS 35742, f. 196).

49. Ibid.
50. PRONI, T/2627/5/Z/12.
51. Geoghegan, *Robert Emmet*, p. 271.
52. PRONI, T/2627/5/Z/18.
53. William Wickham to Armstrong, 20 November 1835 (PRONI, T/2627/5/Z/12).
54. Ibid.
55. See Elizabeth Sparrow, *Secret Service* (Boydell Press, 1999).

Image credits

Index

All places are in Dublin unless otherwise named.

Abbot, Charles 315
Act for the Further Amendment of the
  Administration of the Criminal Law
  (1848) 83
Act of Union (1800) 21, 23–4, 309
Adams, Richard 118, 233–4
Aeolus (episode)
  action in 8
  characters in 96, 118–19, 120, 122
  Childs trial 144–6
  'eloquence' 34–5
Allen, William 235
Anderson, Margaret 254, 256, 257, 258
Angell, John 333
Anglican Church 85
Arch, The (pub) 172
Artane (village) 177, 179
Ashbourne, Lord Edward 34, 99, 113,
  121
Asquith, H. H. 67

Atlas, Nicholas 270
Attorney General v *Delaney* (1875) 112
Attorney General v *Hall and Byrne*
  (1897) 112

Barnacle, Nora 22
Barnes, Julian 74
Barry, Justice 61, 63
Barton, Sir Dunbar Plunket 95, 117
Bengal Terrace, Glasnevin 128, 129,
  147, 155–6
Bergin, Alf (character) 172
Birkenhead, Frederick Edwin, 1st Earl
  of 298–305
Blackstone, Sir William 192–4
Blackwell, Sir Ernley 296
Bloom, Leopold (character)
  Aeolus 156
  background 6–8, 35
  Calypso 173, 226
  Circe 46, 110, 136, 154, 164, 183, 226
  Dignam's funeral 129–30, 163–4, 212
  Eumaeus 12–13, 108–10, 154

father 187, 199–202
freemasonry 182
informers 224
Invincibles 230
Ithaca 166
on James Fitzharris 203–4
and Joe Brady 235–6
Lestrygonians 34, 113, 180
and Martha Clifford 94, 163, 214, 229
religion 111–12, 124–5
and Robert Emmet 213–14
Sirens 107–8
Bloom, Molly (character)
background 6–7, 37–41
and Blazes Boylan 13, 184, 214
and Florence Maybrick 35–6
freemasonry 182
and Paddy Dignam 167, 184
See also Penelope (episode)
Bloom, Rudolph (character) 199–202
Bloomsday 36, 41, 129, 274
Bodkin, Sir Archibald 244, 284–7, 289–6
Bodley Head 217, 284, 300, 302
Boer War 39
Bolton, George 59, 64
Borden, Lizzy 158–9
Borges, Jorge Luis 4
Bowdler, John 246
Boylan, Blazes (character) 8, 184, 214
Brady, Joe 234, 235–6
Brady, Newton 58
Breen, Denis (character) 106
Brennan, Mr 189
Bridgeman (character) 169–71, 185
Bright, Honor 20, 32, 141
British Ireland 20–30
Brooke, Gerald 97
Brooks Divorce Act (1886) 97

Brooks Thomas (building firm) 128, 133
Burke, Colonel Richard O'Sullivan 223, 225
Burke, Thomas 17, 20, 222, 227
Burrowes, Peter 323, 324, 325
Bushe, Charles Kendal 152
Bushe, Seymour
affair 97
background 92, 96, 141, 151–2
Childs trial 34, 128–9, 135
speeches 118–19, 144, 150–1, 153–4
Byrne, Davy 180

Caesar, Julius 79
Calypso (episode) 226
Campbell, John, 1st Baron 245, 246–7
Carey, James 228–30
Carr, Private (character) 46, 47–8
Carson, Edward 99, 298
Casement, Roger 299
Casey family 57, 62
Casey, John (character) 25–7
Casey, Joseph 223
Casey, Patrick 59, 62, 64, 223, 226
Casey, Tom 59
Cassidy, James 156–7
Cavendish, Lord Frederick 222, 227
Censorship Board, Ireland 280, 305
Cerf, Bennett A. 261, 265, 266–7
Chatterton, Hedges Eyre 111, 120–1, 180
Childs, Alexander 141
Childs, Mrs (Samuel's wife) 153
Childs, Rev. Edmund 131, 141
Childs, Samuel 14, 16
See also Childs trial
Childs, Thomas 128, 131–4, 149, 159
Childs trial 33, 76, 86, 99, 127–62
Churchill, Randolph 116
Circe (episode) 45–9

action in 8, 107–8
Bloom in 110, 136, 154, 164, 183
characters in 106, 167
punishments 124
circumstantial evidence 71, 86, 137–8, 144, 159
Citizen (character) 45, 46–7, 100, 208, 213, 216
Clancy, 'Long John' 140
Clarke, Sir Edward 99
Clerkenwell Prison 223, 287
Clifford, Martha 94, 163, 214, 229, 230
Clongowes Wood College, Co. Kildare 21, 112, 120
Clowry, Margaret 95, 100
Cockburn, Lord Chief Justice Alexander 249, 250
Coleman, Sam 255, 269–70, 270–1
Colgan, Terence 327
Collector of Customs (US) 259, 267–8, 273
Collins, Michael 210
Common Law Procedure Act (1856) 195
Conan Doyle, Sir Arthur 52, 65, 72–3, 76
Concannon, Henry 58
Conmee, Fr. John S. J. 179
Conroy, Gabriel (character) 17
Corcoran, Richard 147, 158
Court of Admiralty 104
Court of Appeals
English 32, 78, 82–5
Irish 186, 196–9
US 242, 254, 271
Crawford, Myles 115, 118
Creed Meredith, Justice James 116
Criminal Appeal Act (1907) 82
Criminal Evidence Act (1898) 98–9, 153

Criminal Justice (Evidence) Act (1924) 153
Criminal Law Amendment Act (1885) 101–2
Criminal Law (Suicide) Act (1993) 191–2
Croppy Boy (ballad) 215
Cunniam, Captain Thomas 156–7
Cunningham, Martin (character)
background 168
civil servant 130
Dignam family 69, 167, 177, 178–9
Dignam, Paddy 200
on the law 129, 198
Curran, Constantine 162
Curran, John Adye 236
Curran, John Philpot 118, 308, 314, 321–3
Curran, Sarah
background 207
Cyclops 216
and Emmet 219–20, 309, 311, 319, 321–5
Cusack, John 100
Cusack, Michael 100
Customs Consolidation Act (1876) 284
Customs Court case, US 259–61
Cutting, Bronson 272
Cyclops (episode)
action in 8, 208
characters in 102, 113–14, 168
Citizen 45, 100, 216, 226
and Robert Emmet 206, 213
themes in 23, 80, 105, 123–4, 140, 181

Daily Express 18, 135, 151
Daily Telegraph 72
Dante (character) 25–7
David Drimmie & Sons 182

Davis, Lieutenant Samuel B. 209
Davis, Thomas 17
Dead, The (short story) 17
Deane, Seamus 23
Deasy, Garrett (character) 41–3
Dedalus, Mary (character) 26
Dedalus, Simon (character) 26, 38, 157, 165
Dedalus, Stephen (character)
    Aeolus 119, 145–6
    background 6–8, 41–4, 79
    Circe 46
    Eumaeus 12–13, 108, 154, 232
    Proteus 136–7
    Telemachus 11–12
Defoe, Daniel 174
Delaney v *Burke* (1904) 107
Dempsey, Superintendent 149
Derwent, Lord 280
Dictionary of Irish Biography 84, 210–11
Dignam, Mrs 167, 170
Dignam, Paddy (character)
    alcohol 176, 177, 184
    death 164, 177
    funeral 122, 129–30, 163–4, 212
    insurance 105, 106, 169
Dignam, Patrick (son) 179
Dodd, Reuben J. 113–14, 120
Dodd, Serjeant 131, 142–4
Dreyfus, Captain Alfred 32, 72–3, 76–7
Dublin Castle 130, 168, 227, 308, 309
Dublin City Commission 229, 310
Dublin Metropolitan Police (DMP)
    background 100–2
    Childs trial 76, 133, 148, 149, 154–5, 158
    Henry Flower's trial 92, 95

Dubliners 94, 130, 168, 178, 255, 256
Dying Declaration 57, 58, 62, 100

Edalji, George 20, 29, 70–4, 74, 82, 86
Edalji, Rev. Shapurju 70, 74
Egan, Kevin (character) 223, 224, 225
Egoist Press 283
Eldon, Lord 330, 331
Eliot, T. S. 3–4, 301
Elliott, Marianne 207, 308
Ellis, Dr Havelock 250, 302
Ellmann, Richard 53, 135, 255, 256–7, 274
Emancipation, Catholic 24
Emmet, Christopher Temple 337
Emmet, Robert 28, 123–4, 203–16, 219–20, 307–41
Emmet, Dr Thomas 213
Emmet, Thomas Addis 213, 333, 335
Ennis, Edward 62–3
Ernst, Morris 255, 260–1, 265, 270–1, 275, 281
Erskine, Thomas 330
Et Tu, Healy (poem) 108
Eumaeus (episode)
    action in 79, 104
    characters in 12–13, 118, 154, 232–3
    Parnell trial 108–10
Evening Telegraph 107, 118, 145, 156, 164, 231
Eyre, Chief Justice 330

Falkiner, Sir Frederick 34, 113–15, 120, 121
Fanning, Ronan 67
Farrell, Patrick 316, 327–8
Federal District Court, US 4, 254
Fenianism 84, 221–3, 226–7, 234
Festy King trial 32

Finnegans Wake
  cases in 20, 75
  handwritten letters 76–7
  'heliopolis' 27
  themes in 19, 28, 31–2, 65, 78, 137
Fitz-Patrick, W. J. 204
Fitzgibbon, Lord Justice Gerald 112, 115–17
Fitzgibbon, Gerald (jnr) 116
FitzGibbon, John 328
Fitzharris, James 118, 204, 231, 233
Fitzpatrick, W. J. 329
Fleming, John 327
Flower, Henry 20, 33, 94–6, 98, 99
Flynn, Nosey (character) 106, 180–1
Forster, William Edward 'Buckshot' 227
Foster, Roy 332
Four Courts 103, 212–13
Foyles 301
France, Anatole 10
Free State Offensive, Irish 103
Freeman's Journal, The 127
Friends of the Emerald Isle 217

Gabler, Hans Walter 217
Galway, Ireland 104
Gannon, Bridget 95–6, 99–100
Gardner, Lieutenant Stanley 40
Garryowen (song) 48
Garvin, John 100
Gautier, Théophile 271
Gavan Duffy, Colum 96–7
General Life Insurance Company 171
Geoghegan, Patrick 209, 210
George III, King 24, 331
Geraghty, Michael (character) 102
Gibraltar 40–1
Gibson, Andrew 87
Gibson, Justice John 99–100

Gibson, Rev. 153
Gilbert, Stewart 276
Giltrap, James 155–6
Gladstone, William 16, 24, 110, 227
Glanmire Station, Cork 190
Glasnevin Cemetery 129
God Save Ireland (ballad) 234–5
Godfrey, Sir Edmund 19
Grattan, Henry 323
Great Wyrley Outrage 29, 51, 68–77, 87
Green Street Criminal Court 14, 98, 114, 137–8, 310
Greenbaum, Wolff & Ernst (New York) 253–4, 259, 265–71, 272–3
Gunther, Professor Gerard 278

Hades (episode)
  action in 8
  characters in 122, 164
  Childs trial 69, 144
  law in 186, 198
  Shakespeare in 137
Haines (character) 11–12, 23, 43, 129
Hall, Radclyffe 260
Halsey v New York Society (1922) 271
Hamlet (Shakespeare) 137, 145
Hand, Judge Augustus 4, 262, 278–9
Hand, Judge Learned 262, 263–4, 278–9
Hanily, Sergeant 96
Hardwicke, Elizabeth, Countess of 311–12
Hardwicke, Philip, 3rd Earl of 310, 312, 317
Hardy, Thomas 330
Harrington, Timothy 33, 62, 96, 97–8, 223
Harris, Sidney 284, 287, 288, 290–1, 296
Hartington, Lord 110

Harvey, Charles Meade 103–5, 106, 186–91
Harvey v the Ocean Accident and Guarantee Corporation (1905) 103–5, 186–91
Harvey, William 188, 195
Haynes, Mrs 198
HCE (character) 32, 65, 76, 77
Healy, Maurice 120
Healy, Tim
  background 27
  and Bushe 119
  cases 96, 99, 141, 148, 150–1
  memoirs 62–3, 159–60
  on William Kenny 118
Heaney, Seamus 31
Heap, Jane 254, 256, 258
Henderson, Mr 300, 301–2
Herbert, Dr S. 299–300
Herzog, Moses (character) 102
Heymoolen v United States (1928) 259–61
Hicklin, Benjamin 242, 248–9
High Court 186, 196
Hilferty, Mr 134, 150
Holmes, Lord Justice 196, 197–9
Home Office 284, 297
Home Rule 24, 28, 67, 156, 234
Horner's Weekly 173–4

Il Piccolo della Sera 52–3
Invincibles, Irish National 220–37, 230–1
Ireland 5, 11, 15–17, 23
Irish Christian Brothers 177–8
Irish Independent 16
Irish Parliamentary Party 27, 98, 109
Irish Privy Council 318–21
Irish Republican Brotherhood 223, 226

Irish revolution 221, 226
Irish Times 129, 132, 161, 332
Irish Weekly Independent and Nation 182–3
Isaacs, Rufus 119
Ithaca (episode) 119, 166

Jesuits 178–9, 303
Johnson, Lindsay 73–4
Joy, Henry, Chief Baron 103
Joyce family 155, 165
Joyce, John 56
Joyce, John Stanislaus (father) 31, 33, 34, 98, 120, 156, 223
Joyce, May 178
Joyce, Myles
  case against 57, 62, 63
  conviction 60
  execution 54, 86
  innocence 28, 56, 64, 66
Joyce, Patrick 59, 62, 64
Joynson-Hicks, Sir William 243, 244, 250–1, 287–8

Kelleher, Corney 48
Kenny, Justice William 17, 117–18, 161
Kernan, Tom 123, 178, 205, 206–7, 212
Keyes, Alexander 156, 157
Kiberd, Professor Declan 10, 30
Kiernan, Barney (character) 123, 168, 208
Kilmainham Jail 211, 315, 339
Kilwarden, Lord 318, 337
Kipling, Rudyard 39
Knowles, Enoch 74

Lady Cairns (ship) 104–5
Lady Chatterley's Lover 255
Lambert, Ned (character) 120, 165, 179–80

Land Act (1903) 98
Lane, John 301
Larkin, Michael 235
Lawrence, D. H. 272, 297
Lawrence, George 195
Lawson, James 115
Leavis, Dr F. R. 290, 294–5
Lee, River 190, 195
Leinster Street Baths 164
Léon, Paul 268
Leslie, Shane 287
Lestrygonians (episode) 34, 113, 180–1, 182, 257
libel, and publication 106–7
Liberal Unionist Party 28, 110
Life Assurance Act (1774) 174–5
Limerick, Bishop of 118, 234
Lindey, Alexander 261, 266, 268–9, 272
L'Irlanda alla Sbarra (article) 52, 53–5, 64–6
Little Review, The 254, 256–7, 283
Lloyd George, David 27
London Corresponding Society 330
Lord Chancellor of Ireland 34, 99, 121
Lord Lieutenant of Ireland 55–6, 61–2, 123, 207, 310
Lotus Eaters (episode) 163–4, 171–2
Lyons, Dr J. B. 118

Maamtrasna murders 28, 53–4, 55–64, 76, 86
Mabillon, Jean 19
MacCarthy, Desmond 300
McCourt, John 255
McCoy, C. P. 171–2
MacDonagh, Michael 309, 310–11
McDowell, Professor R. B. 97
MacEvilly, Dr John 64
McHugh, Fr Michael 60, 115

McNally, Leonard
  cross-examination 328
  Dublin Castle 309, 324
  Emmet trial 308, 315, 316–17, 325–6
  pension 328–9
  secret dispatches 322
McNally, Leonard (jnr) 323
McNevin, William 321
Madden, Honourable Dodgson Hamilton 117
Madden, Dr Richard Robert 124, 206, 308, 333
Mallon, John 101, 102
Mallon, Superintendent 236
Manton, Judge Martin 262–3, 278
Maolra Joyces 56–9, 60, 62
Marsden, Alexander 318
Masses, bequests for 111–12
Maybrick, Florence 20, 32, 36, 86, 93–4
McNeill, J. G. Swift 124
Mee, Arthur 297
Menton, John Henry (character) 92, 165
Meyerbeer, Giacomo 214
Mona (ship) 104–5
Moore, Roderick 176
Moore, Thomas 206, 208, 209, 216, 325
Moran, D. P. 13
Morley, John 110, 116–17, 234
Morning Post, The 302
Mosley, Geoffrey 301
Mountjoy Prison 135, 139
Moyers, Sir George 171
Mulligan, Buck 43–4
Munster and Leinster Bank 171
Murphy, William Martin 16
Murray, Josephine 155
Myers, Kevin 332

Nausicaa (episode) 169, 257, 258, 283
Nestor (episode) 8, 13
New Century Loan Society 134, 150
New York World 231
Nicolson, Harold 300
Nighttown 107, 108
Nolan, Emer 48
Nolan, John Wyse 226
Norbury, Lord John 204, 206, 314–15, 325, 334, 336–8
Norris, Margot 80–1
Northern Ireland 15
Norton (Childs witness) 148–9
Noyes, Alfred 298–9

O'Brien Institute for Destitute Children 177–8
O'Brien, Michael 235
O'Brien, Sir Peter 58, 63
Obscene Publications Bill (1857) 245–50
O'Callaghan, Felix 92, 122
O'Conghaile v *Wallace* (1938) 116
O'Connell, Daniel 24, 66–7, 314
O'Donnell, Patrick 229
Odyssey (Homer) 3, 164
O'Grady, Mr 189
O'Grady, Standish 318, 320, 321, 324
O'Hagan, Thomas 103
O'Hanlon v *Logue* (1906) 112
Oldfield, Roger 74
O'Loughlen, Sir Michael 103
O'Molloy, J. J. (character) 92, 106, 110, 122, 145, 154
Order for Destruction 246, 249
Ormond Hotel 38, 107, 213
Orwell, George 78, 138, 141–2, 289
O'Shea, Katherine 'Kitty' 20, 25, 27, 108–10

Oxen of the Sun (episode) 8, 22–3, 128–9, 146–7

Palles, Christopher 111, 115
Parliament, English 83
Parnell, Charles Stewart 5, 17, 24–5, 94, 108–10, 227
Parnell Commission 20
Pearse, Patrick 210
Pearson, Chief Constable R. T. 291, 292
Pelican Insurance Company 175
Penelope (episode) 8, 36, 39–41, 182, 284–6, 288–9
Penguin Books 255
People v *Wendling* (1933) 270
Pepys, Samuel 333
Petrie, James 211
Philbin, Anthony 59, 64
Phoenix Fire Office 175, 176
Phoenix Park murders 32, 65, 101, 222, 227–8, 230–4
Piggott, Richard 94
Pitt, William (the Younger) 23–4, 330, 341
Plunket, William Conyngham 103, 152, 313, 333–4
Plurabelle, Anna Livia 76–7
Policies of Assurance Act (1867) 105, 166–7, 170–1, 181, 185
Popish Plot 19
Porter, Sir Andrew 117, 121
Porter, Charles 290
Portrait of the Artist as a Young Man, A 25–7, 108
Pound, Ezra 256
Power, Mr (character) 129, 130–1, 151, 172, 199–201
Prezioso, Roberto 52
Protestantism 16–17, 23, 141

Proteus (episode) 120, 136–7, 224, 257
Proust, Marcel 10
Punch (journal) 66
Pyrrhus 79

Queen's Hotel, Ennis 187, 199
Queen's University, Belfast 117
Queensbury, Marquis of 99
Queenstown Yacht Club (Cobh) 187–9
Quinn, John 258

R v Bywaters and Thompson (1922)
    20, 32
R v Childs (1899) 127–62
R v Frederick Seddon (1912) 20
R v Hicklin (1868) 242, 248–51, 262,
    263, 276–7
Random House 253, 261, 265, 275
Redesdale, Lord 318
Redmond, John 98
Rehnquist, William 192–3
Reith, Lord 300
Ridgeway, William 332–3
Roberts, Frederick, 1st Earl 39
Roman Catholicism
    death 111–12, 172
    emancipation 5, 23–4
    religious divide 15–17, 85, 141, 248–9
Ronen, Ruth 80–1
Royal Exchange Assurance 175
Royal Irish Constabulary 92
RTÉ Television 315
Rumbolt (character) 217–18
Russell, Sir Charles 94

St Andrew's Church 111, 229
St Catherine's Church 205
St Michan's Church 212
St Patrick's Cathedral 103–4

St Peter's Church 213
Salisbury, Robert, 3rd Marquess of 67
Saulsbury, Willard 209
Scott, Henry 248, 249
Scottish Widows Fund (Mutual) Life
    Assurance Society 169–70, 177
Scylla and Charybdis (episode)
    action in 8
    Shakespeare in 117, 121, 137, 187
    themes in 34
Second Circuit, United States Court of
    Appeals for the 4, 262, 278–80, 301
Seddon, Frederick 37, 92–3
Seward, Professor Albert 292, 294
Shakespeare and Company 283
Shakespeare, William 42, 117, 137, 187,
    246, 273
Shaw, George Bernard 124
She is Far from the Land (ballad) 208
Sheehy, Eugene 135
Sheil, Richard Lalor 103
Sirens (episode) 38, 107–8
Sirr, Major Henry 319, 322, 325
Smith, F. E. 73
Somervell, Sir Donald (David) 302, 304
Special Criminal Court 138
Spencer, John, 5th Earl 55–6, 61–2
Spenser, Lord 229
Stamp Duties (Ireland) Act (1842) 111
Stephen, Sir James Fitzjames 84–5
Stephen, Leslie 84
Stephens, James 221, 222, 223, 224,
    226
Stephens, Sir James Fitzjames 331
Stephenson, P. R. 242–3
Stopes, Dr Marie 260, 275
Sumner, John S. 254, 258, 283
Supreme Court, US 279, 281
Swan, Rev. Brother William 178

Tariff Act (1922) 259, 268, 271–2
Taylor, John F. 119
Telemachus (episode) 8, 11–12
Thomas Street 123, 205, 206, 318, 327, 337
Tilson, Judge 259–60
Times Literary Supplement 290, 297
Times, The 73, 74, 84, 94, 124
Tit-Bits (magazine) 173
Todd Burns & Company 178, 180
Treason Acts 205, 330–1
Trench, Samuel Chenevix 43
Trew v Railway Passenger Assurance Company (1861) 197
Trieste, Italy 22, 33, 53
Trinity College 16, 116, 208, 210
Tweedy, Major Brian (character) 46, 47–8
Tynan, Patrick 231

Ulster Defence Regiment 48
Ulysses
  action in 6–9
  censorship 236–7, 241–51
  characters in 6–9, 33, 46, 108
  classic book 255, 271–4, 276
  context 3–14
  editions 217, 271, 273, 283
  in England 283–305
  and historical facts 81–2
  law and 17–20, 106–7, 113–19, 253–82
  literary technique 139
  punishments in 123–5
  readership 9–10, 30, 303
  suicide in 199–202
  themes in 9, 19, 30, 37, 91, 222
  See also individual episodes

Unionism 17, 28, 234
United Kingdom Temperance and General Provident Institution 176
United States Post Office 256
US v Berg (1934) 270
US v Dennett (1930) 270
US v Kennerley (1913) 263–4
US v One Book called Ulysses (1933) 4, 242, 253–4

Vagrancy Act (1824) 247
Victorian age 78, 139–40, 242–4

Waldron, Fr Jarlath 60
Wall, Thomas 113
Wandering Rocks (episode) 102–4, 123, 178–9, 186, 206–7, 212
Waugh, Evelyn 244
Weaver, Harriet Shaw 283
Wellesley, Marquess of 308
Wesley, John 245
Westland Row 111, 163, 229
Whiteside, Chief Justice James 103
Wickham, William 312–16, 318, 326, 336, 339–41
Wilberforce, William 245
Wilde, Oscar 99, 101
Woolf, Virginia 304
Woolsey, Judge John M. 254, 274–8, 279

Yeats, W. B. 206, 209, 216, 338
Yellow Press (Yellow journalism) 18, 85, 135
Yorke, Charles 317, 326
Young, R. F. 105, 171